The Politics of Religion
and the Religion of Politics

The Politics of Religion
and the Religion of Politics

Looking at Israel

Ira Sharkansky

LEXINGTON BOOKS
Lanham • Boulder • New York • Oxford

LEXINGTON BOOKS

Published in the United States of America
by Lexington Books
4720 Boston Way, Lanham, Maryland 20706

12 Hid's Copse Road
Cumnor Hill, Oxford OX2 9JJ, England

British Library Cataloguing in Publication Information Available

Library of Congress Cataloging-in-Publication Data

Sharkansky, Ira.
    The politics of religion and the religion of politics : looking at Israel / Ira
Sharkansky.
        p. cm.
    Includes bibliographical references and index.
    ISBN 0-7391-0109-9 (alk. paper)
        1. Judaism—Israel. 2. Religion and politics—Israel. 3. Orthodox Judaism—
Israel. 4. Israel—Politics and government. I. Title.
BM390 .S5112 2000
296.3'82'095694—dc21   99-086513

Printed in the United States of America

Contents

Preface

One of the reasons for my coming to Israel in 1975 was to share more fully in the Jewish experience. Then as now, religion provided as much fascination for me as politics. Gradually, I have come to view the two phenomena as being closely related, and equally integral to the human experience.

This book is partly about religion and politics in Israel, but mostly about the mixture of politics and religion. The point is not only that much of politics is about religion, but that the two enterprises are similar in many ways. Politics and religion are prominent among the traits that separate *Homo Sapiens* from simpler animals. Politics and religion depend on one another. They deal with issues that are difficult and intensely important. Politics most clearly indicates *how* we *should accomplish our social goals*, while religion indicates *what those goals should be*. Detailed goals may emerge from political competition with no obvious connection with religion. Politics provides the *who gets what*, and *how they get it*. Religion supplies the underlying themes of justice, equity, and righteousness. It is religion, or something close to it, that is likely to provoke charges of unfairness about how politics distributes resources, jobs, or public services, and to begin yet another round of political activity dealing with distribution.

In contrast to what I shall argue in this book, it is common to see religion and politics as distinct and antagonistic. According to Luke 20:25, we should "pay to Caesar what belongs to Caesar and to God what belongs to God." That sentiment is appropriate for people who composed the New Testament: members of a weak religious community located in a hostile state. It does not describe the contemporary condition in western democracies. Religious leaders urge political behaviors on their followers, and politicians deal with issues that have religious relevance. Both religion and politics employ doctrines and organization in order to advance their causes in competition with rivals. Both promise rewards. Both have their doctrinaire commentators concerned with ideology or theology, as well as pragmatists skilled in finding in the doctrines, laws, and precedents appropriate solutions to difficult problems.

The mixture of politics and religion may be more prominent in Israel than in other democracies. Israel is the Promised Land and much of Judaism has political relevance. Not the least of the issues are *What is the Promised Land?* and *How much of it should Israelis insist upon in negotiating the boundaries of the modern state?* Beyond this are numerous issues of religious law that have guided Orthodox and ultra-Orthodox political parties in their efforts to shape the activities of the modern state.

Elsewhere the overlaps between religion and politics differ in detail but not in substance. The United States is an obvious topic of comparison. There is a celebrated separation of church and state, but the United States stands out for the penetration of politics by religion. For many America is the Promised Land. There are high levels of religious affiliation and intense arguments about abortion, sex education, evolution, and public prayer.

The Argument in Brief

The chapters that follow provide many details. For those who may have trouble keeping their eyes on the linkages between them and the main argument, the following list can serve as a summary of the main theme. It indicates how religion and politics penetrate one another, and resemble one another.

- Religious doctrines are politically relevant, and they influence the policy agendas of western democracies.
- Both religion and politics promise a lot for the near or distant future. For many they deliver continued expectations that the promises will be fulfilled. For others they reinforce cynicism that it is all a performance to quiet the masses.
- Both religion and politics attract majorities. Most people in most western democracies, when asked, say that they believe in God. Most people also do something political, even if it is only to pay some attention to political leaders or vote in elections.
- Parties and religious congregations work to recruit and retain members, reinforce loyalties, and train and select leaders.
- Actions of both religion and politics mix the promotion of spiritual and symbolic goals along with material payoffs for the faithful.
- In western democracies, there is ritualized, low-intensity affiliation with both religion and politics, as well as a tendency for affiliation to be inherited within families.
- Both religions and political leaders tolerate abstentions. Many people who say that they believe in God seldom attend religious services. No democracy imposes severe punishment for the failure to vote.
- For both politics and religion organizational self-interest, as opposed to purported doctrines, may provide the best clues as to how leaders will act.
- Both religious and political leaders are creative. They invent new doctrines and rituals, borrow attractive features from other sects or parties, split off

one from another, and distinguish themselves from their previous allies and current antagonists.

- Despite claims about absolute values, ambiguity is part of the success and failures of religion and politics. A lack of clarity in doctrine aids in recruiting support, but also assures frustration in judging accomplishments.
- Despite unclear doctrines and a looseness of affiliation, there is a history and a continuing potential of intense loyalties in both religion and politics, with a capacity to provoke violence.
- In Israel and other western democracies, religious issues are likely to be the subject of political dispute. However, the demands of religious activists of different perspective come up against one another and against those who are secular or anti-religious. The result is generally a stand-off, with neither religious nor anti-religious activists able to overcome the other.

Several of these points are not self-evident. Some contradict conventional wisdom (i.e., that religious and political doctrines are loosely defined and loosely held by adherents) or seem to contradict one another (i.e., the loosely held together doctrines co-exist with a history of intensity and potential for violence). While the deeply committed among religious or political activists may never be convinced of these or other points, it is the task of subsequent chapters to flesh out this summary list, illustrate its components, and identify their implications.

I consider this book to be an essay composed of several parts that illustrate the similarities between religion and politics. The principal, but not the only, point of reference will be the particular religion and polity that I know best: Judaism and Israel.

I have sought to avoid writing a diatribe against either religion or politics. The two activities are not identical. There does not seem to be an equivalent of direct primaries among religious congregations, or an air of sacredness in politics that resembles what Jews experience at the Western Wall, Christians at the holy sites of Jerusalem, Bethlehem, or the Vatican, or Muslims at Mecca.

My purpose is to focus on the similarities between religion and politics, and to learn from each about the other. Politics is not entirely free of personalities or ideas that are revered by party faithful. Charisma appears in both fields. When a political party wraps itself in a religious symbol, like the defense of the Land of Israel, the sacredness of life and family, or the impropriety of certain sexual activities, the resemblance to religion comes to the fore. We must remind ourselves of the wide variations among religious and political movements. Both have examples that emphasize the visceral or cerebral. A revival meeting resembles a party convention. And a rabbinical discussion of religious law is not all that different from the deliberations of policy analysts and lawyers about program details.

We will see that politics as well as religion can justify its place on the moral high ground. Both religion and politics are involved in the shaping of our values and our standard of living. We can choose our sources for the norms of justice, equity, and righteousness from the Hebrew Bible, Greek philosophy, the New Testament, or more recent sources. Neither religion nor politics can claim a monopoly of virtue or to be free of evil. Political demagogues have their religious equivalents in self-serving prophets and false messiahs. Both politicians and religious leaders have been found violating the morality that they preach.

The history of both religion and politics teaches the value of deliberate thought and doubt in the face of claims that are far reaching. The continued pursuit of knowledge and intellectual self-confidence are useful in defense against being swept up in momentary passions that are either religious or political, or that cross the boundaries between the two realms. In Israel and other Western democracies, the most prominent religious and political leaders seem to have learned these lessons. Despite occasional bursts of intensity, we enjoy a moderate and tolerable mixture of religion and politics. Some of this moderation derives from religious values in behalf of peace and fairness, and the realization of religious and political leaders about the dangers inherent in other religious claims about absolute truths and in favor of ethnocentrism. The moderation may also depend on the prosperity that has generally prevailed in the west since World War II, as well as to lessons absorbed by religious and political leaders from the Holocaust. It is in the nature of both religion and politics that readers from either the religious or the anti-religious ends of the spectrum will view this conclusion about moderation as overly optimistic.

Conditions are different outside of western democracies. Former parts of Yugoslavia, as well as Afghanistan, Iran, Sudan, and Lebanon illustrate immoderate religion and politics, and the violence that draws on religious conceptions of us versus them. Many people in Northern Ireland aspire to moderation, but others do what they can to frustrate the peace. Extremists among both Israelis and Americans justify violence in the name of causes that derive from religion, but authorities in both countries have limited the damage.

Those familiar with my earlier books and articles will recognize some themes and details that repeat themselves. In reaching the conclusions presented here, I have worked my way through *Ancient and Modern Israel: An Exploration of Political Parallels*; *Israel and Its Bible: A Political Analysis*; *Rituals of Conflict: Religion, Politics, and Public Policy in Israel*; *Policymaking in Israel: Routines and Coping for Simple and Complex Problems;* and *Ambiguity, Coping, and Governance: Israeli Experiences in Politics, Religion, and Policymaking,* as well as articles in several academic journals. I have sought to describe and explain Israel's politics, a prominent aspect of which involves wrestling with the aspirations and burdens of its Judaic heritage. Coping, as opposed to solving problems fully and finally, marks a situation of conflicting norms and other vexatious problems.

My offering in this book is the observation that religion and politics have a great deal in common. And while both carry the seeds of absolutist certainty in one's convictions and a justification for doing great harm, both also provide the means to urge temperance, patience, humility, and living together in peace. None of this is new in Judaism or other religious traditions, but it is sufficiently blurred by other themes as to justify yet another book in order to identify and assess the possibilities.

Chapter 1

Religion and Politics Cannot Be Separated, in the Holy Land or Elsewhere

Politics and religion make life worth living and death tolerable. Both speak in terms of absolute truths, but intellectuals should know better. Artful theologians justify distinctions in doctrine by finding clear contrasts in writing that others see as fuzzy. Long before the insights provided by "postmodern" literary criticism, students of the Bible and other sacred texts recognized the multiplicity of meanings. Basic doctrines are obtuse, and interpreters tell as much about themselves as about the religious or political documents under consideration.

Both religion and politics promise a lot for the near or distant future, and for many they deliver continued expectations that the promises will be fulfilled. For others they produce frustration and cynicism. By some rules of courtesy, neither politics nor religion make for polite conversation. Arguments get out of hand and lead to violence. In both politics and religion, there can be too much of a good thing.

The essences of politics and religion are similar. As the title of this chapter indicates, much of Israeli politics is about religion, there is a great deal in Jewish doctrines and traditions that is relevant to politics, and the general idea is applicable beyond Israel and Judaism. However, our concerns go beyond the political disputes that are about religion.

It is the similarities between the enterprises we call religion and politics that comprise the theme of this book. In both religion and politics leaders use doctrines in an effort to justify actions and to cement affiliates to their organizations. Religion supplies much of the morality involved in political ideals. In both religion and politics the doctrines are ambiguous and interpretations creative and flexible. In neither religion nor politics is the enterprise entirely about doctrine or issues. Keeping the group together often seems more important than maintaining purity of doctrine. The organization in politics as well as in religion is likely to be more central than adherence to theology or ideology.

The importance of the community, movement, or party is not the only similarity between politics and religion to be developed in this book, but it provides a good starting place for the argument. It also is especially prominent in Israel, insofar as Judaism combines ethnicity with doctrines. Maintaining a degree of unity in order to protect Jews (the atheists as well as the ultra-Orthodox) against outsiders is a cause especially important to a community that has suffered so much and so recently. Yet the concern for the group is true not only of Jews. Christian denominations of all varieties, and other sects as well, are concerned to defend their members against outsiders.

It is appropriate here to sample the issues that mix politics and religion in Israel. We shall return to these items time and again in order to show the complexities of detail, the implications for both religious doctrine and political behavior, and the similarities in the endeavors we call religion and politics.

Israel's Jews do not agree as to who is a Jew. Nor do they agree as to who has the authority to perform a conversion to Judaism. Orthodox rabbis insist on preserving their monopoly on conversions in Israel, and reject the claims of Reform and Conservative rabbis that they can perform the task properly. Prime minister Benjamin Netanyahu appointed his minister of finance, an Orthodox Jew, to chair a committee to produce a solution. The committee proposed a joint activity, involving cooperation by Reform, Conservative, and Orthodox rabbis. The government endorsed the committee's report. Ultra-Orthodox rabbis ridiculed it, and the Orthodox Chief Rabbinate was laconic in its response.

Religious Zionists with a commitment to Jewish sovereignty in the Land of Israel complained that the right-wing Netanyahu government did not do enough to expand Jewish settlements in territories that had not been turned over to the Palestinian Authority. They also complained that Israeli security forces were not doing enough to assure their safety in their settlements, and on the roads connecting the settlements with Israel. Some of these Jews destroy the property of Arabs, and some participate in random assaults on individual Arabs. Religious nationalists in Palestinian organizations, in contrast, demand all of Palestine for Islam. Their principal weapon in recent years has been a suicide bombing in the midst of an Israeli crowd. They promise the bomber an eternity in Paradise, and threaten the peace process that manages, despite all the religious and nationalist extremists, to keep itself going.

Jewish and Muslim extremists are not simply items in a survey of religious oddities that have survived to the lisp of the twenty-first century. Their importance is greater than that of the Shakers, witches, devil-worshippers, or the followers of cult leaders who participate in collective suicide. Jewish and Muslim fanatics threaten the peace of a region that can ignite catastrophes further afield.

Members of the ultra-Orthodox Lubavitcher community concluded that their late Rebbe, Menachem Mendel Schneerson, was the Messiah. Some did not lose hope when the Rebbe died quietly without world-shaking events. Among the spiritual, death may be only a temporary detour of the divine plan.

Competitors among the ultra-Orthodox communities ridicule the Luba-vitcher, and add them to the list of followers after false messiahs who have brought catastrophe. Most readers are familiar with Jesus Christ and the problems that his adherents have caused the Jews. Somewhat less known is Sabbatai Zevi, a Levantine Jew of the seventeenth century, whose claims to be the Messiah split Jewish communities into advocates and opponents. Zevi himself converted to Islam when given a choice between that and execution by Ottoman authorities. Yet another messiah claimant was Jacob Frank, who found adherents from the remnant of Zevi's followers. Frank became known for sexual promiscuity, and for his own conversion to Islam and then to Christianity.

Ultra-Orthodox Jews resist being counted due to a plague suffered after a census taken during the time of King David. However, estimates are that they comprise less than 10 percent of the country's Jewish population. They may be 25 percent of the Jewish population in Jerusalem. Their neighborhoods spread across a large part of the city, and abut major roads that they demand be closed on the Sabbath. One secular complaint is that the ultra-Orthodox do not contribute their share to the support of the endangered state. Most ultra-Orthodox men take advantage of exemptions from compulsory military service given to full-time students in religious academies. Some remain in the academies until they become fathers of enough children to qualify for exemptions due to family size.

Another complaint is that the education of ultra-Orthodox children is entirely religious, and does not provide them with the knowledge to prepare for employment that will be meaningful economically, or to choose intelligently between a religious or a secular life. The Ministry of Education has not dared impose even minimum standards on the curricula of ultra-Orthodox schools. One anthropologist (himself religious but not ultra-Orthodox) observed a group of ultra-Orthodox twelve-year olds who were highly trained in the exegesis of religious texts. When he asked them to draw a map of Israel, none of them knew what he meant by a map. None could name Israel's neighbors. One thought that the Philistines were still a problem. When asked to indicate how long it takes to travel from Beer Sheva to Jerusalem (83 kilometers), several said that the biblical Abraham had done it in three days, and since he had the Lord's help it must take longer now.[1]

One of my own relatives tells what happened while riding a bus in Jerusalem. When the hourly news broadcast reported something about Libya, an ultra-Orthodox man sitting alongside of him asked "What is Libya?" "A country in Africa," was the response. The next question was, "What is Africa?" A study of ultra-Orthodox women has the informative title, *Educated and Ignorant*. It emphasizes the paradoxical contrast between intensive schooling and a community organized to exclude outside influences or individual initiative.[2]

These are only a few of the points that touch religion and politics in contemporary Israel. It is the Holy Land, and the focus of religious dispute over the ages. The Jews are currently in charge, and Jewish sacred texts include numerous reports and discussions about what moderns call politics. Israel provides a setting where these overlaps between politics and religion are especially apparent, but they appear wherever God and governments claim adherents.

A Note on Terminology: Orthodox, Ultra-Orthodox, and Traditional, Religious and Political

The terms "Orthodox" and "ultra-Orthodox" are the most conventional and useful of designations for two clusters of religious Jews. They represent one side of the great divide between what most Israelis consider "religious" and "secular." The Orthodox and ultra-Orthodox together represent the orthodox side of Jewry, and the religious sector in Israeli politics. Jews who are progressive religiously tend to affiliate with Conservative, Reform, and Reconstructionist congregations. They are well represented in North America, but are a struggling minority in Israel. "Secular" Israelis are the near majority of Jews who affiliate with neither orthodox nor progressive congregations. Also prominent in Israel are Jews known as "traditional." They tend to be Middle Eastern in origin, and observe some but not all of the religious commandments. They may attend synagogue frequently, eat only kosher food, but drive on the Sabbath to attend family picnics, an outing at the beach, or a football game. Survey research has found about 10 percent of the Jewish population in each of the "Orthodox" and "ultra-Orthodox" categories, perhaps 30 percent "traditional," and about half who consider themselves secular.

In contrast to what the labels suggest, there is no intention here of designating the ultra-Orthodox as more religious than the Orthodox. As subsequent discussions will show, Judaism (like other major faiths) is too complex for a simple rendering of congregations as more or less religious. Each of the Orthodox and ultra-Orthodox are themselves composed of separate congregations and movements whose members differ on points of doctrinal interpretation, ritual, and custom. The dress and the political style of the ultra-Orthodox tend to differ from the Orthodox, but there are numerous individuals who dress and behave in ways to confuse the distinctions.

Just as we must avoid precise definitions of Jewish religious movements, so we should avoid wrestling with definitions of "religion" and "politics" or their derivations like "religious" or "political." We shall see shortly the problems in specifying the terms as used by moderns. There are additional problems in using the terms in reference to ancient times. Rather than tripping through efforts to clarify what is not likely to be made crystal clear, it is best for author and reader to rely on the context in order to make the discourse sufficiently clear. Recall that a principal message of the book is that the boundaries between religion and politics are fuzzy, with considerable overlap.

A Long History of Interwoven Religion and Politics

We can date the onset of politically relevant religious events, or religiously relevant political events in the Holy Land, with the invasion led by Joshua. Scholars dispute whether the story portrayed in the Books of Joshua and Judges really occurred as reported. However, those who view the sources as at least partly realistic date it about 1200 BCE. The story is religious due to its source in the Hebrew Bible and its connection with the Promised Land. It is also inherently political insofar as it describes ethnic rivalry and the conquest of territory.

> So Joshua smote all the land, the hill-country, and the South, and the Lowland, and the slopes, and all their kings; he left none remaining; but he utterly destroyed all that breathed, as the Lord, the God of Israel, commanded.[3]

The Book of Judges suggests that complete conquest was more an aspiration than an accomplishment. Many Israelites did not accept doctrines of ethnic purity or the rituals demanded by their leaders. They dwelt among, and married with Canaanites, Hittites, Amorites, Perizzites, Hivites, and Jebusites.[4]

> Because the Israelites worshipped the gods of those people, . . . the anger of the Lord was kindled against Israel; and he said: "Because this nation have transgressed my covenant . . . I also will not henceforth drive out any from before them of the nations that Joshua left when he died."[5]

Much of the Hebrew Bible describes the continuing efforts of its heroes to achieve control over the Land of Israel and the Israelites. It is a story of aspiration and frustration. There was always a more powerful enemy gathering in the field or just over the horizon, as well as other cultures to tempt God's people. As chapter 4 of this book indicates, both the Bible's description of the Promised Land and the quality of the promise have left much work for interpretation. In modern Israel they provide the stuff of both religious and political dispute.

According to the Bible, Samson and then Saul fought Philistine incursions into the land claimed by the Israelites. David took Jerusalem from the Jebusites at about 1000 BCE. In the year 722 BCE the Assyrians conquered the northern kingdom of Israel that had emerged from a division between Israel and Judah following the death of David's son Solomon. The Books of Jeremiah and Lamentations describe the destruction of Jerusalem a century and a half later by the Babylonians.

Two of the last books in the Hebrew Bible describe heroic efforts to rebuild Jerusalem by those who returned from exile in Babylon under the leadership of Ezra and Nehemiah.[6] The dominant empire then was that of the Persians. Later the Greeks came on the scene, and the Books of Maccabees, added to some versions of the New Testament but not the Hebrew Bible, tell the story of conflict between Jews who had adopted the culture of the Greeks against those who stood as zealous Jews, as well as between Jews and Greeks. The celebration of Chanukah simplifies this story into a heroic struggle between faithful Jews and Greek oppressors.

For the next chapter in this story of conflict we rely on the work of the Jew who was born as Joseph ben Matthias and became the Roman Flavius Josephus. He describes how Jews attracted to the culture of Rome fought against Jews who insisted on living according to Jewish law. Again there was a mixture of civil war and a rebellion of Jews against the imperial power. This time the foreign empire proved stronger and more persistent than the Greeks. Roman legions overcame two major Jewish rebellions that began in 63 CE and 132 CE, and they followed their victories with substantial slaughter, property confiscation, and selling captives as slaves. Over the next few centuries there was a gradual petering out of Jewish settlement in the Holy Land as a result of poverty and out-migration.

This ancient history was political as well as religious. The control of territory by a religious or ethnic community is by nature associated with government and politics, as is the manner in which authorities rule the territory. A political reading of the Hebrew Bible sees regimes led by kings and priests, with prophets accorded special status as individuals who spoke the words of the Lord while criticizing kings, priests, and other elites.[7]

The ancient narrative also shapes current politics and religion. One feature of Judaism is a view of its people as chosen by the Lord, with its history shaped by the Almighty's protection or anger. Jews continue to celebrate key events in their collective memory. The exodus from Egypt is a central point in the ritual calendar marked by the holiday of Passover. Chanukah recalls what is said to be a Jewish victory over Greek oppressors. The ninth day in the Jewish month of Av is a day of mourning for the destruction of Solomon's Temple by the Babylonians and Herod's Temple by the Romans.

After seventeen centuries or so of exile and political dormancy, the story of the Jews heated up with the Enlightenment and the onset of modern Zionism. The Enlightenment combined freedom granted to the Jews by certain European governments together with the initiative taken by Jews in those countries and elsewhere to leave their closed societies and acquire the education that allowed them vastly wider choices as to how to live. Many left the Jewish concentrations of Eastern Europe for America. Others became socialists or free enterprise liberals. The Zionists were a group of liberated Jews who sought their future in a Jewish society on the site of the ancient homeland.

The Zionists' slogan, "A land without people for a people without a land" was only partially accurate. Jews arriving in Palestine from the late nineteenth century clashed with indigenous Arabs, as well as with Arabs who came to Palestine in order to take advantage of the economic growth associated with Jewish migration. Some religious Zionists view the Arabs as remnants of the Amalekites. They were a tribe who frustrated the movement of Israelites to the Promised Land under the leadership of Moses, and earned the most fulsome of biblical curses.

> Thus saith the Lord of hosts, I remember that which Amalek did to Israel, how he laid wait for him in the way, when he came up from Egypt. Now go and smite Amalek, and utterly destroy all that they have, and spare them not; but slay both man and woman, infant and suckling, ox and sheep, camel and ass.[8]

This passage causes no end of emotion to Jewish humanists. In individual cases it is difficult to determine if the emotion is revulsion or pleasure: revulsion at finding signs of genocide in the Holy Bible, or pleasure in being able to use the holy text in anticlerical campaigns against what they perceive as the potential domination of Israel by primitive believers.

There are no simple interpretations of a history so long as that of the Jews, and involving so many clashes with outsiders. Modern Israelis divide between those who celebrate the stand of zealots against the Romans, and those who consider the zealots to have been foolish in mounting rebellions that failed so drastically and caused all the later disasters associated with exile.[9] The dispute is not academic, but has direct relevance to the policies pursued by modern governments. Those who admire the ancient rebels against Rome counsel an uncompromising stand against the Palestine Liberation Organization (PLO), Arab governments, and western governments that urge compromise. Those who condemn the ancient rebels cite the costs of not going along with international realities dominated by the great powers.

The Holocaust and the establishment of the Israeli state are recent events whose assessment provokes dispute. Ultra-Orthodox and other Israelis argue as to whether it is proper to employ religious symbolism on the annual Holocaust memorial day organized by the State of Israel to honor the victims. Some ultra-Orthodox commentators put the blame for the Holocaust on German Jews who created Reform Judaism, and thus provoked the anger of God. Secular Jews see this as a ridiculous manipulation of history for political purposes (i.e., the conflict between orthodox and progressive Judaisms). They point to ultra-Orthodox rabbis whose blind faith in the Lord kept them from acknowledging a danger on the horizon and leading their followers from Europe. While many of Germany's Reform Jews escaped prior to the Holocaust, higher proportions of the ultra-Orthodox Jews of Eastern Europe found themselves trapped and then exterminated by German forces.

Ultra-Orthodox Jews have come only partially and reluctantly to accept the institutions of the Jewish state. The state is not governed by the Torah and was not clearly ordained by the Lord. The ultra-Orthodox have been steadfast in avoiding military service, and ignoring national days of mourning or celebration created since the establishment of the modern state. Yet they use their voting power to increase their allocations of state resources for ultra-Orthodox schools and other social programs, plus construction in what are planned as exclusively ultra-Orthodox neighborhoods. Each year the days set aside to commemorate those who lost their lives in the Holocaust or Israeli security forces, as well as Israel Independence Day, generate explicit displays of ultra-Orthodox indifference, and secular anger about the ultra-Orthodox.

Conflicts between Jews and Arabs since the 1920s have been more often the result of contrasting national aspirations than religion per se. Usually of lesser prominence are disputes involving other religious communities with claims over part of the Holy Land. One winter rainstorm damaged the roof of the Church of the Holy Sepulcher and produced an argument between Christian congregations as to which should have the privilege of undertaking repairs. Damage to a wall in the same section of town caused a quarrel between Christian and Muslim authorities. In the year before the celebration of the millennium, the Christian-dominated local government of Nazareth decided to create a plaza on a site where local Muslim wanted a mosque to commemorate the tomb of an ancient hero. Each of these issues reached the peaks of religious organizations and the table of the Israeli government, whose members were anxious to keep things on a low flame. Earlier problems involving Christians and Muslims gave rise to the word, "crusade," and quarrels between Roman Catholic and Greek Orthodox Christians in the nineteenth century provided fuel for what became the Crimean War.[10]

Israeli officials work to stifle inter-community religious controversies involving Muslims or Christians. The possibilities of Christian crusade or Muslim holy war are too awesome to be ignored. When Jewish hooligans damage Christian or Muslim religious sites there are efforts to apprehend and prosecute them, and to proclaim once again Israel's intention to protect the religious rights of non-Jews.

There have been ugly inter-communal incidents. When a Greek Orthodox priest was brought to a Jerusalem hospital with bullet wounds, a police investigation found that he was part of group of clerics who had banded together to protect themselves against Muslim attacks.[11] A local newspaper in Jerusalem used the headline, "New War" for an article that described incidents of tension and violence involving Palestinian Christians and Muslims in Bethlehem and Nazareth. The article itself reported numerous events that seemed less than a war: family disputes between Christians and Muslims that led to violence and even killing; groups of Christian and Muslim youths that engage in levels of violence toward one another in their villages, including damaging one another's religious structures.[12]

A religious Jewish soldier entered a church in Jaffa, asked the one person present to leave, and then turned his automatic weapon on the sacred statuary. The priest of the Jaffa church issued a sweeping denunciation of Jewish bigotry and the inadequacies of Israeli education.[13] Roman Catholic Monsignor Hilarion Capucci was convicted in 1974 on charges of smuggling arms for Palestinian terrorists. He was released from prison and expelled from Israel several years later in response to a request that Pope Paul VI wrote to the Israeli president.[14]

Religious Jews may have been deliberate in their provocation when they moved into an empty building near the Church of the Holy Sepulcher just before Easter in 1990. They put Jerusalem Mayor Teddy Kollek in a delicate position. He chastised Jews for choosing Easter as the season to become neighbors of the Holy Sepulcher, while defending the right of Jews to live anywhere they could legally secure residence in Jerusalem. The action led to a condemnation from Greek Orthodox clergy that recalled the historic Christian practice of permitting no Jews to live in Jerusalem when the Crusaders controlled the city, and throwing stones at Jews who wandered near the Church of the Holy Sepulcher when Muslims were in charge. In a public letter to the Greek Orthodox clergy, Israel's President Chaim Herzog expressed his anguish at the Christian response:

> The sight of a priest in clerical garments, standing on a ladder, ripping down a Star of David from a Jewish residence, cheered on by an enraged mob, is a horrible reminder of what our people lived through in history on many sad and tragic occasions.[15]

A moderate degree of conflict among Jews does not threaten the state or society. Officials of the state allow the tensions to play themselves out. As a result, disputes between Jews become the most prominent of Israel's religious conflicts. Not all concern religion in the narrow sense, but everything concerning Jews may concern religion in the larger sense. Antagonists on matters of social policy argue as to what is best for the *Jewish* state, or consistent with *Jewish* morality.

The overlap between religious and national values is not restricted to Israel.

> What it is to be Polish, or what it is to be Irish is inextricably bound up with a religious identity. In a similar fashion it is difficult to separate the identity of secular Israel from the identity of a profoundly Jewish experience.[16]

The conflict in Northern Ireland between Protestants and Catholics is one of the most publicized and bloodiest of recent conflicts with a flavor of religious war. Yet it is as much political as theological, concerned with which cultural group and whose organization achieves control of territory. There is no denying the prominence of religious symbols in the dispute. But the element of us versus them drowns out whatever differences can be found about religious doctrine.

Chronic dispute may be endemic to Judaism. As a national identity as well as a religion, the Jews include individuals with a wide variety of beliefs and practices. There are agnostics and atheists, believers who affiliate with Reform or Conservative movements, as well as the Orthodox and ultra-Orthodox. Jewish history assures a high incidence of politically relevant issues associated with matters of faith. Arguments about the Holy Land of Israel and the Holy City of Jerusalem exist on the conceptual boundaries between politics, nationalism, and religion. Jewish involvement with foreigners from biblical through modern times has left unpleasant memories involving Egyptians, Babylonians, Persians, Greeks, Romans, Christians, Muslims, Spaniards, Germans, Russians and Eastern Europeans, British, Americans, and others.

Ancient animosities toward Egypt received reinforcement in the wars of 1948, 1956, 1967, and 1973. Israeli attitudes moderated substantially with the visit of Anwar Sadat to Jerusalem in 1977 and the peace treaty signed in 1979, but turned sour again with indications that this would be a cold peace with few signs of accord from the Egyptian government, Egyptian enterprises, or intellectuals. Relations between Israel and Spain, Germany, Russia, and other Eastern European governments are correct and occasionally warm, but reflect the ambivalence of Jews who remember their history. There are Israelis who will not visit Germany or buy German products, and insist that Israeli orchestras or radio stations not play the music of Richard Wagner. Wagner was an anti-Semite, and the Nazis used his compositions as their themes. Israelis argue as to whether the most dedicated anti-Semites are the Germans, Poles, Ukrainians, Croats, Latvians, or some other tribe. The record of British and American governments includes points of insensitivity to Jewish suffering in Europe, and low priorities for Jews seeking refuge. All of this works its influence on the Foreign Ministry, which must be sensitive to Jewish feelings in the materials prepared for encounters between ministers, trade delegations, or cultural exchanges. Outsiders may think that these are manifestations of nationalism and not religion. To Jews, however, there is an overlap between their national history and their religion.

The legalism of Judaism provides its own impetus to political dispute. Religious laws govern what observant Jews may eat and wear, when they can work and travel, what medical services they can use, with whom they can marry and under what conditions they can divorce and be buried. All of this creates demands for secular authorities to use religious laws in their regulation of industrial production, shop hours, transportation, and imports; to prevent abortions; as well as to avoid creating procedures for civil marriage, divorce, and burial.

Judaism's overlap between doctrine and ethnicity justifies religious symbolism for virtually every Israeli political issue. The use of Hebrew is arguably a religious act even while anti-religious Israelis conduct their campaigns in the holy tongue. Hebrew is the language of the Bible, and educated Israelis (anti-religious as well as religious) illustrate their conversations with biblical quotations. The Zionists' concern for revitalizing Hebrew as a national language and teaching it to immigrants evoked spiritual affinities with the ancient people. (Although Aramaic had become the national language by the start of the Common Era, and it is prominent in the Talmud which is central to the education of religious Jews.)[17] There are religious Jews who prefer to use Yiddish for mundane matters, and to preserve Hebrew for ritual. Yet most of the ultra-religious have acquired enough of the Zionist enterprise to become fluent in Hebrew for conversation. The country's Arabs also use Hebrew for many activities. Arabic has status as an official language, but few Israeli officials are fluent in the language. Arab intellectuals complain that their younger generation is becoming too Israeli in dress and other customs, as well as in language.

The Commonalitics of Politics and Religion

Perhaps the most fundamental reason for there being a thick mixture of politics and religion in Israel is that there is a great similarity in the underlying characteristics of religion and politics.[18] Their mixture is apparent elsewhere, but is especially pronounced in the Holy Land. By examining their intertwining in Israel, we should become sensitive to their fundamental likeness, which occurs wherever people attend to matters of politics and faith.

Both politics and religion have wide adherence. Most people in most western democracies, when asked, say that they believe in God. Most people also do something political, even if it is only to pay some attention to political leaders, or vote in elections.

Both politics and religion are organized. Parties and religious congregations look after the loyalties of those they consider to be members, seek to educate a younger generation for roles as followers or leaders, have programs to select and train leaders, and choose who to assign positions of large responsibility. Congregations compete with one another as do political parties in order to increase the number of their affiliates, or the closeness that their affiliates feel toward the organization.

Both political parties and religious communities employ doctrines to attract affiliates and separate themselves from competition. While the doctrines of religion tend to promise rewards in the world to come, those of political parties promise benefits closer to the here and now, or the near future. Yet doctrines of both mix spiritual along with material payoffs. Comradeship, being on the right side of a worldly or spiritual competition, and the promise of a better future are the stuff of both religious and political messages. According to the psychiatrist Anthony Storr, both religion and political doctrines serve the existential human need to impose order on chaos. Both religious and political leaders provide explanations for troublesome events. Both offer guidance about appropriate actions in the face of personal and collective crises.[19]

Both religion and politics deal in the mundane as well as the lofty. Not only a better future, but an immediate job or a contract may be on offer in exchange for political support. Religious leaders offer to serve as intermediaries with the Almighty to obtain material benefits, as well as finding a marriage partner or helping in the birth of a healthy child. At times the quid pro quo is immediate. Missionaries offer food and medical attention in exchange for participation in religious services. In less developed corners of western democracies, there is still money exchanged for votes.

Political demands may have a religious component. Justice and righteousness have biblical roots. Freedom from domination draws on the story of Exodus and its flight from slavery. That precise definition is not apparent in either the religious or political expressions of justice, righteousness, or freedom does not diminish their appeal, and their capacity to motivate mass movements.[20]

Both religious and political doctrines are loosely held. Neither religion nor politics has achieved the various forms of paradise that they promise. The flexibility of doctrine helps sophisticated theoreticians and crafty leaders in both realms who are skilled in convincing simple believers that the future will be better. Church goers are not likely to know the ins and outs of dogma that separate their congregation from near competitors. The party faithful are not likely to know much about the positions held by candidates for minor offices, or even all the postures held by candidates for the most prominent offices. It may be desirable that adherents do not take too seriously the messages conveyed by religious or political leaders. Both religion and politics can incite hatred of outsiders as well as intense loyalties to insiders. Moderation of belief, or even routine mouthing of slogans, may be more healthy than doctrines sincerely believed by many followers.

Routinized affiliation is consistent with yet another commonality of religion and politics: the tendency of affiliation to be inherited within families. The learning of slogans and ritual often comes from home, as well as from the school and social circles associated with home and neighborhood. There are cases of individual rebellion against the family's religion as well as its politics. Recruiters in parties as well as religious communities seek young people at impressionable ages, and hope that a successful recruitment will lead to a life-long affiliation passed on to the next generation.

It is tempting to distinguish the monotheistic religions (Judaism, Christianity, and Islam) from politics by the statement that one is monolithic and dogmatic while the other lives by the give-and-take of bargaining and compromise. Yet neither religion nor politics has a monopoly of tolerance or dogmatism. The monotheistic faiths have their contending branches and leaders, with some explicitly accepting doubt and dispute. And political movements in democratic countries may find themselves with popularly elected leaders who are authoritarian in their inner circle and tolerate no criticism from aides and subordinates.

Both religious and political leaders are creative. They invent new doctrines and rituals, borrow attractive features from other sects or parties, split off one from another and distinguish themselves from their previous allies and current antagonists. "Religious cannibalism" refers to the borrowing of interchangeable parts. "Hackers of the supernatural" putter around in others' beliefs to find something useful. The process is not new. Scholars of the Hebrew Bible identify components of doctrine and legend that came from other peoples. "The Middle East was always the California of the ancient world."[21]

Christianity was one of several sects that emerged from first-century Judaism. Among what we learn from Josephus and the Dead Sea Scrolls are details about the Essenes and other groups who distinguished themselves from the Judaic establishment.[22] It did not take long for the followers of Jesus to split themselves into competing divisions. The New Testament condemns those of his own disciples who denied him, and led contrary movements after his death.[23] In this it follows the style of the Hebrew Bible in identifying other communities of faith, and seeing them as threats to the proper way that the Lord's people should devote themselves to the Almighty and holy law.

Tribes that encountered European missionaries adopted basic features of Christianity, but mixed them with elements of existing traditions. Critical studies of the Book of Mormon find implausible the claim of the Church of Jesus Christ of Latter-day Saints that it was translated from golden plates written in ancient Egyptian. It seems more likely to have been created by Joseph Smith, who was influenced by the prose of the King James Version of the Bible. Contemporary Europeans and North Americans who search for something new take elements of Hindu, Buddhist, Confucian, or a pagan tradition, and cook up their own creeds and rituals. A sizable number of African Americans have adopted forms of Islam. Individuals in other cultures may gather a following around their own interpretation of western faiths. The pursuit of creed and ritual that answers one's need is as prominent as the globalization of commerce, industry, finance, and mass communications.[24]

Politics is a credible substitute for religion, or an article of faith unto itself. Individuals show levels of dedication to party activity not inherently different from what others show with respect to their congregation. Seeking to achieve political consensus through persuasion while avoiding violence is not morally less attractive than behaviors that are more formally religious.

Both religion and politics are dynamic. Individuals and organizations change their postures. The literature of political science features the concept of "realigning elections," when large numbers of citizens seem to change their party affiliation and begin a new era in politics and public policy. Such an election occurred in 1932 in the United States, and in 1977 in Israel. Studies of religion in the United States show a dynamic by which "mainline" Christian and Jewish denominations are losing members, while "conservative" denominations are growing. In this American research, it is Reform and Conservative Judaism that fit the conception of "mainline," while Orthodox Judaism is considered "conservative".[25] Israelis speak about a similar rightward movement as secular Jews discover religion, and the moderate Orthodox become more like the ultra-Orthodox in religious law and ritual.

The implication of dynamism in both religion and politics is that a current trend may come to an end and even reverse course. Conditions change, generations replace one another, and public opinion on both religious and political issues varies from one period to another. While both religious and political movements claim adherence to established principles and evoke the memory of their founders, it is seldom clear that the founders—should they return—would recognize the movements that claim to be what they created. Subsequent chapters of this book detail political tensions surrounding issues of religion in Israel. Some recent changes in policy have favored religious demands, while others have favored secular interests. While it is not feasible to predict a dramatic change in attitudes about any particular issue, it is not wise to assume that there will be no change, or that change will flow in one direction or another.

Both religion and politics have their mainstream and their extreme elements. And in both, there is a tendency for the extremists to adhere to positions that seem guaranteed to mark them as outsiders. "I'd rather be right than President" is the hallmark of the political leader with principles or ideology, but without a chance of victory. Mainstream organizations are flexible, whether they be political parties or religious organizations. Outsiders are not only stubborn but they also play on their status to enhance their suffering and their view of the establishment (religious or political) as demons intent on bringing them harm. R. Laurence Moore describes the functionality of being outsiders for Mormons, Jehovah's Witnesses, Christian Scientists, and other American sects.[26] We shall see the relevance of Moore's point both for the ultra-Orthodox and the ultra-anti-religious in Israel. Moore also writes that diversity in religion, like politics, can provide a social balance that keeps extremists at bay. He compares James Madison's concern for the plurality of political interests in Federalist #10 with the plurality of American denominations, and he argues that each manages to limit the fanaticism that can emerge in politics or religion.[27]

This insight also has validity for Israel. There is hope for continued competition and moderation in a situation where no political party has ever achieved a majority in a parliamentary election, and where the major religious segments (Orthodox and ultra-Orthodox) are each no greater than 10 percent of the Jewish population.

Ambiguous Definitions

Definitions of both religion and politics provoke more questions than they answer. According to one scholar,

> 'religion' refers to a vast and ill-defined collection of beliefs and activities and practices and exercises related in complex ways, . . . the various ensembles or beliefs and activities we call 'religions' are often radically different from each other, and . . . there is a large gray area where we do not know whether or not we shall describe a given ensemble of beliefs and practices as a 'religion.'[28]

The *Oxford English Dictionary* provides eight definitions for religion and a like number for politics. It tells us that religion includes actions, belief, and reverence focused on a divine ruling power. It treats politics as the science and art of government, with an eye toward the unfavorable as well as the lofty: conduct of affairs, management, scheming.

Scholars of religion or politics who seek to precisely define their subject typically embark on a lengthy discussion that twists and turns and ends with little more than an appearance of precision. The elements of religion include profound values, beliefs and interpretation, community and authority, learning and dispute, conformity and apostasy, spiritualism, traumatic life experiences, the search for answers to penetrating questions, magic and ritual.[29]

Political scientists consider politics to be the management of dispute via persuasion followed by voting when argument seems to have reached the limits of its capacity to change minds. Ideally politics manages conflict verbally, but violence may be somewhere in the picture to control those who will not go along with the rules and the consensus. If the essence of politics is persuasion, it comes close to a rabbinical norm that it is desirable to engage in consultation in order to seek God's will and not one's own.[30] Influence has a role in persuasion, with power going to those with wealth, information, skills of expression and organization, and personal magnetism or charisma. It is not clear which of these factors is more important in politics, and which in religion.

Politics and religion are often mixed, as when political ideas carry religious messages. Morality and righteousness as well as justice figure in religious and political discussions. In the United States, abortion, school prayer, the teaching of evolution, and home teaching are political topics with religious roots.[31]

The prohibition amendment to the United States Constitution was largely the work of Protestant ministers and their followers. Residents of some countries that are officially Roman Catholic, like Ireland and Italy, have concerned themselves with divorce as well as abortion. Islamic Fundamentalists pressure governments throughout the Middle East to implement religious law. When Israelis argue about the boundaries of their state, some base their claims on what they perceive to be what the Lord promised Abraham in the Book of Genesis.

An article in *The Economist* illustrates the seamy sides of both politics and religion with a comparison of how American and German authorities have treated the Church of Scientology. At one time both considered it a business and demanded tax payments accordingly. Later the United States government recognized it as a religion, which means greater status and lower taxes. Then the United States government criticized Germany for failing to grant it similar recognition. According to *The Economist*,

> it is hard to argue that (Scientology) does not meet the dictionary definition of a religion—any system of belief in a higher unseen controlling power . . . Scientology tries to turn its followers' minds and part them from their money . . . it will try to change their lives forever. But so do lots of religions. Scientology's founder, L. Ron Hubbard, taught that humans are clusters of spirits that were trapped in ice and banished to earth 75m years ago by Xenu, the ruler of the 76-planet Galactic Confederation. Some religions teach stranger things. Some Christians, for instance, teach that God created the world in a week. This weekend others will be eating bread and drinking wine in the belief that these are Christ's body and blood.[32]

A person familiar with organizations and markets should not be surprised at the similarities between religion and politics. Both depend on organizations. Both involve competition, recruitment of the disinterested, and the continued reinforcement and strengthening of loyalties. Both deal in the intangibles of truth and promises. Neither offers something that can be tested immediately and concretely. The better party or the more appropriate faith is something to be known by trust and feeling rather than weights and measures.

Religious organizations, like political parties, offer a wide range of services to separate the insiders from the outsiders. Political parties sponsor newspapers, sport clubs, and picnics, as well as campaign rallies that resemble revival meetings. Religious congregations seek to occupy their members beyond their meetings for prayer. Jewish ghettoes have at times been voluntary mechanisms to separate the faithful from the Gentiles, as well as forced segregation by hostile governments. The ultra-Orthodox in Israel aspire to live in their own neighborhoods where their celebration of the Sabbath and religious holidays is not troubled by outsiders, and where the religious need not be disturbed by women who dress immodestly, the sight of secular newspapers and television, or the sound of secular radio.

The Mormons are noted for their busyness. Separate nights of the week are dedicated to family activities, visits to the homes of other families in the congregation, as well as separate organizations for the men, women, older and younger children of the congregation. There is no professional priesthood, but it has been estimated that there are enough offices in the church or its affiliated organizations for 55 percent of the membership over the age of twelve. "The church has provided a job for everyone to do."[33] Many teenagers spend fourteen hours per week in Church activities.[34] As a result of all this activity among members of the Church, there may be little time for social contacts between Mormons and non-Mormons.

An article about communities of the "Christian right" in a suburb of Kansas City emphasized efforts to separate themselves from others in order to preserve a threatened lifestyle.

> Olathe's evangelical churches sometimes seem as much community centers as houses of worship. Olathe Bible Church, for instance, offers more than 40 "small groups"—organized by age, marital status, and interest—in which adults meet once a week in congregants' homes to pray for one another. Children have their own small weekly meetings called "cell groups." Olathe Bible also runs parenting classes; separate men's and women's weight-loss programs; aerobics classes; a weekly dinner for older members; father-and-son camping expeditions; a men's only "Sports Blowout"; family swim nights; and a group called "Moms in Touch," in which mothers pray for their children. A church pamphlet titled "Created for Community" explains that socializing with other Christians is not a "spiritual extra or an add-on" but is central to God's plan and the church's work.[35]

It is not only difficult to define "religion" in the abstract. It is also difficult to define the core meanings of particular religions. Judaism no more nor less than Christianity has plural manifestations, with each variety complex in its rituals, doctrines, and traditions. The histories of both Judaism and Christianity feature borrowing of ideas and practices from prior traditions, and a continuing evolution of practice and interpretation.[36] Spiritual leaders have been trained to distinguish their variety from others, but the complexity of their arguments leaves many to wonder. What is essential and what is marginal to each enterprise? Are there commonalities that unite the different traditions? How much of the distinctions are motivated not so much by intense belief as by concerns to separate communities and to justify differential feelings toward insiders and outsiders?

Similar questions may be asked about the major political parties that compete near the centers of the ideological spectra in democratic countries. Democrats and Republicans in the United States, Labour and Conservative in the United Kingdom, as well as Labor and Likud in Israel have numerous overlaps in their doctrines, and no shortage of obfuscation in their campaign tracts.

Those convinced of both eternal truth and political certainty will read these lines with something akin to disbelief, ridicule, or even anger. Maybe the author has fallen on his head. Perhaps his distinguished university made a mistake in granting tenure and letting him teach its students. An early retirement might be the appropriate response, or something like the sentence handed down against Salman Rushdie.

If these are, indeed, the responses from readers committed to religious and political realms, they demonstrate yet another commonality. Both religion and politics have a history of certainty and insularity. If the critics read on, they may come to see the advantages in viewing religion and politics as involved in similar activities. The preacher and the politician, the believer and the voter seek the good in a context of beliefs and facts that are not completely clear as to their meaning. Claims of both religious and political leaders fall short of objective proof. They all exaggerate the certainty with which they express their loyalties. Skepticism is an appropriate antidote for those who would examine either religion or politics.

Continuous Argument About Problematic Doctrine

Ambiguity is part of the successes and failures of religion and politics. A lack of clarity in goals aids in recruiting support, but also assures frustration in judging accomplishments. The payoffs are never as great as the promises. An Israeli popular song complains that the Messiah has not come, and has not even phoned in order to explain the delay. There are never enough resources to satisfy all those who look to government for their salvation.

Religions claim to purvey revealed truth, sometimes of the most absolute variety. Yet the history of their doctrines and commentaries is one of continuous argument. Among the quarrels are whether miracles central to their doctrines really happened or are metaphors for the power and glory of the Almighty. "Stories for children" are the way some commentators describe biblical testimonies of the unbelievable, i.e., tales that are meant to convey great ideas to individuals of limited capacity. Others assert that everything described in the Bible is true and really happened the way it is portrayed. The parting of the Red Sea and the epiphany on Mount Sinai are important landmarks in Judaism, while the virgin birth and the resurrection are central points in Christianity that are arguably miracles or metaphors.[37] Judaism offers a creation story that Christianity adopted, but does not sit well alongside modern science. One scholar writes that the ancient audiences who listened to oral renditions of biblical episodes were made up of more- and less-sophisticated persons, with the more sophisticated able to tell the difference between the report of a historical record and the use of a literary device.[38] The differentiation exists today. Arguments continue as to what is fact, or fiction meant to enlighten. The phenomenon has its parallel in political audiences that differ as to how much of a campaign speech they view as serious promise as opposed to uplifting rhetoric, or how much of new legislation they expect to be implemented.

Holy texts purvey absolute certainty but illustrate contradictory themes. Against the power and omniscience of God portrayed in the Hebrew Bible are stories that show God to be unsure of himself and willing to bargain with humans, as with Abraham in the case of punishments to be meted out to residents of Sodom[39] and Moses concerning the punishment of wayward Israelites in the desert.[40] The Almighty was concerned to avoid a head-on confrontation with adversaries who may be too powerful, [41] and blustered at Job rather than answered his challenges in detail.[42] Each of these problematic episodes has been subject to commentary time and again by those who find cause for skepticism, and those who read the same words in a way to justify the view that the Lord is absolute in his power and justice. When all else fails for religious commentators who wish to explain away a difficult element of Holy Scripture, they remind us that God is incorporeal, and that God's ways are inscrutable to mere humans.[43]

Meanings found in the New Testament are no more certain than those from the Hebrew Bible. A commentator wrote about one unclear passage, "there are probably as many approaches to the . . . problem as there are New Testament scholars."[44] A group of Christian scholars sought to put some order in the speculative and contentious research by *voting* about numerous episodes concerning Jesus, and expressing their judgment as to the degree of certainty that they really occurred. A considerable number of religious scholars view details about Jesus' virgin birth and his resurrection, as well as descriptions of his arrest and trial, as mythic inventions composed sometime after his death.[45]

Criticism of the historicity of events described in the Hebrew Bible or the New Testament does not imply a rejection of the spiritual messages found in them. Individual Jews and Christians who question the accuracy of details are inspired by principles that they find imbedded in the stories.

The varied messages in religious doctrine support a wide range of political movements. The political right, left, and center each have their religious voters who call upon their view of the Almighty. The Christian tent in the United States is wide enough for Pat Robertson on the right and Jesse Jackson on the left. Christian history ranges from the righteous slaughter of the Crusades to the morality of American Abolitionists.[46] Orthodox Israeli Jews can choose between the fervor of those who would kill Arabs selected at random in order to firm up Jewish claims on the land, and the movement of Rabbi Yehuda Amital (Meimad) that elevates peace over land. Some ultra-Orthodox rabbis concern themselves largely with issues of Sabbath and modesty in Jerusalem, and scorn the actions of the Israeli state on both sides of the 1967 border.

The Problems and Benefits of Ambiguity in Politics and Religion

The problems of ambiguity in politics are well known. Voters are never sure which campaign promises are credible. Legislators negotiating the contents of a law do not know which provisions will be implemented more or less completely. Even with the best of intentions, unanticipated shortages in resources, an international crisis, or a change in priorities can explain the alteration of commitments. There are no fixed boundaries or guidelines to behavior that can be described as legitimate, reasonable, or acceptable. Ambiguity produces the stress of not knowing one's own limits or those of one's adversaries.

The situation is similar in religion. In the case of well-established faiths, adherents must study for years to learn the acceptable interpretations of ambiguous or contradictory doctrines. And even then they may be led by error or intention to express something that is unacceptable to someone. Ecclesiastical trials, excommunication, banishment, and worse have been the fate of heretics and apostates.

The other sides of these coins are the opportunities to recruit widely on the basis of doctrines that are attractive without being precise. Salvation and paradise in religion have their political equivalents in the promises made by political leaders who advocate collectivism and individual freedom. There are political as well as religious mantras designed for ritualized repetition. A little boy at Sunday School once defined "faith" as "believing firmly what you know isn't true."[47] Political commentators perceive widely different themes in agendas such as the New Deal, Fair Deal, New Freedoms, New Federalism, de-colonial-ization, and peace with honor. They all promised more than they delivered. In their time, however, they served as the slogans of movements that attracted followers. Prime Minister Benjamin Netanyahu won the 1996 Israeli election by promising peace with security as well as a united Jerusalem. His opponents assert that he made peace insecure and assured the division of Jerusalem.

In this situation of multiple uncertainties, believers in conventional re-ligious doctrines may have an advantage over activists in democratic polities. Religious Israelis, like their counterparts elsewhere, can fall back on centuries of well-formulated explanations for the delay of salvation. They say, for example, "The Jews once again demonstrated by improper behavior that they were not ready for the coming of the Messiah." Political activists have no such easy excuse about the assertions of competing parties, with each claiming that it could accomplish more in the interval between the upcoming election and the one after that.

* * *

Religion and politics are similar but not identical. There does not seem to be an equivalent of direct primaries among religious congregations, or an air of sacredness in politics that resembles what believers experience at their holy sites. Yet it is our task to focus on the similarities, and to learn what we can from them to inform us about religion and politics.

It is not the purpose of this book to provide a full survey of religion and politics in Israel or elsewhere. It is, rather, to examine several sides of the similarities between religion and politics, and their intermingling in specific controversies. Most of the chapters concern political struggles in contemporary Israel. Insofar as these have ancient roots, it is appropriate that we delve into historical episodes that have had a lasting impact on both religion and politics. We also make numerous points of comparison with other national settings and religions.

A reader should view this book as an extended essay about religion and politics. Insofar as it deals with issues of such emotional charge, deep roots, and fuzzy doctrines, it is not appropriate to expect clear conclusions. Some will object to treating such seemingly different realms as similar. Religion and politics are studied in faculties of humanities and social science. The style as well as the substance of this book fit somewhere on the boundary between the two kinds of discipline. It is as more an exploration than a systematic analysis. It seeks to as sess its central ideas with a wide variety of relevant information. We concern ourselves with struggles and debates of long standing that will continue into the future. In politics as in religion, the journey seems to be more important than the destination. This book will not write finis to any of the disputes to be examined. If the book is successful, it will cause its readers to reflect on several general points, and to question some details of history, doctrine, and the preaching of both religious and political activists.

The most general point in the book is the lack of certainty that should attend all religious and political claims. Truth, justice, and righteousness lend themselves to many perspectives. Each slips from attainment, especially in the presence of different views of what happened in the past, what is occurring now, and who should get what.

Many who are knowledgeable about religion and politics may see these as trivial points, well known and obvious. Yet the shrill rhetoric and the blood still spilled in behalf of political and religious claims indicates that we can afford to make the points once again, and to illustrate them in Israel where politics and religion are virtually complete in their overlap. In fact, the weight of reality is on the side of moderates who take a skeptical view of both religious and political intensity. Most of the time, in most western democracies (including Israel), most people seem willing to temper their political and their religious feelings and thereby avoid the ugliness of confrontation and violence.

Subsequent chapters flesh out the perspectives introduced here. They offer ideas and details, using them to show that politics adds to our understanding of religion, and religion our understanding of politics. Stories about individuals as well as political parties and religious leaders, plus a reading of historic texts and social science research, contribute to our themes.

Chapter 2 considers the complexities encountered in the study of religion and its relevance for politics. Chapter 3 explores how issues in both politics and religion affects what seems to be the simple statement that Judaism is the prevailing religion of Israel. Being multifaceted is not unique to Judaism, but it is more obvious in a religion defined by ethnicity rather than only by adherence to doctrine or ritual. The noise of Israel's politics owes something to the inclusive nature of its national religion. It has a place for the indifferent and the anti-religious, as well as the ultra-Orthodox. Chapter 4 explores the mix of religious and political doctrines involved in the concept of the Promised Land. Chapter 5 examines the political chaos and religious fluidity apparent when Christianity emerged from Judaism, focusing on the mysteries of Christ's elevation to the status of Messiah. Chapter 6 describes parallels in ancient and contemporary Jewish conflicts over modernization and orthodoxy. Chapter 7 depicts the overtly political side of Orthodox and ultra-Orthodox Judaisms, as well as Israeli anti-religiosity. Chapter 8 emphasizes the ambiguity common to religion and politics. Finally, chapter 9 looks for reasons to explain why religious conflict remains moderate in modern Israel and other democracies.

Chapter 2

Studying Religion and Its Relevance for Politics

Religion appears as the subject matter in university courses in social science and the humanities. Professors of sociology, psychology, economics, history, literature, art, and of course religion and political science consider themselves experts. The Hebrew term for the humanities: *מדעי הרוח* (*madai haroach*), provides an insight into the frustrations of those who expect clear answers about religion. It can be translated into English as "science of the spirit," or science of the wind."

Whether from one faculty or another, there is a lot to read about religion and its relevance for politics. One can begin with the Hebrew Bible and Plato, or even earlier fragments from other cultures, and work forward to the latest pamphlets and professional journals. There are exegeses, tracts and pamphlets by theologians and philosophers, preachers and common folks, believers, doubters, and anti-deists who have been fascinated with religion. No less numerous are the composers of political doctrines and leaders of small or large groups who have sought to use the power of the state to advance their course or oppose someone else's.

Social scientists who would study religion face a daunting task. The magnitude of ideas and activities represented by religion, as well as their profundity, challenges any who would describe or understand it. One scholar calls religion one of the most deeply rooted, profound, awesome, mysterious, spiritual of human phenomenon, dealing with the big questions, one of the great binding forces; dominant ruler of daily life.[1] Another describes religion as a web of symbols and ritual that links humans to the ground of human existence.[2] These sentiments can also be directed at politics. Like politics, religion can be uplifting, enlightening, humane, and outward reaching with universalistic sentiments; and it can be parochial, concerned only with those who are dedicated to its doctrine, and hateful of outsiders.

Also challenging is the prospect of putting some order into the variety and constantly changing collection of beliefs and practices. Diversity has repeated itself from ancient times to the present. George Bernard Shaw wrote, "There is only one religion, though there are a hundred versions of it."[3] U.S. President Dwight D. Eisenhower expounded a similar theme when he spoke of religion as fundamental to the American way of life, "Our government makes no sense unless it is founded in a deeply felt religious faith, and I don't care what it is."[4]

We find a bizarre assortment of religious practices and commentaries even when we confine ourselves to the most highly educated, culturally and politically "advanced" countries of North America and Western Europe. "Religion's diversity . . . appears limited only by . . . the outer boundaries of human inventiveness . . . even within a single tradition." [5] Self-described pagans among our contemporaries have revived worship of the sun, wild animals, and vegetation along with witches, warlocks, and Satan. Ronald Reagan stood with conservative Christians and Jews against abortion and in favor of prayer, but allowed his wife to schedule White House events in consultation with a San Francisco astrologer.[6]

With all the diversity and dynamism, there is much that is similar from one religious community to another. Claims to have discovered new truths usually prove to be repackaging or recombined versions of old traditions. Perhaps the most apt quotation is the famous line from Ecclesiastes: "The thing that hath been, it is that which shall be; and that which is done is that which shall be done: and there is no new thing under the sun."[7]

Rabbi Harold Kushner uses up-to-date language and concepts of caring in his *When Bad Things Happen to Good People,*[8] but does not move far beyond the Book of Job. Bad things do happen to the good and to the innocent, and there is no clear answer as to why. The Book of Job itself was not the first writing to ponder this issue and to produce more questions than answers. Scholars find evidence that it relies on even more ancient tales from non-Judaic cultures.[9]

Modern scholars caution one another against the ridicule of religions. In the politically correct jargon of academia, no religion is more or less deserving of worship or serious study than any other. It is politically uncorrect to speak derisively of paganism or witches. "Wiccans" is the accepted way of labeling groups that practice witchcraft. In the pages of the *Journal for the Scientific Study of Religion,* which serves the academic community of social scientists, the truth of religious doctrine is less at issue than describing and analyzing the behavior of the faithful.

Religiosity and Secularization

One of the issues in the study of religion is how the enterprise is faring. Some surveys find a decline in church attendance and other indicators of religiosity. Yet others show that while some denominations are losing "market share," others are gaining. The picture writ large shows majorities in most democratic societies professing a belief in God and a religious affiliation.

Academics know well that large numbers of people profess to having religious beliefs, but they also are learning that the connections between believers and their congregations—or those between believers and their beliefs—may be loose. Surveys find variations in the interpretation of key doctrines.[10] The parallel appears in politics where activists manage to justify a great variety of proposals within their interpretation of party dogma. The political equivalent of secularization is a drift of parties from the right and left toward the center.

It may be inaccurate to describe a process of "secularization." Religiosity prevails, along with much dispute about the meaning of doctrine for specific instances, and schisms among those who do not go along with the prevailing views. It may be more accurate to describe what one scholar calls "neo-secularization." This is a lessening in the scope of religious authority. Individuals remain nominally affiliated, but are less inclined than in the past to rely on religious authorities to govern their beliefs or behaviors.[11] This begs the question as to whether masses of church-affiliated ever did know, and subscribe, to the official beliefs of the congregations that counted them as members. "Nominality." may always have been the norm for most people, especially for those who remained in the religion to which they were born, that which prevailed in their immediate surroundings, or was imposed on the population by the ruler.

A study of religion and politics in Springfield, Massachusetts, found a moderation in both the intensity of religion and the vigor of its leaders' pursuit of religious goals in local politics. In other words, both religious leaders and their followers, in this American setting during the 1980s, seemed to be less strident than in the past with respect to their concern for a religious agenda in the political sphere. There remained intensity on some issues, such as opposition to abortion and the distribution of condoms in public schools. Leaders of the Evangelical churches were most concerned about promoting this agenda. Catholic clerics expressed an official church position, but also indicated their recognition of others' concerns. Catholic lay members resembled non-Catholics in their acceptance of birth control and abortion.[12] A study of religion in Muncie, Indiana, which includes a retrospective look at earlier community studies (Muncie is the Middletown of the sociological classic that described life in small town mid-America)[13] found religion in the 1980s less parochial and less strident than in the 1920s. Members of the dominant Protestant majority were more tolerant of those who subscribed to different religious traditions. Views of religion were less likely than in the past to emphasize what is forbidden, and more open to an acceptance of recreation as well as religion on Sunday. The authors found a generalized view of moral virtues, rather than a concern with the doctrines formally associated with members' denominations.[14]

A persistent question asks why religion has not declined further. The great challenge of the last 200 years has been the advancement of science. Astronomers, physicists, biologists and others have not solved the great question of how life began and how the earth and its inhabitants came to be. However, they have learned enough to deny the details provided in, as well as other miracles reported in, the Hebrew Bible and New Testament.[15] Neither enlightenment, nor atheistic and anti-clerical regimes have destroyed traditional faiths. Many people admit a lack of religious affiliation and untold others do not subscribe to all the doctrines taught, but religion remains a thriving enterprise.

The authors of Genesis and the Gospels may be justly accused of a creative use of metaphors for their spiritual feelings. They did not describe reality with scientific accuracy, but they purveyed a message that attracted a large following in ancient times, and continues to do so today. The Bible's authors provided something to help ancients and moderns cope with mysteries of life and the challenges of death. "Everywhere belief in religion arises from attempts to save man or console him from the consequences of his own and other peoples' impulses, desires, fears and actions."[16]

The biblical injunctions and prohibitions provided a framework of morality that remains useful even if the Holy Books do not answer all of the questions they provoke. The contradictions are not the discovery of recent generations, but have caused millennia of pondering by rabbis and church scholars. If God is just why did he not provide a more direct answer to Job? If murder is forbidden, when is killing justified? The problems raised by questions like these stretch one's powers of reckoning that is part of the religious experience. Somewhat lower on the scale of quandaries is the distinction between bearing false witness and telling a falsehood meant to facilitate social or political discourse. Or when is the failure to fulfill a campaign promise an act that should be forbidden or excused?

Within a large picture of continuing religiosity, the details change constantly. We may think of God as everlasting, but God's representatives have shown no end of creativity in devising their descriptions of the deity and ways to serve. Even the traditional faiths of Judaism, Christianity, and Islam have shown much diversity in their ancient and modern versions. There was a school of Shammai that interpreted the law severely in Judea, and a school of Hillel that was known for flexibility. The Talmud is a loosely edited portrayal of disputations among rabbis of different perspectives. A cynical view of the Reformation, presumably one of the great divides in religious history, is that it did little more than replace a pope in Rome with a variety of national and local popes, each claiming authority to lead a flock in the proper way.[17]

Changing political styles from outside the congregation has proved able to alter the content of traditional rituals. Progressive Jews have composed prayer books for celebrating the Passover Seder that link the story of the Exodus with the freedom of racial minorities from persecution, and the ascendance of feminism. Although animal sacrifice was a central feature of Judaic rites at the Temple and remains part of the Passover ritual for some Jews, there is a vegetarian version of Passover for those who would protect all of God's creatures. Politically and religiously progressive Christians see rebellion against a religious establishment as part of Christ's story. Some of them stand against conservative fellow religionists who adhere to what they defend as the essential elements of their faith. One study of Protestant and Catholic congregations in a Chicago neighborhood affected by demographic change and political controversy found that some congregations made efforts to adapt rituals to the moral issues raised in the community, while others maintained traditional rituals unchanged. Where there was change, it seemed to hurt. The researcher describes controversy, anxiety, and resistance, as well as ritual changes that were gradual and piecemeal. Here as elsewhere in the religious world, as in the political, there are likely to be tensions between traditional and progressive perspectives, plus strong feelings about one or the other. As in politics, moreover, many people seem oblivious to what appears as crises to others, and go on with conventional behaviors.[18]

The Social Science of Religion

The mysteries of adherence to any religion, as well as the workings of particular communities, do not succumb easily to the tools of social science. Scholars concerned with religion use survey questionnaires, but they are limited in their capacity to probe the intensities or subtleties of religious feelings. Questions designed with an eye to probing religiosity in the Roman Catholic tradition may not work among Evangelicals or Jews. What may work with Orthodox Jews may not be suitable to Reform Jews. And nothing may work with groups that do not trust outsiders, like ultra-Orthodox Jews.

Ultra-Orthodox Jews are intense in avoiding anything that looks like a census. II Samuel 24 describes a census urged upon David by God, but followed by a plague. Commentators have not definitively answered the puzzle as to why a census ordered by God would be punished,[19] but the ultra-Orthodox are taking no chances. When Israel's Central Bureau of Statistics was preparing the national census in 1995, the rabbinical tribunal of one ultra-Orthodox community, Edah Ha-Haredit, ruled that counting Jews was against religious law and would cause a plague, as in the case of King David. The rabbis of other ultra-Orthodox communities also opposed the census, but accepted a proposal by the Central Bureau of Statistics to remove a question of religious affiliation from the questionnaire. This would turn the census into a counting of Israelis and not a counting of Jews. For the rabbis of Edah Ha-Haredit, this was not sufficient. They continued in their opposition to any census. As in years past, the census appeared likely to undercount ultra-Orthodox Israelis who worried about the catastrophe that accompanied the actions of King David.[20]

Despite the problems associated with questionnaires about religion, there is no end of research about personal traits associated with indices of religiosity.

Some findings confirm expectations, some are worrisome, and some are curious or trivial. Perhaps to be expected, individuals with a high degree of religiosity admit less than others to be users of illicit drugs, and they are less likely to approve of sex outside of marriage. Reflective of the narrowness and parochialism, as opposed to the outgoing and encompassing sides of religion, is the finding that religious people, especially those affiliated with conservative Protestant movements, are less likely than others to score high on "humanitarian" indices that reflect tolerance for minorities or divergent beliefs, or a concern for the less well off. On the trivial side, or begging further explanation, are findings that pet owners tend to value religion less than nonowners; that members of conservative churches lock their cars during Sunday morning services more often than members of liberal churches; and that those who partake frequently in religious services are less likely to die of certain heart diseases.[21]

Researchers with an eye to economic models examine "demand-side" and "supply-side" explanations of why some religious communities grow more than others. They find themselves severely criticized for overlooking the spiritual elements of faith, but they can produce at least partial explanations of why some congregations grow while others stagnate or decline.[22] Not too dissimilar is an organizational approach to religion, which concerns itself with concepts developed in dealing with business, social, and political organizations to investigate religious leadership, the recruitment and retention of affiliates, and relationships between congregations and denominations.[23]

"New religious movements" (NRMs) is a label designed to replace the negative terminology of "cult" and allow dispassionate social scientists to examine movements that develop outside of, or on the edge of, established religions. NRMs represent what may be cases of intense affiliation at the opposite end of the spectrum from routine religious membership. One book-length annotated bibliography limited itself to new religious movements in Western Europe, and listed 3,000 books and articles that the compilers selected from an initial pool of 8,000 items.[24] These movements have spawned a substantial industry of cult experts and de-programmers who hire themselves out to family members concerned to recapture children (and older adults with money to bequeath) who seem to have been isolated and brainwashed by cult leaders. Considerable research among these groups suggests that intense, but temporary affiliation is more prevalent than lasting commitment. There are tragic stories of ruined lives and even mass suicide in this corner of the religious world. The term "religious pathology" is used to describe the especially eccentric or anti-humane doctrines and behaviors.[25] However, another pattern is the abandonment of NRMs by those who had been converted, sometimes as the individuals search out additional alternatives.

Contentious Scholarship

Dispute is endemic to the study of religion. Not only do many of the basic texts require translation to a modern tongue, but they are made obtuse by illusion and metaphor. There is also the problem of interpretations rendered authoritative by the traditions of various congregations, and guarded over by mentors who are unfriendly to innovation. The same perspective applies to politics, with movements having their own obtuse doctrines as well as competition about acceptable interpretations.

Arguments about the origins of the Bible illustrate the clash between doctrine on the one hand, and inconclusive scholarship on the other hand.[26] Rabbinical commentators agree that the Torah (or Pentateuch, Genesis through Deuteronomy) was provided to Moses by God. There is less certainty about other parts of the Bible, but religious Jews tend to agree that the Book of Joshua was composed largely by Joshua; that the Books of Judges, Ruth, and Samuel were composed by Samuel and his students; that the prophets or their students composed the books attributed to them by name; that Jeremiah composed the Book of Kings and Lamentations; that Solomon composed Ecclesiastes and Song of Songs; that the scribe Ezra composed the book that carries his name as well as the Book of Chronicles; and that Nehemiah composed the book identified with his name.[27]

A problem for some of these assignments is that the texts show numerous layers that seem to have been composed at various times. Ecclesiastes includes language forms that developed only centuries after it was supposed to have been composed by King Solomon. According to one scholar, the claim that Solomon wrote the book "is like saying . . . that a book about Marxism in modern English idiom and spelling was written by Henry VIII."[28]

Secular scholars have struggled with detailed analysis and artful hypotheses in order to identify who wrote or edited various books and passages. One critic of their work calls it an

> exercise in futility . . . detective ventures . . . kept going only by recourse to unwarranted assumptions, ad hoc epicycling, non sequiturs, and other offenses against logic and common sense that could provide matter for a textbook on fallacies.[29]

It is likely that the composition and editing of the Hebrew Bible was a long process, involving oral and written traditions, with quarrels among editors and compilers. The Books of Job and Ecclesiastes found their place in the Bible even though they were suspect for ideas considered heretical by virtue of their questioning of faith and the justice of God. The Book of Ecclesiastes benefited greatly from the claim that Solomon was its author. The Book of Ezekiel was worrisome for its explicit descriptions of God. Some rabbis prohibit anyone under the age of thirty from reading certain portions.[30] The Song of Songs appeared to some readers then, as now, to be too worldly, if not downright pornographic. It benefited from the argument that Solomon was the author, and that its proclamations of love were not so much carnal descriptions as an allegory for the love between God and Israel.[31]

The Book of Esther has offered several problems for those who ask why it was included in the Bible. Its shrill nationalism was problematic for the rabbis when they were still suffering from the losses to Rome and working out the posture of passivity with respect to secular powers.[32] The Book has been faulted for not mentioning God. Esther did not act like a nice Jewish girl when she participated in the contest to select a member of the king's harem. Yet she used her charms for the sake of Israel.[33]

Among the mysteries of the Hebrew Bible are different versions of the same events. The Books of Samuel and Chronicles have contrasting reports as to whether it was David who killed Goliath.[34] Kings and Chronicles differ as to whether Solomon gave or received parts of the Galilee in a deal with Hiram of Tyre. The chronologies offered in the books of Exodus through Kings exceed by far the 480 years said in I Kings 6 to have transpired between the exodus and Solomon's construction of the Temple.[35] The thirteenth chapter in the First Book of Samuel seems to state that Saul was one year old when he became king. This statement has been viewed as a simple error in transcription that somehow became fixed in the text. Yet some deny that anything in the holy book could be a mistake. The Jewish commentator Rashi read the passage as referring to events during the first year of Saul's kingship.[36]

Problems of interpreting the Bible are made even more difficult by the efforts of some ancient authors to obscure the meaning of their work in order to protect themselves and their listeners from retribution. The Book of Daniel is said to employ a setting in Persia three or four centuries before the Book's composition in order to write about contemporary conditions.[37] Chapter 6 in Daniel tells about intrigues among the advisors of the king to concoct a situation in which Daniel will be killed on account of following Judaic rituals. The story ends by showing the weakness of worldly politicians against the influence of God.[38] This seems to be making a point about foreign government like that of Antiochus IV Epiphanes, which was in power about the time the book is said to have been written. Those who purveyed the tale of Daniel might have suffered at the hands of the regime if the story had been written explicitly with contemporary details. Commentators on the New Testament make a similar point about the parables of Jesus: that he provided his lessons by means of veiled stories in order to foil the efforts of Jewish or Roman authorities to accuse him of fomenting rebellion.[39]

The Book of Isaiah illustrates the complexities and implications for the further development of religious doctrines in assessing the meaning of key biblical passages. Isaiah is a collection of what may be the work of two, three, or more authors.[40] Different sections seem to have been written as early as the middle eighth century BCE while Israel was under pressure from Assyria, and as late as the latter part of the sixth century BCE when Judean exiles had returned from Babylon. Some traditional Jewish commentators concede the multiple authorship of Isaiah, saying that there was an Isaiah school which continued the perspective of the prophet over the course of several generations. Other religious Jews insist that the whole Book of Isaiah was the work of the prophet himself, who forecast the Babylonian exile and the return to the Land of Israel which was to occur more than 100 years after his death. A variant on this view is the explanation that Isaiah did not reveal the latter part of his book to the public, but provided it to disciples who were to publicize it when it proved to be accurate.[41] In contrast is the irreverent language of a modern commentator who refers to the Book of Isaiah as a "garbage can of prophecy" on account of its numerous authors and themes.[42]

Early Christians found in murky passages of Isaiah what they claim is the Lord's prediction of Christ's coming. Isaiah 52-53 tells of a man to whom the power of the Lord was revealed, who was despised and wounded for the people's iniquities. A modern Christian translation that the man was "pierced"[43] fits the story of the Crucifixion but is not supported by the Hebrew words מכה (*macha*) or מחלל (*mchalal*) that appear in the text of Isaiah. Traditional Jewish commentators view the suffering servant as a symbol for the Israelite nation or as Isaiah's view of himself.[44]

The rich messages of the Bible change with each reading. The images outweigh the words. All this makes for a great deal of excitement for those who are curious, but annoying for the faithful who cannot tolerate ambiguity. Interpretations began to vary from the very beginning, while the later books of the Bible were still being written. Perhaps the concern was to create something that was religiously correct. The Books of Chronicles repeat much of what appears in other books, with changes in detail that put a better face on Judaic heroes. Chronicles skips lightly over the life of Saul with few uncomplimentary details. It does not mention young David's offer to fight against the Israelites alongside the Philistines, or the older David's adultery with Bathsheba. Neither does it dwell on Solomon's foreign wives, or his acceptance of their gods. Chronicles also changes the story of Solomon giving Galilean towns to Hiram in payment of debts.[45] Readers interested in an irreverent account about the editing of sacred texts that may stand as a fictionalized account of writing Chronicles should read Stefan Heym's *The King David Report.*[46]

Christian sects have publish edited versions of the Psalms and prophets that include creative translations of the original Hebrew, remove all reference to their Judaic context, and add references to Jesus.[47] The Mormons have an inspired "translation" of the Book of Genesis as revealed to Joseph Smith that begins with a conversation between God and Moses about Jesus.[48] Muslims agree with the Jews that God revealed his word to Moses, but contend that the Hebrew Bible does not record the word accurately. According to one story in the Koran, it was Ishmael (rather than Isaac) who was offered for sacrifice by Abraham. In the Muslim source, Abraham and Ishmael are said to have built the Kabah in Mecca. Muslims cite this story to question the biblical claims to Israel made by the Jews.[49]

Authors of the New Testament set a standard for sectarian wrangling that resembles the brickbats hurled by Reform and ultra-Orthodox Jews of today at one another. In both cases a student of organizational theory can see the workings of group self-interest, and appeals to the crowd by trying to reduce the value of one's opponent. At the time of the New Testament's composition, the prominent rival of the new religious movement of Christianity was the old religious movement of Judaism. The Pharisees (predecessors of rabbis) were symbols of the establishment.

The Gospels are especially shrill. They refer to Pharisees as vipers[50] and blind guides;[51] and hypocrites who preach one thing and do another.[52] Jews are said to have demanded the death of Jesus, while the Roman official Pilate saw him as innocent of a capital charge.[53] Jewish priests are described as bribing Roman soldiers to testify that disciples stole the body of Christ from his tomb, in order to create the image that he had not risen from the dead.[54]

In a later portion of the New Testament, the disciple Paul took aim at the legal details in Judaism: "it is written in the law of Moses, Thou shalt not muzzle the mouth of the ox that treadeth out the corn. Doth God take care for oxen?"[55]

Some biblical scholars seek to resolve the smallest details about the Bible's meaning by assembling numerous kinds of evidence: historical records and artifacts from archeological sites, the examination of word usage and other clues to the period when a particular biblical passage was written. However, their works are marked by numerous instances when they must speculate because of evidence that is obscure or incomplete.[56] It is impossible to be certain as to the intentions of the Bible's authors. Consistent with this is research that pursues not so much what the Bible expresses, as how interpretations of its meaning have changed from one post-biblical period to another, and according to the cultures of those who study it.[57]

* * *

The following chapters examine additional points of controversy in religious scholarship. In keeping with the theme of this book, the focus will be on those issues that comprise the fuzzy boundaries between religion and politics. Some of the problems described are those of interpreting ancient texts, and some the significance for doctrines of problems presented by current politics. Not only is there a great deal to read on the borders between religion and politics, but there are likely to be numerous ways of reading each document.

The looseness of religious doctrine and scholarship, and the adherence of many affiliates for nondoctrinal reasons, raises basic questions about the religious enterprise. Ethnic-encompassing Judaism includes within its fold atheists and agnostics, as well as a wide range of belief and practice. Other communities have their nominal members who do little more than participate in ceremonies of birth, marriage, and death, or who even avoid these but who identify themselves as "Catholic," "Protestant," "Christian," or "Muslim" when asked.

Here as elsewhere, we encounter the "softness" of our knowledge about religion. While some scholars might be faulted for naive ideas, loose conceptions, or poorly designed research, a major problem is the subject. "(Religion) is hardly a phenomenon easily amenable to concrete objectivity, and dispassionate rigor, and some of its aspects are particularly elusive."[58]

For many, a religious identity is something to maintain, like wearing clothes, driving on the proper side of the road, and observing conventional courtesies in public. Yet unlike these other activities, religion has the power to excite and incite. It remains an open question—unproved by anything in the many literatures about religion—whether the hateful sides of religion have contributed more sorrow to human history than the humane and compassionate sides of religion have contributed to conditions of understanding and peace.

Chapter 3

Where Judaism Prevails

Depending on what we mean by "prevail," Judaism either dominates or struggles in Israel. The story is as much one of politics as of religion. If anyone doubted the overlaps between the religious and the political enterprise, Israel's experience should deal with the skepticism. The overlap between religion and politics may be greater in a Jewish state, insofar as ethnicity is inherently involved in the conception of Judaism, and ethnicity touches on elemental features of politics: citizenship, and preferences in the distribution of benefits.

Israel's history may add to this confusion of religion and politics insofar as the state is new, and its people have come from numerous lands and cultures. Their Judaism, as a result, is not all of one piece. Moreover, state building, or the creation of national institutions, has been delayed by several wars, large waves of immigration, and more recently a drawn-out process of making peace with Arab states and the Palestinians. Among the issues in the politics of peace are religious concepts concerned with the Promised Land and the Holy City. After more than fifty years, Israel still does not have clearly defined boundaries, international agreement about the location of its national capital, or a constitution. Numerous other issues of religion remain unsettled and maintain prominent places on the national agenda. Continuing disputes about the Sabbath affect the livelihood of people who would work, the convenience of people who would shop, and the profitability of the national airline that currently does not fly on the Sabbath. Issues of modesty affect the pictures included in advertisements. Among the problems of Jews who wish to practice non-Orthodox Judaism in Israel are the monopolies of Orthodox rabbis to decide who may marry, as well as who may be converted to Judaism in Israel. The rights of women are matters of dispute with respect to the divorce proceedings, as well as the style of prayer permitted in public places.

If our concern is only the simple one of numerical preponderance, there is no question that Judaism prevails in Israel. Official reports are that about 5 million Jews comprise 79 percent of the population. This makes Israel more homogeneous than a number of other western democracies in terms of the nominal religious affiliation of its residents, as well as the only country in which the Jews comprise a majority. Israel is approaching a situation where more Jews live there than in any other country. A decade ago there was no question that the United States was home to more Jews than Israel. There were 3.6 million Jews in Israel and perhaps 5.5 million in the United States. With the continuing immigration to Israel from the former Soviet Union, and the continued intermarriage and assimilation of American Jews, Israel may now be the country with the largest number of Jewish residents. There are, to be sure, unresolved questions about the number of immigrants from the former Soviet Union who really are Jews, and the fate of American Jewry. Here we mention the questions to indicate we should know of their existence, without bothering to probe them.

Israel's Declaration of Independence proclaimed it to be a "Jewish state." The state seal, as well as the flag and coins carry religious symbols. The Sabbath is protected by state law, and Jewish holy days provide almost all of the national holidays. The Hebrew Bible is a required text in secular schools, which educate some 72 percent of Jewish primary and secondary school pupils. Twenty percent of Jewish youth study in "state religious schools" that combine substantial religious instruction along with secular subjects, and the remainder in "independent" schools associated with ultra-Orthodox congregations. In these schools there may be little or no secular education. In the most extreme, there may be only the rudiments of arithmetic to supplement religious education.[1]

A more demanding conception of "prevail" includes elements of "control," and here the picture is more complicated and relevant to the themes of this book. Both religious and secular Jews consider themselves restricted by the other. Struggle is chronic, with each side citing religious and political doctrines in its own favor and employing its weight in the Knesset and the governing coalition. A fair reading of the outcomes is that neither religious nor secular perspectives prevails over the other.

A minor theme in the story of struggle pits religious, but non-Orthodox, Jews against the Orthodox and ultra-Orthodox. This theme has a limited effect on Israeli politics because of the few non-Orthodox religious Jews in the country. The conflict gets considerable attention from overseas Jews, especially in the United States, where the non-Orthodox are a majority. American Jews enlist American officials in what they describe as a struggle against Israeli authorities and their practice of religious discrimination. We return to this story in chapter 6.

We also must remind ourselves that struggles among Jews occurs in a setting closely watched by Muslims and Christians. They are concerned that the Jews do not take all of the Holy Land for themselves.

What Is Judaism?

A description of Judaism could begin with the 613 commandments said to be derived mostly from Numbers, Leviticus, and Deuteronomy, and elaborated in the post-biblical Mishnah, Talmud, and 1,700 years of additional rabbinical commentaries. Religious Jews adhere to these rules when preparing food, choosing their clothes, engaging in economic transactions, performing their prayers, or interacting with a spouse or someone else of the opposite sex. There are likely to be more than 613 combinations of how Jews interpret and observe—or fail to observe—these commandments.

Conversely, a description of Judaism might begin with the sentiments in behalf of freedom, justice, righteousness, and peace that appear in Exodus, the prophets, and other books of the Hebrew Bible. Some commentators make the point that the people called Hebrews, then Israelites, then Jews were not Greeks.[2] By this they mean that Judaism lacks a primal concern for doctrinal consistency. While this is true, and while there were ancient animosities between Greeks and Jews, there was also strong empathy for Greek culture among Jews who "Hellenized." Commentators concede some lasting impacts of Greek thought even on documents with Jewish religious significance. Ecclesiastes found its way into the Hebrew Bible despite its skepticism with respect to faith and justice, as well as its relativity (everything has its season).[3] It is read in synagogues annually during the festival of Succoth.[4]

The ethnic element in Judaism, as well as the lack of Jewish preoccupation with doctrinal niceties, allows the argument that Judaism is what Jews do! Even though there may be only 14 million or so Jews in the world (still below the 17 million prior to the Holocaust), this is enough to array a great variety of doctrines, rituals, legends, and customs. The range of beliefs and behaviors among Jews seems no less than those associated with other humans who claim some religion, or no religion at all.

Judaism endures competing claims of legitimacy by various adherents of orthodoxy and reform. There is no central authority to resolve disputes. Ultra-Orthodox congregations declare individuals to be banned and forbid contact with them. However, there is now little difference between Judaism and other major faiths with respect to their modern tendency to overlook heresy or blasphemy. Jews and Gentiles who violate the Lord's commandments do so at the risk of being ignored.

Heterogeneity in a Homogeneous Country: Almost All Are Jews, but That Does Not Bespeak Unity

Israel's Jews are anything but a homogenous or harmonious community. We have already introduced the categories of ultra-Orthodox, Orthodox, "traditional" and secular. One survey employed a continuum from "strictly observant" to "totally nonobservant." Fourteen percent of the respondents defined themselves as "strictly observant," 24 percent "observant to a great extent," 41 percent "somewhat observant," and 21 percent "totally nonobservant." Another survey found that 18 percent of the sample said that they "observe most of the commandments," 40 percent "observe some of the commandments," and 32 percent "do not observe any of the commandments."[5]

Insofar as living in Israel is one of the commandments, the responses of 32 percent of this sample raise questions about the standards employed for religiosity. Even Israeli Jews who proclaim themselves most removed from religious concerns have absorbed a good deal of knowledge about Jewish history, doctrine, and ritual from their school years and programming in the mass media.

Part of Israel's distinction among nations, and its role in Jewish history, is to serve as a refuge for Jews and Judaism. To date, it has absorbed close to half of the Jews in the world. Most have arrived not primarily out of passion for religion or living in the Promised Land, but because they found life unbearable where they were. They came in waves: Germans after the Nazis came to power in the 1930s; the remnant of the Holocaust and refugees from Arab lands in the 1940s and 1950s; Hungarians and Romanians in the 1950s; Soviet Jews with the temporary opening of their regime early in the 1970s and in much larger numbers with the collapse of the Soviet Union in the late 1980s; Ethiopians in the 1980s and 1990s; and occasional spurts of migrants from Argentina, Brazil, Uruguay, and Chile when those countries turned in authoritarian directions.

These migrants and their descendants differ on the desirability and the meaning of Israel as a refuge for Jews and Judaism. The explanation of their attitudes may have something to do with economic development. Israelis are no longer desperately poor. There has been a lessening of the security threat. Israelis are now a full generation from the Holocaust and the pogroms that swept periodically through Eastern Europe and Arab countries. There has not been a concerted attack by Arab countries since 1973. Many Israelis want to make their country like others: liberal, pluralist, secular and democratic. Some would flee their Judaism without leaving Israel. Among the Jews who come from wealthy countries of the Diaspora are those who would import their varieties of Judaism to Israel. Religious Israelis look on these movements askance. Some of the ultra-Orthodox see in secular Israelis and liberal Judaism the seeds of national destruction.

A History of Conflict

Conflict is not new to Judaism, nor is it unique to Judaism. The development of Christianity began in conflict, i.e., with a group of Jews who found reason to set themselves off from the religious establishment. Those who term Paul as the first

Reform Jew[6] miss the point by a century and a half. An earlier wave of reform set those Jews who wanted to behave like Greeks against a group of zealots. Indications of even earlier struggles appear in the biblical Books of Ezra and Nehemiah. They tell of authentic Jews (i.e., those who won the struggle and gave themselves the label of authenticity) who returned from exile in Babylon to find a loose-living population that had not been sent out of the land. Leaders of the returnees forbade marriage with these locals of doubtful Judaic lineage, and ordered that existing marriages be ended. A close reading of the biblical text raises doubt as to the power of the leaders to enforce their edict. The tenth chapter of Ezra names some individuals who divorced their wives and others who promised to do so and paid a fine for having trespassed. It does not indicate that these divorces occurred. Then the chapter concludes with another list of men who married improper wives, without indicating that they divorced them.

Even earlier rebellions are recorded among the Israelites of the desert. At one point the Almighty expressed dismay at his people's behavior. "Ten times they have challenged me and not obeyed my voice."[7] Later he found his servant Moses guilty of an infraction severe enough to deny him entry to the Promised Land.[8]

There was rebellion within the first families. Those who doubt Judaism's familiarity with dispute need only read the Book of Genesis, with its tales of family problems involving Adam and Eve, Cain and Abel, Noah and his sons, and—once the story of the Hebrews begins—Jacob and Esau, then Joseph and his brothers. Abraham has special status as the first of the Hebrews. Jewish legends elaborate the few words in the Bible [9] and create a story of a son rebelling against a father who was a maker of idols. More than three millennia later, some of the young Jews of Eastern Europe who left their bourgeois families for a life as Zionist pioneers described themselves as descendants of the rebellious Abraham.

Several biblical episodes portray the problems of individuals who face great conflict with themselves or others, wrestle with difficult conditions, and cope by means of decisions that are manifestly imperfect. All this stands against the caricature of the Hebrew Bible as a source of absolute and fundamental truths. It foretells the practice of modern Israeli leaders who cope with the contrary pressures of religious and anti-religious Jews by granting to neither what they demand.

Ambivalence, rather than certainty, appears at crucial points in the history told in the Bible. Moses was anything but certain in the face of an awesome boss and a difficult task. The assignment was no less than to bring forth the Israelite slaves from their bondage. This would require Moses to overcome his fear of being under a sentence of death for having killed an Egyptian,[10] make a direct approach to Pharaoh, and remove human assets of sizable proportions from the Pharaoh's economy. The story also indicates that slaves are likely to be a passive lot. Moses was unsure of his ability to persuade them that he would lead them to a better life. "Who am I, that I should go unto Pharaoh, and that I should bring forth the children of Israel out of Egypt?"[11]

God sought to strengthen Moses' resolve with training in magic that would demonstrate the power that he represented, as well as by indicating that Moses will go to Pharaoh in the company of the elders of Israel.

The continuation of the encounter involving God, Moses, and Pharaoh reveals a lack of absolute authority in the behavior of the Almighty as well as Moses. Both God and Moses appear to be stressed in anticipation of persuading Pharaoh to give up his slaves. They cope by lying. God instructed Moses not to ask for the slaves' freedom, but only for a holiday so the slaves could go to the wilderness for a religious feast. [12]

The Hebrew Bible is at its literary richest in its story of David. He is not the stereotype of a hero or villain, but rather a complex individual who shows strength and weakness in the presence of temptation and stress.

Early in his story, when he was pursued by the mad king Saul, David recognized the reality of his weakness. He sought to maintain and build his strength with the opportunities available. At one point he assembled a band of what may have been desperadoes, outlaws, or bandits and sold protection to landowners, as portrayed in the episode of Nabal and Abigail.[13] During this period of weakness, David subordinated himself to Achish, the son of a Philistine king, and received for his services the town of Ziklag.[14] One passage indicates that Achish asked David to join him in a campaign against the Israelites. As would be expected from a vassal who had been awarded a town, David agreed.[15] Before the battle could be joined, however, other Philistine commanders refused to fight alongside an Israelite.[16] Subsequent episodes in David's life include his adultery with Bathsheba and his involvement in the death of her husband, as well as problems with destructive offspring. On the positive side, he greatly strengthened the Israelite state, and is credited with humility toward his subordinates and a profound love of the Almighty.

There is no more prominent expression of ambivalence in the Hebrew Bible than the Book of Ecclesiastes. The preacher (*Kohelet*) who speaks through the book expresses the self-doubts that many moderns seem to hold with respect to religious faith. Everything is ephemeral. Wisdom is to be preferred to foolishness and is better than money or possessions. However, the pursuit of too much wisdom, or too much of anything, is like chasing the wind. One should not be overly righteous or overly wise. Why make a fool of oneself? It is best to enjoy what can be attained and to live the best life possible.[17]

God is not to be denied, but God is also a subject of the preacher's ambivalence. The author of Ecclesiastes wrote that man has a sense of time past and future, but no comprehension of God's work from beginning to end.[18] It will be well with those who fear God and obey his commands.[19] God knows all our secrets, and brings everything we do to judgment.[20] Yet God is inscrutable, and one should not be overly righteous. The preacher repeats that death is the end of the just as well as the unjust.[21] The prime of life is to be enjoyed, but it will pass and seem in retrospect to be emptiness.[22]

The final portion of Ecclesiastes not helpful to the reader who wishes to know just what are the most important values of the writer. It says that the speaker turned over many maxims in order to teach, and chose words carefully in order to give pleasure, even while teaching the truth. The third verse from the end is the classic remark against too much study, "the use of books is endless, and much study is wearisome."[23] The last two verses urge the reader to fear God and obey his commands.

We can date the disputes of modern Jewish history from the onset of the Enlightenment. The term summarizes several events marked by the ascendance of science and education, and an expected retreat of religion. It is common to focus on the late eighteenth century, but important episodes were apparent as early as the sixteenth century, and continue to the latter part of the twentieth century. Copernicus and Galileo did their work in the sixteenth century, Newton in the seventeenth century, Darwin, Freud, and genetic engineers in the nineteenth and twentieth centuries. Parallel to all of this have been developments toward greater individual freedom in the political sphere associated with the American and French Revolutions. More people came to realize that concepts like *good* and *justice* do not come fully prescribed from the Almighty, but vary in character from one cultural setting to another.[24] The status of Roman Catholic control over Western Europe weakened. France and then other countries gave citizenship to Jews. Even where they did not receive explicit rights, Jews began to leave their enclosed communities for new locales and cultural experiences.

Organizations sprang up to advocate different and contradictory ways of dealing with the new opportunities and residual problems of European Jewry: to learn Gentile languages and pursue a greater integration into a European nation; to learn Hebrew and prepare for migration to Palestine; and to promote Yiddish and keep the Jews where they were but as a distinct community that would pursue its interests within the framework of a European state. Many Jews became enthusiastic socialists, and some became explicitly humanistic, agnostic, atheistic, and anticlerical. Others were attracted to liberalism, or remained religious and aloof from secular issues. Among the religious, there were choices from Hasidic and anti-Hasidic congregations. Especially in Western Europe and North America, there were also Jewish religious variations from orthodoxy.[25]

Chronic Dispute in Israeli Politics

A fundamental feature of Israeli politics complicates the task of religious parties, or any other organized interest. Divisions among the Jews have created a situa-

tion where no political party has ever won a parliamentary majority. Every government since the founding of the state has been a coalition between parties that
seek to advance their own interests and frustrate others, even while they formally
govern together. Religious parties have increased their representation as a result
of the 1999 election, winning twenty-seven out of 120 seats. They have done
well in advancing some of their causes and holding back anti-religious efforts.
From their own perspective, however, the religious have never done well
enough. We return to the problems of determining "who is winning" relig-
ious-secular disputes in chapter 7, where we discuss the tactics of the religious
parties.

Dispute among the Religious

Orthodox and ultra-Orthodox movements unite in seeking to advance religious
interests, but also compete with one another. Competition among Orthodox and
ultra-Orthodox political parties ranges from mundane concerns to outdo one
another in patronage appointments to explicit and veiled insults directed against
one another's rabbis to violence and vandalism of one another's property.

The ultra-Orthodox SHAS and the Orthodox National Religious Party
(NRP) delayed confirmation of the government of Prime Minister Benjamin
Netanyahu over a dispute as to which of them would get to name the first minister of religions after they had agreed to rotate the position between them after
two years. (Israel's prime minister and Knesset serve for a maximum of four
years.) SHAS was operating an illegal radio station when the Ministry of Communications indicated that it would pursue a policy to regularize the multiplicity
of political, religious, and commercial stations without licenses. Suspicious
about who would be let in and left out, the parliamentary leader of SHAS threatened to bring down the government if other religious stations received broad-
casting licenses and his did not.[26] On the eve of the 1999 elections, the SHAS
chair of the Knesset Finance Committee said that he was holding up allocations
for institutions associated with the NRP, because the Ministry of Education,
controlled by an NRP minister, was limiting its allocations to schools associated
with SHAS.[27]

Orthodox and ultra-Orthodox rabbis have issued contrary rulings as to
whether it is permitted under Jewish law to move remains from one grave site to
another for the purposes of construction. One newspaper account included in its
headline, "Who Is He in the Eyes of the Burial Societies?" The message was that
one rabbi's pronouncement in support of moving remains would not convince
the rabbis who operate the burial societies.[28] The continuation of this story produced threats of violence between followers of rabbis taking different positions
with respect to the movement of graves, wall posters in religious neighborhoods
that referred to a rabbi who would permit moving the graves as a "whore," and

the hiring of security guards by one group of ultra-Orthodox who felt themselves in danger from another group of ultra-Orthodox.[29]

When the deputy minister of housing, affiliated with the ultra-Orthodox United Torah Judaism, indicated that a new neighborhood would not be designated for ultra-Orthodox families, activists in SHAS began signing up families. "Why should the voters of NRP be the only ones to benefit?" was the question asked by one of the organizers.[30]

During the summer of 1998, the newspaper of the NRP lined up with those politicians favoring the compulsory recruitment of students in religious academies to the military, while ultra-Orthodox papers opposed it strongly. An article in an ultra-Orthodox newspaper called the NRP paper an agent of the secular Satan, while the NRP paper claimed that one-half the prostitutes in Israel were graduates of ultra-Orthodox schools for girls, and that most of their customers were ultra-Orthodox men.[31]

Religion and Politics at Israel's Jubilee

The twinned occasions of Memorial Day for those killed in defense of Israel and Independence Day in 1998 provided several insights into religious and political dispute. As in the past, the days followed directly on one another on the fourth and fifth days in the Hebrew month of Iyar. Because the Hebrew calendar is lunar, its dates vary from one year to the next with respect to the secular calendar. In 1998 Memorial Day and Independence Day occurred from Tuesday sundown on the 28th of April through sundown on Thursday, the 30th. Insofar as this was the fiftieth Jubilee Anniversary of the state's independence and May 1 fell on a Friday, which has become a half-work day for virtually all of the public sector and much of the private sector, the government proclaimed an extra day of celebration. As a result, there was a long period from Tuesday evening through Saturday evening for religious and political issues to work themselves into a boil.

The country's fiftieth anniversary had a religious as well as nationalist flavor. According to the 25th chapter of Leviticus:

> Ye shall hallow the fiftieth year, and proclaim liberty throughout all the land unto all the inhabitants thereof: it shall be a jubilee unto you; and ye shall return every man unto his possession, and ye shall return every man unto his family.

A memorable feature of Jubilee Weekend was a clash between ultra-religious and secular sensitivities surrounding the central celebration in Jerusalem. The ultra-Orthodox deputy mayor of Jerusalem objected to a performance of the prestigious Bat Sheva dance troupe that included one scene of dancers stripping to their underwear while music and voices adapted a portion of a festive hymn sung in praise of the Lord as a supplement to the Passover seder (*Echad Mi Yodea*). The Orthodox NRP minister of education and culture sought a compromise. Negotiations about a change in the dance routine chaired by the president of Israel seemed to succeed the afternoon before the performance, but then broke down as the first events of the evening's program were getting underway. While television honored guests (Israel's president and prime minister, the chair of the Knesset, the vice president of the United States and their wives) being escorted to their seats, off-camera journalists reported changing sentiments about the compromise among members of the dance troupe. Ultimately the troupe's artistic director announced his resignation as a protest against censorship and the dancers left the site without performing. Then other artists scheduled for the evening dithered about their support for artistic freedom or the country's fiftieth anniversary. Some performed and others did not.

The scandal sent political and religious figures into action, with no clear indication which comments were solely political and which mixed political calculations with religious sentiments. Public figures seemed to position themselves with one eye to their primary community (religious or secular), and another eye to the party coalitions that were necessary. The ultra-Orthodox deputy mayor of Jerusalem said that the need to keep the holy city clean of secular trash was only part of a larger campaign that was necessary in a country where a majority could not recite the prayer that is central to Jewish rituals ("Hear O Israel, the Lord our God the Lord is One."). The secular left stood four square for freedom and against religious dictates. Politicians seeking a middle ground spoke against censorship, but in favor of nonoffensive performances at key national celebrations.

Media discussions revealed a range of opinion about the performance that was canceled. There was anything but an obvious or agreed interpretation of the artistic adaptation of the Passover hymn. Some secular and religious observers thought the dance inspired and uplifting, while others saw it as insulting to the tradition. One ultra-Orthodox position was that Jerusalem's deputy mayor had made a strategic error in raising the issue. He had thereby involved the ultra-Orthodox in secular Israelis' Independence Day, and risked making the state and its celebrations part of what is important to the ultra-Orthodox.

Tel Aviv's Jubilee celebration on Saturday evening after the end of Sabbath provided that city's mayor with an opportunity he could not miss. During the previous week he had suffered a set back in interparty maneuvers toward the next municipal election. Saturday night he served as master of ceremonies for a free concert in the park that attracted 150,000 people for a performance of the Israeli Philharmonic with Yitzhak Perlman and a number of other ranking stars. The evening's finale would be Tchaikovsky's 1812 Overture with cannon and fireworks. The mayor arranged a brief video snippet of the dance routine that had been canceled at the Jerusalem celebration. He reminded the crowd that Tel Aviv was the cultural capital of Israel. He overlooked the attractions of the musical program, and claimed that the huge crowd spread out on the lawn had come to identify with his protest against religious dictates. Two days later the mayor called a press conference and said that he would not run for another term in the municipality. He would form a new centrist party and become a candidate for prime minister. He emphasized the scandal of the dance troupe in his announcement, and indicated that he would campaign against religious dictates from the ultra-Orthodox. A month later, the *Christian Science Monitor* reviewed the mayor's moves, and concluded that he was an opportunist who so far had not found leading figures willing to support his candidacy.[32] As the national election campaign moved forward the then former mayor of Tel Aviv joined with three other figures to create a new Center Party. The former mayor did not become the party's candidate for prime minister, and his anti-religious inclinations did not stand up against his colleagues' desire to avoid offending religious voters. The Center Party's candidate for prime minister was photographed kissing the beard of the ultra-Orthodox figurehead of SHAS.

Some days after the Jubilee weekend, the Ashkenazi Chief Rabbi of Israel Israel Lau expressed himself. Lau is known as a humane individual who has used his office to help individuals who find themselves in unpleasant situations because of religious law. He also speaks out frequently in behalf of Jewish unity and accommodation between secular and religious Jews. In the case of the dance troupe, however, his posture was not friendly to artistic freedom. He cited reli-gious law against undressing in public, and said it was a religious duty to issue warnings about such violations. He noted that religious explanations about the Book of Job say that Job suffered because he had been an advisor of Pharaoh who did not warn Pharaoh against his evil actions. In response to this statement, the Knesset leader of the left-wing Meretz Party said that he doubted Job would agree with this commentary.[33]

The Jerusalem Foundation, created by former mayor Teddy Kollek and with a record of supporting cultural programs as well as refurbishing religious sites, announced that it would subsidize a performance of the dance in Jerusalem's largest concert hall as a statement against censorship.[34]

On the first workday after the long period of celebration, both religious and secular leaders spoke about the dangers of a *kulturkampf* and urged restraint. They also reiterated the positions of their camps with respect to the principal occurrence surrounding the dance troupe.

A week later another round of the *kulturkampf* began. An Israeli singer, who had been a soldier in the Israeli army and then had a sex-change operation, won the Eurovision international song competition. Critics argued as to whether the performance or the personal story of the artist was responsible for the success. The Israeli television account of the singer's victory was accompanied by footage of a celebration by transvestites and homosexuals in Tel Aviv. According to Eurovision rules, the next annual competition would be in Israel. The same deputy mayor of Jerusalem who led the campaign against the Bat Sheva dance troupe announced that he would not allow the Holy City to be dirtied by Eurovision. The response of Jerusalem's mayor was swift. Perhaps he feared being upstaged by Tel Aviv's claim to being the cultural capital. He overlooked his own long-standing alliance with the ultra-Orthodox and called the deputy mayor a chatterbox and his remarks stupid. He promised that the Jerusalem Municipality would not censor artistic expression, and that the next Eurovision competition would be in his city.[35] When interviewed on a nightly television news program, a Knesset member of SHAS said that it was forbidden to listen to a female singer, but that the winner of the Eurovision competition was not really a woman.[36]

On the Boundaries of Religion, Ethnicity, and Politics

As Israelis were preparing to celebrate the Jewish New Year in September 1998, several figures identified with movements of religious and not so religious Moroccans engaged in a frenzy of mutual accusations surrounding the blessings bestowed by an aged rabbi, Yitzhak Kaduri. A reader should be wary of reaching profound conclusions from the story, except to see yet another mixture of religion and politics, spirituality and self-interest, all in the context of competition for ethnic and/or religious leadership and votes. The antagonisms may be heightened by the nature of the Moroccan community, one of the largest among Israel's Jews. Many Moroccan families are poor and traditional Jews. Even those who acquired advanced education and entered prestigious occupations may be sensitive to their families having suffered poverty and a lack of respect at the hands of the European Jews who dominated Israel when they arrived in the 1950s. The community is open to political appeals that emphasize religiosity, traditional cultural values that are not necessarily religious, as well as a concern for social services, and a simpler but usually implicit message that Moroccans should vote for Moroccans.

Member of Knesset David Levi, formerly a minister and leading figure in Likud and more recently head of the Gesher party, claimed leadership of socially concerned but not necessarily religious Moroccans. Levi accused his ethnic and political competitors of exploiting the Rabbi Kaduri. According to Levi, the rabbi was so old and feeble that he did not know where he was taken and who he was blessing. Levi had a history of personal conflict with Prime Minister Benjamin Netanyahu. It did not take Netanyahu long to say that he drew inspiration from the rabbi, and that he found his mind clear. A newspaper photo showed the prime minister receiving a New Year's blessing from the rabbi. When Levi heard that Netanyahu had found the rabbi's mind clear, Levi said that it was a cause to doubt the prime minister's judgment on other matters.

SHAS leader Ariyeh Deri, whose own background and much of his following is ultra-Orthodox and Moroccan, led the charge against Levi. Deri asserted that Rabbi Kaduri was a holy man in full command of his faculties, took an active interest in issues of politics and public policy, and used his blessings with wisdom as well as compassion. Rabbi Ovadia Yosef, the spiritual leader of

SHAS, said that Levi's comments represented a "great sin and crime that cannot be forgiven." Individuals identified as close to Rabbi Kaduri said that David Levi's son had been refused when he asked for the rabbi's blessing as a candidate for mayor of his home town, and that David Levi's brother, also a member of Knesset, had sought the rabbi's blessing when he had a toothache. Yet another religious figure, the current head of a family dynasty of holy men with roots in Morocco, whose brother had led a now defunct ethnic-religious party in the Knesset, said that "they are making a circus of Kaduri." The NRP (Orthodox) minister of education urged limitations on the rabbi's political activities.[37]

Religion and Politics in the Run-Up to the 1999 Election

With the national election campaign already underway, issues of religion and democracy claimed their place on the national agenda. Leading ultra-Orthodox rabbis criticized the Supreme Court in the harshest of terms. Its justices, according to them, were engaged in a frontal assault on the Torah, and had already brought down the Lord's wrath on the people of Israel and perhaps the entire world. Rabbis called upon the faithful to resist the Court's intrusion in religious issues, in ways that recalled the mythic resistance of the Jews against ancient Greek proclamations that forbade circumcision and introduced pagan ceremonies into the Jerusalem Temple.[38]

The immediate issues were recent or pending decisions concerning non-Orthodox conversions to Judaism and the entry of non-Orthodox representatives to local religious councils (topics to be covered in chapter 6). Perhaps more important was the upcoming election, and the need for an issue to excite religious and traditional voters to support parties that would see to the preservation of Judaism. For the leadership of SHAS, there was the further problem of Ariyeh Deri, the party's leading parliamentarian and former interior minister. His first of perhaps three criminal trials for a series of alleged offenses was drawing to a close. SHAS leaders seemed intent on flexing their muscles in order to impress the judges trying the case and those on the Supreme Court in anticipation of an appeal.

Ultra-Orthodox leaders proclaimed a mass protest before the Supreme Court. An organization of law professors proclaimed a threat against the rule of law and democracy, and organized a counter-demonstration. The police began to assemble their forces in order to keep the groups apart, and to protect the Supreme Court building.

Security forces indicated that they were expanding further the protection of individual justices, which had already been increased as a result of earlier threats. Police and Justice Ministry officials indicated that they were examining the comments of the rabbi identified with SHAS for indications of indictable offenses with respect to incitement, rebellion, and insult of government officials. In response, SHAS politicians threatened revolution if the police moved against their rabbi. Secular parties took aim at what they termed religious extremism and fanaticism. For some, it was a time for outright conflict against the ultra-Orthodox, with violence if necessary, in order to protect law and democracy.

Caught in the middle were the Orthodox of the National Religious Party. The chief rabbis, traditionally aligned with the Orthodox but not the ultra-Orthodox, indicated support for the demonstration before the Supreme Court. However, leaders of the Knesset delegation of the NRP indicated their support for the Supreme Court, and their opposition to the demonstration.

Israel's president and prime minister pursued separate campaigns to establish a dialogue between Supreme Court justices and religious leaders, both with the hope of bringing about a cancellation of potentially explosive demonstrations and counter-demonstrations and returning the issues involved to the back burner of simmering but not boiling controversy.

The demonstration and counter-demonstration went forward with a great deal of media attention, the presence of some 2,000 police, dislocation of traffic in Jerusalem, but without untoward behavior. Ultra-Orthodox leaders claimed the presence of 600,000 of their followers, but this seemed to rely more on biblical imagery than an accurate number. By tradition 600,000 gathered at Mount Sinai to receive the Torah, but that is larger than conventional estimates of the entire ultra-Orthodox population in Israel. More modest estimates were 250,000 at the ultra-Orthodox demonstration, and 50,000 at the counter-demonstration.

The ultra-Orthodox had several advantages to explain their greater numbers. A sizable portion of the country's ultra-Orthodox live within walking distance of the demonstration site in Jerusalem. Moreover, the organizers tied up much of the country's available buses to transport their people from Bnei Brak and other ultra-Orthodox locales. By the time the leaders of the counter-demonstration began to organize, there were a limited number of buses that could be rented.

A few weeks later, Ariyeh Deri's trial ended with a verdict of guilty, and a prison sentence of four years that would be delayed pending appeals to the Supreme Court. Rabbis at the center of the SHAS establishment proclaimed Deri's innocence, and attributed the court's action to corruption in the Israeli Ministry of Justice and Courts. The media campaign of SHAS in the weeks before the election featured a united SHAS leadership behind Deri, portrayed as being hounded unjustly by an anti-religious establishment.

A Knesset committee began deliberating the suspension of Deri from the parliament, but the process was not completed before the election. Soon after the court issued its verdict and sentencing, the head of the left-of-center Meretz party condemned any willingness to deal with a convicted felon. It was not easy for the heads of other parties to deal with the situation. SHAS had a block of ten seats in the Knesset elected in 1996, and the intensity of its activists seemed capable of increasing its representation as a result of the current election. Most likely, SHAS would be an element in the post-election maneuverings to create a governing coalition. It took several days for the heads of Labor and Center parties to formulate a posture that would bar them from negotiating with Ariyeh Deri after the election, but would allow them to reach accommodations with his political party. Netanyahu proclaimed his support for the rule of law, and indicated that he would deal with Deri so long as the Supreme Court had not ruled finally on his appeal (a condition that might give him a year's grace). A few days later, Deri proclaimed his party's support for Netanyahu's candidacy.

Who Is a Religious Jew, and Who a Secular Jew?

The contrary stereotypes that religious and secular Israelis express about one another's success and the verbal warfare between religious and secular activists suggest two contrary camps. In reality, however, it is difficult to define the labels "religious" and "secular." The categories blur when we look at specific behaviors, or try to probe the meaning of behaviors for individuals.

While only some 20 percent of Israelis identify themselves as Orthodox or ultra-Orthodox, substantial majorities of Israelis observe at least some customs that can be called religious: a Sabbath meal with members of the family that includes lighting candles and traditional prayers, a Passover seder, fasting on Yom Kippur, and saying that their Jewishness is important to them. Substantial numbers claim to eat only kosher food.[39]

It is easier to raise questions about these findings than to find answers that are fully satisfying. Should the Sabbath meal or Passover *seder* enjoyed by Israelis who call themselves secular be categorized as part of the national culture as opposed to a religious ritual? And what about the extensive support of the Israeli military within the society, with Orthodox if not ultra-Orthodox activists investing the military with a quasi-religious function to protect the holy nation and guard the sacred land? Does this signify only that Israelis like many other nationalities are patriotic, or does it reflect the development of an aged religion to meet contemporary conditions?[40]

Israel's Yom Kippur presents its own fascinations for religious analysis. Airports and seaports close. There is no Israeli radio or television. Synagogues are crowded and road traffic virtually halts except for emergency vehicles. There is an awesome feeling of a nation honoring a sacred day. However, major streets in secular neighborhoods ring with the sounds of children playing and riding bicycles, skateboards, roller blading, and generally carousing on the streets where normally there is heavy traffic. Stores and automats renting videos do a brisk business prior to Yom Kippur, and there is international telephone and the Internet for those who want to remain in touch. When the national radio comes back on the air an hour after sundown, the first news is likely to report the number of children injured during the holy day, as well as the number of adults who took ill while fasting and had to be conveyed to hospital.

What Keeps Secular Jews in Judaism?

Numerous religious Gentiles have wondered about the staying power of the Jews. From a Christian perspective, the community went bad two millennia ago, and should long have conceded its error and disappeared into the universal faith. Even Jews wonder at their own persistence. Jewish comics thank God for choosing them as His people, but cite the problems involved and ask God to choose someone else.

A subset of Jewish wondering deals with the capacity of Jews to survive as a ruling people in their own land. The Israeli novelist and essayist A. B. Yehoshua notes that Judaism developed for more than two millennia in situations where its people were ruled by others, and that Judaic doctrines do not provide clear answers for Israeli Jews wanting to know how to rule non-Jews, especially in conditions of hostility and with the Promised Land at stake. There are reli-gious doctrines that grant rights and protection to non-Jews. But there are also doctrines that sanctify preferences for Jews and assert Jewish domination over the Land of Israel. Yehoshua laments that Israel's leaders have not learned to balance the contradictions. He asked, when he wrote thirty years into the Zionist experience, if Judaism is suitable only for the Diaspora.[41]

For religious Jews the question that heads this section is no issue, or borders on apostasy. Jews are the Chosen People, and must uphold their ancestors' agreement to honor the Lord's commandments. Yet we cannot overlook the large number of Israeli Jews who are secular. Their lifestyle suggests that they do not accept the burden of the ancient covenant. Even the outward appearance of being religious may tell us little of inner feelings. Jewish ethnicity may keep people identified with the community even if they reject Jewish religious doctrines that require or forbid various behaviors.

Inertia plays its role in Judaism as well as other religions. Most Jews are born into the community and most die in it. At least nominal loyalty is easier than rebellion, especially in the homogeneous population of Israel. Being a member of a threatened community contributes to group adherence. The socialization of school, national media, and military service reinforces adherence. The Holocaust, wars, and terror attacks provides more than enough cement to keep people in the community. For some, to be sure, the pressures associated with the same events push them away from Israel and away from Judaism.

Israeli Jews, like those of the Diaspora, draw inspiration for the long history of their people, their survival, and notable accomplishments. They cite Israel's achievements and those of Jews in the United States and other western countries. American Jews are better educated and enjoy higher incomes than virtually all other religious or ethnic groups in the country. They are greatly over-represented in distinguished occupations and as recipients of prestigious awards, despite being only a few decades removed from a condition when distinguished universities imposed quotas on Jewish applicants to their student bodies and let only the most select Jews onto their faculties.

Surely there must also be a contribution to the adherence of secular Jews from ancient doctrines. Notions of Chosen People, Promised Land, demands of the prophets for righteousness, and the sentiments of Psalms work their mystery on Gentiles of numerous denominations who look to the Hebrew Bible for inspiration. The ideas attract people who search for meanings that they cannot find from modern science and technology. If it is good enough for the Gentiles, it must also explain part of the continued affiliation shown by Jews who indicate by word or behavior that they are not religious. The ethnic element of Jewishness requires only that an individual not renounce the heritage. The lack of renunciation in itself signifies a bit of what others might call religiosity.

A Light unto the Gentiles

The significance of Israel and the Jews in the history of religion invites us to consider what issues concerned mostly with Judaism mean for religion generally. According to the Book of Isaiah, the Lord said that he will give Israel "for a light unto the Gentiles, that thou mayest be my salvation unto the end of the earth."[42] It would not exceed the flexible rules of biblical interpretation to read this to mean that what we learn about religion and politics in the Promised Land may help us understand parallel phenomena elsewhere.

What Are the Lessons to Be Learned from Israel with Respect to More General Issues of Religiosity?

First, we see that substantial numbers of people are prepared to believe what normal science indicates is unbelievable, and they curse those who question what they proclaim. The language used by religious Israelis against those who call themselves Jewish humanists, or secular Jews who would ride, purchase goods, or work on the Sabbath, is no less unpleasant than what some North American and European Christians use against those who they call ungodly or worshipers of the devil, or murderers for their support of abortion. The head of SHAS's rabbinical council said that he would "declare a celebration and throw a banquet the day that wicked woman Shulamit Aloni dies."[43] When Aloni headed the overtly secular Meretz party, her statements against religious leaders made her a symbol in their eyes for evil incarnate.

Outside of Israel, religious fanatics include cult members who murder one another and commit suicide in order to hasten their meeting with what they believe to be divine spaceships or other heavenly manifestations. Israel's extremists include the religious Jew who felt that Prime Minister Yitzhak Rabin should die for bargaining away parts of the Land of Israel, and other Jews who admire the killer.

Surveys routinely find sizable majorities in advanced, western societies who express a belief in God. Substantial numbers pray or attend religious services regularly, and believe that God has answered their prayers. It is no easy task deciding how to define conventional religion, or where to draw the line between religion, cult, and sect. One divide is between the established and the new, with the established including those once-new organizations like Christian Science, Mormons, and Jehovah's Witnesses, that have passed through at least one leadership transition from charismatic founders. A more simple division separates those who accept what the evaluator calls the cardinal principles of faith from those who do not. Some Christians use a standard like this to decide that Mormons, Jehovah's Witnesses, Christian Science, and Unitarian-Universalists are outside their camp.[44] Israel's Orthodox and ultra-Orthodox rabbis use a similar rule against Conservative and Reform Judaism. Ultra-Orthodox and Orthodox activists are even less well disposed to Reform or Conservative Jews than to Jews who are secular. Reform and Conservative activists are not indifferent to issues of practice and doctrine, but challenge the learning of Orthodox rabbis that has represented their status among believing Jews for two millennia.

There can be no doubt that God is alive and well, at least in the beliefs of most people. The Almighty is also a factor in the politics of democracies whose economies are well developed and whose populations highly educated. Even where the churches are mostly empty, as in Scandinavia, public funds support the clergy, national flags carry a religious symbol, people express affiliation with a religion, and many say that they believe in God.[45]

A second lesson to be learned from Israeli materials is that only a minority of those counted as religious adherents may be systematic and serious in their beliefs. While 79 percent of Israelis are Jews, only some 20 percent of them are Orthodox or ultra-Orthodox. Perhaps most people in Israel and elsewhere carry a religious identity that is only nominal, and are not schooled in the details of doctrine that concern clerics and scholars. We do not know how many of the Orthodox and ultra-Orthodox remain in their communities because it is the easiest way to live and remain with their families. Students of other religious traditions have commented about the unknown numbers who adhere to a faith in order to be on the safe side.[46] Perhaps there is a heaven and hell, or at least some places more and less pleasant where we will spend eternity. Death remains an unpleasant mystery. The political parallel to this routine affiliation are the traditional supporters of political parties who do not probe too deeply into the candidates' records.

Individual Americans and Israelis, as well as Irish, Italians, and Spaniards pay more than lip service to the Almighty. Yet except for a very few who would kill in order to accomplish their view of God's will, religious extremism is not a public problem in democratic societies. Likewise, overt and enthusiastic atheism is passé. The problems associated with theism no longer draw wide interest. Religion surrounds us. It demands a place on the public agenda, and intense advocates assure a certain level of noisy debate. Yet religious claims of revealed truth do not preoccupy a majority of voters or public officials.

Chapter 4

The Religious and Political Significance of the Promised Land

A state's territorial boundaries are implicitly political. The issue affects the reach of the government, the classification of individuals as citizens or something else, and relations with neighboring countries. In the case of Israel, the issue is also religious. National boundaries are among the most difficult items on the problematic agenda of negotiations toward peace.

This chapter deals with those elements in the Judaism of Genesis that express an adherence to people and place. As we shall see, however, the discussion cannot proceed far without reference to other elements of Judaism that are more spiritual and universal.

Very early in the Hebrew Bible there is a promise of progeny and land.

> Look now toward heaven, and tell the stars, if thou be able to number them: and he said unto him, So shall thy seed be. . . . I am the LORD that brought thee out of Ur of the Chaldees, to give thee this land to inherit it . . . from the river of Egypt unto the great river, the river Euphrates.

In the same portion there is a warning of problems to come. "Know this for certain, that your descendants will be aliens living in a land that is not theirs."[1]

The Book of Joshua claims the total conquest of the Land by the Israelites after the Exodus from Egypt, but indicates that foreigners remained among them. The Book of Judges reinforces the image of an incomplete conquest and describes foreigners who continued to threaten the Israelites.[2] The Israelites were chronically threatened by more powerful empires. There were exiles after conquests by Assyria and Babylon. The Book of Jeremiah reports that the prophet was taken to Egypt along with a group of Judeans after Jerusalem fell to the Babylonians.[3] Jeremiah also urges the exiles to build houses and seek the welfare of their place.[4] Roman forces took many slaves and exiled other Jews after the end of the period described in the Hebrew Bible. And from time to time there were voluntary migrations of Jews who went abroad in search of opportunities.[5]

The Books of Ezra and Nehemiah describe the return of Babylonian exiles, but their authors seem to have relied more on wish than reality. Most of the exiles may have remained in Babylon, and most of the world's Jews may have lived in the Diaspora during the period of the Second Temple (537 BCE - 70 CE).[6] One estimate is that one million Jews lived in Judea during the reign of Herod (37 - 4 BCE), while four million lived in Syria, Asia Minor, Babylon, and Egypt.[7] Another estimate is that only 10 or 20 percent of the Jews actually lived in Judea during the lifetime of Jesus.[8]

What Is Promised Land?

Like other concepts central to religious belief, the Land of Israel is subject to varying interpretation. With respect to the designation of territory, the Book of Genesis itself provides several options. The borders mentioned in chapter 15: "from the river of Egypt unto the great river, the river Euphrates" are not precise enough to guide a surveyor. Is the river of Egypt the Nile, or perhaps only an outlet to the sea at El Arish? The difference between the two is a matter of 100 kilometers or more along the Mediterranean Sea, depending on which outlet of the Nile is chosen.

The problem becomes more complex by the 17th chapter of Genesis, when the Lord promises to Abraham "all the land of Canaan" without setting out the boundaries. The 34th chapter of Numbers provides enough clues to keep historians and cartographers busy matching places with the lands of ancient peoples.

> Command the children of Israel, and say unto them, When ye come into the land of Canaan; this is the land that shall fall unto you for an inheritance, even the land of Canaan with the coasts thereof. Then your south quarter shall be from the wilderness of Zin along by the coast of Edom, and your south border shall be the outmost coast of the salt sea eastward. And your border shall turn from the south to the ascent of Akrabbim, and pass on to Zin. and the going forth thereof shall be from the south to Kadesh-barnea, and shall go on to Hazar-addar, and pass on to Azmon. And the border shall fetch a compass from Azmon unto the river of Egypt, and the goings out of it shall be at the sea. And as for the western border, ye shall even have the great sea for a border. This shall be your west border. And this shall be your north border. From the great sea ye shall point out for you mount Hor. From mount Hor ye shall point out your border unto the entrance of Hamath; and the goings forth of the border shall be to Zedad. And the border shall go on to Ziphron, and the goings out of it shall be at Hazar-enan. This shall be your north. And ye shall point out your east border from Hazar-enan to Shepham. And the coast shall go down from Shepham to Riblah, on the east side of Ain; and the border shall descend, and shall reach unto the side of the sea of Chinnereth eastward. And the

border shall go down to Jordan, and the goings out of it shall beat the salt sea; this shall be your land with the coasts thereof round about.[9]

The eastern boundary of the Promised Land indicated here (the east shore of the Chinnereth, i.e., the Sea of Galilee), is far short of the Euphrates as promised in Genesis and somewhat less than what modern Israel has managed to acquire.

The entire Israelite enterprise never amounted to much in a material sense. The Jewish homeland was poor and marginal. The description recorded in the Book of Numbers of a land "flowing with milk and honey"[10] was a judgment made by spies who had come from the desert. The Judaic heartland was in the mountains, away from more powerful people along the coast. It lacked an abundance of water and rich soils. It never developed the agricultural wealth or the large populations associated with the Nile River of Egypt or the Tigris and Euphrates Rivers of the eastern empires. It also lagged behind other empires in the sophistication of its governmental structure and administrative controls, and it is affirmed that "the country was always a cultural backwater, impoverished artistically as well as economically."[11]

The location of the Land of Israel was problematic and invited invasion. It was on a land bridge between Asia Minor, Mesopotamia, Africa, and Arabia, "a meeting place between continents and civilizations."[12] It was the corridor through which Egypt attacked Assyria, Babylon, or Persia, or by which those powers attacked Egypt. It was on the route that the Phoenicians used in trading with Africa, Arabia, and India via the Red Sea. Caravans crossed the land from Mesopotamia to Egypt, and from Arabia to Asia Minor. The Israelites were mostly set upon by others and concerned to protect what they had. Usually they paid tribute to one or another imperial capital. Occasionally they sought to play off one empire against another. This led to national disaster on more than one occasion.

Joseph Heller dealt with the problem of geography in his novel, *God Knows*. He has David proclaim: "I had taken a kingdom the size of Vermont and created an empire as large as the state of Maine!"[13]

As might be expected, modern Jews do not stand united in their view of the Promised Land. Most committed are those who are members of spin-offs from the movement founded by the late Rabbi Meir Kahane, the right wing of the National Religious Party (NRP) and the movement that calls itself Gush Emunim (bloc of the faithful). They are highly represented among the Jews who settled in the West Bank and Gaza after the 1967 war. Some of the most vocal describe acquisition of the Land of Israel as integral to the salvation of the Jewish people, as well as their own material safety, and oppose all territorial concessions to Arabs. A few of these people express the view that the Arabs are descendants of the Amalekites, subject to the biblical curse demanding their total annihilation.

Not all supporters of the NRP, affiliates of Gush Emunim, or settlers in the West Bank and Gaza think alike. Individuals balance Judaic norms of land against Judaic norms of peace and reciprocity. Some are willing to trade land for firm guarantees of peace, while others are anxious to rid Israel of control over land heavily populated by non-Jews. They vary in the assurances of peace they are willing to accept in exchange for land. Rabbi Yehuda Amital is dean of the Har Etzion yeshiva in Gush Etzion, located in the West Bank between Bethlehem and Hebron, and prominent in a movement of religious Jews that is left of center on territorial issues (Meimad: The Movement for Religious Zionist Renewal). He sees the deliverance associated with Zionism as strong enough to tolerate the removal of a few Jewish settlements that will be done for the sake of peace. He speaks moderately and rejects the dire prediction of crisis. A small proportion of the settlers may have problems, he says, but most will adapt to the new reality. He urges settlement leaders to discard delusions that they will overthrow the government, and to work within the framework of the agreement with the Palestinians to include as many settlements as possible into the boundaries of what will become a new map of Israel. For him, the spiritual values associated with the Land of Israel are more important than where exactly within the Land the Jews can settle.[14]

While the Land of Israel is an issue of intense religious and political importance to supporters of the NRP, it seems only secondary to the ultra-Orthodox. Part of the explanation may be political competition. Issues that the Orthodox of NRP support, the ultra-Orthodox may oppose. Ultra-Orthodox doubt that the Lord's hand is apparent in the work of Zionists, including the creation of the Israeli state or its rule over the Land of Israel. Many ultra-Orthodox are explicitly fixed in the attitudes, interpretations of law, and dress which they say prevailed when their congregations were founded in central and eastern Europe as much as 400 years ago. Most of them came to Israel not out of nationalist passion, but because the Nazis destroyed their academies and killed most of their people in Europe.

Some ultra-Orthodox rabbis have been explicit in saying that peace is of greater weight in religious law than land, and have sided with the peacemakers. Others have taken positions closer to the right wing of the NRP, without indicating any affiliation with Zionism per se.

Beyond the overtly religious camps secular Israeli Jews appear at all points of the spectrum involving land and peace. Their arguments may be nationalist, but not explicitly religious (assuming the two streams can be separated in the case of Jews). Among the claims of those called "hawks" are:

- We took it. It is ours.
- The 1967 war was defensive. Why should we give back what they risked when they sought to annihilate us?

- It is important for our defense.
- We cannot trust the Arabs to honor peace agreements.

Reflecting other perspectives are positions no less nationalist. And because they concern Israel, they also carry at least a tinge of religiosity:

- Israel will suffer a loss of democratic and social morality if it must govern a hostile population of non-Jews.
- It is more efficient, in the long run, to rid ourselves of territory that we cannot govern easily or well.
- Arabs hate us, and go over quickly to violence. It's best for us to separate from them and the land they occupy.

Problems and Opportunities Associated with the Holy City

Jewish sentiments toward Jerusalem are no less complex than those concerned with the entire Promised Land. Like the Promised Land, the issue of Jerusalem has roots in religion and impinges on contemporary politics.

Jewish connections with the city begin with David's defeat of the Jebusites and his establishment of a home and the center of his kingdom, as described in the Books of First and Second Samuel. The Bible credits David's son, Solomon, with turning Jerusalem into a world center of opulence and wisdom. The Book of First Kings provides an idealized description of great wealth and domestic harmony:

> Solomon ruled over all the kingdoms from the river unto the land of the Philistines and as far as the frontier of Egypt; they paid tribute and were subject to him all his life . . . All through his reign Judah and Israel continued at peace, every man under his own vine and fig-tree, from Dan to Beersheba.[15]

In reality, both the Promised Land and Jerusalem were less central to the world than they are described in the Hebrew Bible. One writer expresses their marginal character by describing Babylon's destruction of Jerusalem as a routine maneuver to punish rebellious peoples on the borders of its empire.[16] From the perspective of the Jews, that routine act was the greatest of historical catastrophes. Another writer states that Alexander the Great "incidentally wrest Judea . . . away from Persia" as part of his eastern conquests.[17] For the Jews, the Hellenization of Jerusalem after Alexander's conquest was a period of profound historical significance and a national trauma.

Despite its chronic weakness, Jerusalem was a symbol of hope. After the desolation left by the Assyrians in the northern kingdom in 722, the prophet Isaiah saw Zion (Jerusalem) as the salvation of God's people.

> Your country is desolate, your cities lie in ashes. Strangers devour your land before your eyes. . . . Only Zion is left, like a watchman's shelter in a vineyard . . . In days to come the mountain of the Lord's house shall be set over all other mountains. . . . All the nations shall come streaming to it . . . out of Jerusalem comes the word of the Lord.[18]

Assyria weakened by the end of the seventh century BCE, but the geopolitical setting of Judah remained unenviable. It became subject to the competition between Egyptian and Babylonian regimes. The prophet Jeremiah perceived that Babylon was the coming power, and that Judah had better align itself with the winner. He cursed King Jehoiakim and his court for exploiting the people economically, and introducing pagan observances to the holy city. Jeremiah's prophecy of what Babylon would do to Jerusalem if it did not pay tribute to that power (perhaps written after Babylon's conquest) ranks among the goriest sections of the Hebrew Bible.

> Says the Lord . . . I will make Jerusalem heaps, a lair of jackals . . . the cities of Judah a desolation, without an inhabitant.[19] (Jerusalem will be) an astonishment, and a hissing; every one that passeth thereby shall be astonished and hiss because of all the plagues thereof . . . (the city's residents will) eat the flesh of their sons.[20]

Jewish miseries at the loss of Jerusalem occupy the entire Book of Lamentations, said by religious commentators to be the work of Jeremiah. "How solitary lies the city, once so full of people! Once great among nations, now become a widow; once queen among provinces, now put to forced labor!"[21] The 137th Psalm was written from the perspective of the exiles in Babylon who yearned for Jerusalem. It has been read over the years in numerous other Diaspora communities.

> By the rivers of Babylon we sat down and wept when we remembered Zion. Our captors called on us to be merry: "Sing us one of the songs of Zion." How could we sing the Lord's song in a foreign land? If I forget you, O Jerusalem, let my right hand wither away; let my tongue cling to the roof of my mount if I do not remember you, if I do not set Jerusalem above my highest joy.

Ambiguity Can Help

As in the case of the entire Promised Land, Israeli Jews express widely different perspectives about Jerusalem. Many reject any compromise about the city. It is holy, even in the eyes of individuals who are secular, and vital for Israel's pride and security. Ultra-Orthodox, in contrast, may be oblivious to what goes on so long as they are allowed to pursue their religious lives within neighborhoods built around religious academies and settled almost entirely by ultra-Orthodox families.

Part of the complexity of Jerusalem lies in its numerous meanings. This renders the city problematic, but also provides opportunities. Multiple designations facilitate the use of ambiguity as a coping mechanism, even as it makes it impossible to find any clear or absolute resolution of the tensions. This section will describe the blurred designations for the Holy City. The issue straddles the boundaries of religion and politics, and shows their commonalities in a place of special religious and political significance.

The names for Jerusalem include Holy City, City of Peace, Spiritual City, Everlasting City, City on the Hill, Zion, Heavenly City, Jerusalem Above. These evoke messianic aspirations of a time to come, or an end of time when a messiah will come, or return, and put things right. Loosely defined areas labeled East Jerusalem, West Jerusalem, New Jerusalem, Arab and Jewish Jerusalem carry meanings that are more nationalistic and political than religious. East Jerusalem and Arab Jerusalem on the one hand, and West Jerusalem, New Jerusalem, and Jewish Jerusalem on the other hand, refer to areas that Jordan and Israel controlled during 1948-67 between Israel's War of Independence and the Six Day War. The same terms are used for Arab and Jewish residential areas of the present Israeli municipality, even though there are Jewish areas in the eastern part of the city, and Arab areas in the west. The Old City is surrounded by a wall and seems to be well defined. However the Jewish, Muslim, Christian, and Armenian Quarters within the Old City have been dynamic and are subject to different specifications. Some think of Mount Zion as part of the Old City, even though it is outside the walls. And the walls themselves varied in their location several times between 1000 BCE and their most recent reconstruction about 1540 CE.

Not all of Jerusalem is holy. Only scattered parts would seem to justify dispute at the highest level of intensity. Israel has provided de facto control to Muslim authorities over what they call Haram Esh Sharif (the Jews' Temple Mount), and has left the Church of the Holy Sepulcher to a number of Christian organizations that have been more or less tolerant of one another. Some Muslim fanatics continue to charge Israel with atrocities on account of the clearing in 1967 of a plaza before the Western Wall, but most of the world seems likely to accept that as part of an evolving status quo.

Jordanian Prime Minister Dr. Abd-al-Salam al-Majali spoke about the several meanings of "Jerusalem" and hinted at what they offer to those who could determine its future by negotiations. He said: "The word Jerusalem is derived from sanctity or places of worship. . . . Political Jerusalem is different from the religious Jerusalem that is sacred to the three religions. Thus, a political solution is possible."[22] Such honesty and modesty is not typical in the setting of Jerusalem.

The ethnic picture throughout metropolitan Jerusalem is mostly Arab to the north, east, and south of the Israeli municipality, and within the municipality in the neighborhoods to the east and north of the Old City; and mostly Jewish in the western and southern parts of the municipality. However, there are pockets of Jewish settlement in the area that is mostly Arab and pockets of Arab settlement in the area that is mostly Jewish.

The on-and-off development of a new Jewish neighborhood called "Mount Homa," became a matter of controversy in 1997, partly because it was to be built on what some called "Arab land," and partly because it would add a Jewish neighborhood within the area of Arab settlements that Palestinians saw as assuring a geographical continuity with their more eastern territory. From another perspective, however, Mount Homa would be just one more Jewish settlement on land that in a previous regime had been under Jordanian control, and one more spot on a map characterized by a mixture of patterns showing Jewish and Arab residential areas alongside and between one another.

The Israeli government has expanded the city it controls. The 1949 boundaries followed the cease-fire lines that ended the 1948 war. Israel extended its municipal boundaries to the west in 1952 and again in 1963 to include developments for a population that grew by more than 96 percent between 1948 and 1967. Soon after the 1967 war, the Israeli government increased the municipal area from 38,000 to 108,000 *dunams* (1 *dunam* = 1,000 square meters). Included within the new boundaries were the Old City, Arab neighborhoods to the north of the city walls and a number of Arab settlements immediately to the east of the Old City, as well as extensive open areas to the north and south formerly under Jordanian control but outside Jordan's boundaries for Jerusalem. The new city boundaries included unpopulated areas that would lend themselves new housing for Jews and industrial development. The most recent annexation in 1992 added another 13 percent to the city's area. It was undertaken to facilitate building for Jewish residents, away from areas likely to provoke Arab opposition.

There is no obvious or natural meaning of "Jerusalem" in its variety of concepts and geographical designations. The boundaries prior to the 1967 war are no more natural or suitable for setting the city's future than those of any time prior to 1967 or since then. However, the pluralities of conception and borders present as many opportunities as problems to Israelis, Palestinians, and others who would help them negotiate its near-term future.

Especially appealing is that most amorphous of concepts and places: metropolitan Jerusalem. Like many other urban places, Jerusalem draws workers, shoppers, and visitors from smaller cities, towns, and villages in its periphery. Metropolitan Jerusalem spills over the as-yet unclear boundary between Israeli and Palestinian territory.

Keeping things ambiguous while accommodating some demands of one's adversaries is a way of coping when it seems impossible to reach mutually agreed, precise, and clear-cut decisions. Untangling Arab and Jewish settlements and neighborhoods in the small space provided by Jerusalem and its environs is likely to foil the most clever cartographers. Moreover, it seems that both Arab and Jewish communities will profit from continued economic exchanges. Thus, even success in separating some of the residents —were it to occur—will come up against interdependence for commerce, medical care, visits to religious sites, and the interactions necessary between officials of Israeli and Palestinian authorities.

Both Israeli and Palestinian officials have mixed far-reaching declarations of their minimum demands with a pragmatic acceptance of realities that, upon inspection, seem to clash with those demands. Palestinian officials make pronouncements about Arab land, but they show no signs of expecting Israel to vacate areas occupied in 1967 that are now home to more than 130,000 Jews. The Israeli regime has insisted that it controls a united city, but has accepted less than full sovereignty at sensitive points. Muslim and Christian religious authorities have been given de facto control over their holy places. Israeli authorities have prevented Jewish prayers on what Jews call the Temple Mount in order to avoid offending Muslim sensitivities for what they call Haram Esh Sharif.

The real intentions of Prime Minister Benjamin Netanyahu during his period in office from 1996 to 1999 were unclear, but that is in the nature of politics in general and the recent history of Jerusalem in particular. Long assumed to be the most intractable issue of the Israeli-Arab conflict, Jerusalem may have been solved, quietly, more or less. The problem is that the solution may fall apart if Israelis or Palestinians boast about it, or even declare it accomplished. It is something that has to be worked on and nurtured, perhaps forever. This place of intense spirituality and its history of bloodshed will test politicians' capacity to cope. The measure of success is not overt accomplishment, but rather in not making things worse.

The situation is delicate in the extreme. Intemperate politicians of all Israeli and Palestinian factions may be unable or unwilling to see the realities and possibilities. Activists in both nations aspire to place the best above the good, and have tried to end the peace process with one provocation or another. There is no shortage of foreign actors wanting to cause trouble in order to serve their own agendas, or naively anxious to make things right in the Holy Land.

The makings of an ambiguous peace begin with the status quo. Those who proclaim Israeli exploitation of a Palestinian population miss several important points. The Arab residents of East Jerusalem benefit from Israeli social programs (medical insurance, child support payments, old age pensions) as well as reliable public utilities. They are also left with substantially more community autonomy than either Israeli or Palestinian authorities are willing to admit. These include:

- Israeli officials have allowed Palestinian businessmen and professionals to practice under Jordanian licenses and the supervision of Arab associations, rather than force them to accept Israeli licensing and the rules of an Israeli Chamber of Commerce or professional societies.
- Palestinian residents of the city vote in elections for the Palestinian Authority.
- Municipal and national education authorities fund schools in the Palestinian sector and formally appoint the teachers and administrators, but consult with representatives of the Palestinian Authority on issues of importance to them.
- Israeli health officials report that they limit their supervision over a major East Jerusalem hospital that has been taken over by Palestinian authorities.
- Arabs living in East Jerusalem report problems among themselves to Palestinian authorities, and bring disputes to traditional Muslim courts for adjudication.
- Israeli insistence that the Palestinian police not operate in Jerusalem are at odds with reports that Palestinian opponents of the PLO have been picked up in the city by Palestinian security operatives and transported elsewhere for detention and investigation.[23]
- Despite shrill calls for a totally Israeli administration in Jerusalem, including the closure of Orient House and other institutions of the Palestinian Authority, Israeli authorities have looked the other way with respect to implementation.
- Hathem Abdel Kader, a member of the Palestinian Legislative Council, provoked an incident by receiving constituents in his Jerusalem home. To members of the Israeli Cabinet, this was a step on the way to a Palestinian capital in Jerusalem. The Israeli minister of security reached an accord in which Kader said that he would not conduct business of the Palestinian Authority, per se, in Jerusalem. The "policy" being followed seemed to resembled that of the United States military with respect to homosexuals: we won't ask; you don't tell.[24]
- According to some reports, Palestinians are building a structure for their parliament right over the boundary of the Israeli municipality. For some Israeli officials, it was ideal. The Palestinians could say that they had a capital in Jerusalem. Israel could accept the new fact, but would not have to concede the point. It was not in their Jerusalem. Right-wing Israeli activists ob-

jected. They perceived that the building proved the duplicity of Netanyahu. The new building was closer to the Western Wall than the Israeli Knesset. The prime minister was dividing Jerusalem. Palestinians also had a problem with the building. Ardent nationalists saw it as betrayal. Arafat was agreeing on a capital only in the suburbs of Jerusalem, and not in the city itself. Arafat waffled. PLO sources said that the building was not the parliament. It was a public facility. Perhaps a university. Then it was said to be for Arafat's offices.

The status quo fails numerous tests of justice. Neither Israelis nor Palestinians realize all of their national or religious aspirations. Yet policymakers can profit from a slogan used some years ago in one of Israel's campaigns in behalf of road safety. The message was not to insist on all one's rights when an accident is imminent. Don't be right, be smart!

History Repeats Itself, with Modifications

Geographic realities seem to have returned to Israel from its distant past, with some of the same effects. Not only is the location of modern Israel largely identical with that of its historical antecedent, but much of what else that is parallel between modern and ancient Israel is linked, either directly or indirectly, to the common place. As in the past, characteristics of the place contribute to insecurity amidst chronic disputes. Most of the world's Jews live outside of Israel, and show no signs of moving to their homeland. The Jewish country depends on great powers that take an unusual interest in its affairs. In both ancient and modern times, there has been a diverse population and conflicts between Jews and non-Jews, as well as between cosmopolitan and zealous Jews.

Israelis exhibit a style of policy advocacy that resembles that of the biblical prophets. We can argue if the trait derives from religious or cultural sources. Prominent individuals criticize in the sharpest of terms behavior that departs from what they see as the appropriate path of history. Modern critics who gain a wide hearing differ from the biblical prophets in not claiming to be speaking for the Lord, but they resemble the prophets in threatening national catastrophe if their advice is not accepted.

The late Yehoshafat Harkabi was head of military intelligence, and became professor of International Relations at the Hebrew University of Jerusalem. He warned Israelis against those who revere the heroic religiosity and nationalism of the Bar Kokhba Rebellion against the Romans in 132-35 CE. To him, they overlook the virtually total destruction of Jewish life in the region of Judea following the rebellion.[25]

According to Harkabi, Bar Kokhba was guilty of irrational warfare that was bound to end in disaster. He failed to take account of the prevailing peace in the

Roman Empire, the capacity of the Empire to focus massive resources in squelching the rebellion, and the Romans' concern not to let a rebellion against the Empire go unpunished. By appearance, Harkabi was a secular Jew. Yet he evoked the Almighty in his writing. He thereby testified to the overlap between religion and politics, and the problems in deciding what is a political statement and what is a religious one.

> It is as though God himself had said to the Jewish people, "Since, in your anger at Hadrian's intention to erect a shrine on my holy mountain, you showed no compassion for the lives of my children in pursuing the Bar Kokhba Rebellion, I have decreed that the Temple Mount not be in the your hands."[26]

According to Harkabi, modern fanatics are the nationalistic and religious Jews who would decide by themselves that the West Bank will be Israel's possession. [27]

> The contention that without ruling the West Bank Israel cannot survive weakens Israel's very right to exist . . . such a stance may conjure up and inject new life into the old anti-Semitic image of Jews' claiming for themselves exclusive rights.

Harkabi predicted disaster if the zealots do not stop, or if they are not stopped by more reasonable Israelis. [28]

> The existence of the Jewish people is not a given. . . . Our deeds and our blunders will have considerable impact not only on the fate of those who dwell in Israel, but in a large measure on the entire Jewish people. Having chosen statehood, our destiny is, to a considerable degree, in our own hands, more than at any time since Bar Kokhba. This new situation demands not myths, but sobriety, much self-criticism, and severe critiques of the historical circumstances in which we find ourselves.

The late Yeshayahu Leibowitz was a religious Jew whose prophecy resembled that of the ancients in challenging both the religious and secular establishments. Leibowitz began to warn Israelis about the moral costs of military occupation soon after the end of the Six-Day War in June 1967. To him, it would be impossible to realize Jewish values in a binational state, especially where the Jews are military occupiers. He directed his harshest tones at religious and nationalist Jews who advocated the settlement of Jews in the occupied territories or the absorption of those territories into Israel. He projected a scenario of continued Jewish-Arab conflict, and a brutalizing of the Jewish state by those who seek to achieve an upper hand by force. "Internally (Israel) will become a state . . . with concentration camps for people like me, and externally it will sink into apocalyptic wars with the whole Arab world from Kuwait to Morocco."[29]

Limits on the Comparison of Modern Israel
with the Ancient Country

We can pursue a comparison between modern and ancient Israel only so far. The condition of the Jews now is better than at any time since the collapse of the kingdom ruled by David and Solomon in 927 BCE. Lest this sound too sanguine for the realities of the Middle East, it is written against 3,000 years of gloomier history.

Despite chronic tensions among the Jews of modern Israel, they have stopped short of the all-or-nothing arrogance that marked ancient disputes. A model of how not to behave appears in I Kings. Jeroboam spoke as the head of a northern delegation to Rehoboam, who was Solomon's son and designated successor. "Your father laid a cruel yoke upon us; but if you will now lighten the cruel slavery he imposed on us and the heavy yoke he laid on us, we will serve you."[30]

Rehoboam's response is a classic example of disdain for accommodation. "My father made your yoke heavy; I will make it heavier. My father used the whip on you; but I will use the lash."[31]

The northern region's declaration of independence was succinct. In this passage from I Kings, the reference to David is the southern kingdom of Judah, which had been the base of David's power. "What share have we in David? We have no lot in the son of Jesse. Away to your homes, O Israel; now see to your own house, David."[32]

Contemporary Jews' learning from this history is both religious and political. The source of this example from 1,027 BCE in sacred texts gives it weight among the religious who would be accommodating with respect to Israel's neighbors and secular Jews. The central role in Jewish history of the ancient division of the kingdoms and their subsequent weakness also serves as warning for secular nationalists.

The usually moderate *Economist* waxed eloquently just before Israel's fiftieth anniversary celebration.[33]

> Israel has much to be proud of. Not the least of its achievements is survival itself, a feat that could not be, and was not, taken for granted for much of its life. It has prospered, too, in spite of the continuing heavy burden of defense . . . the Jewish state has remained true to the democratic ideals on which it was founded. . . . Lastly, Israel has fulfilled much of the Zionist dream of reuniting the scattered Jewish people in their biblical homeland.

The modern state is a democracy with an elected government rather than a monarchy or theocracy ruled by a high priest. Political change has been orderly in modern Israel, without the killings that marked the ruling families of biblical

Israel. The vast majority of the modern population lives in urban apartments or suburban cottages rather than village huts. Most wage earners are involved in the provision of services or industrial activity. Agriculture is the work of a small minority, and is done mostly by collective settlements (kibbutzim and moshavim) rather than by individual peasants. For education, health care, and income security the modern Israeli family looks to a sophisticated state, rather than to itself.

Modern Israel has been stronger militarily than its immediate neighbors. The great powers of today are not Israel's neighbors. This difference provides modern Israel with more room for maneuver in international politics than its predecessor.

The military hardware available to modern Israel is vastly different from that of ancient times. Israel has used sophisticated weapons to compensate for its disadvantages in population size and economic wealth. Yet what Israel has its enemies can acquire. The day may come when Israelis may wish that the available weaponry would revert to the cumbersome tools of old that could only kill one person at a time.

Modern technology facilitates communication between Israel, the Diaspora, and friendly governments, and allows the rapid mobilization of whatever help may be forthcoming. Of course, the globalization of politics and economics does not only help the Jews. The enemies of Israel also have friends throughout the world, as well as economic resources and political appeals that they use to cement their own alliances.

Attitudes and political behaviors differ from those of ancient times. The Jewish people have seen two millennia of miserable history. Israeli leaders are trying to find a way amidst their difficulties. Jewish civil wars, false messiahs, statelessness, and the Holocaust lessen the hope for heavenly intervention in Israel's behalf, and lessen the tendency of prophetic-like social critics to elevate the temperature of policy debates by claiming to speak in God's name.

Benefits and Problems Associated with the Promised Land

The concept of Promised Land is not an unmixed set of problems. It provides part of the cement that has held the Jewish people together through three millennia of difficult history. It is central to religious doctrines that religious and not-so-religious Jews call upon as a guide or as a source of strength and hope in adversity. The Promised Land is also responsible for the interest and support that Gentiles and their governments provide to Israel. The nineteenth-century American explorer Edward Robinson expressed a view said to be especially widespread among Protestants, in keeping with the centrality of the Bible in their own history: "From the earliest childhood I had read of and studied the localities of this sacred spot; now I beheld them with my own eyes; and they all seemed familiar to me, as if the realization of a former dream."[34]

Church historian Philip Schaf expressed a concern for both the place and its Judaic occupants. "The scene at the Wailing Place was to me touching and pregnant with meaning. God has no doubt reserved this remarkable people, which like the burning bush is never consumed, for some great purpose before the final coming of our Lord."[35]

One can argue several explanations through an entire volume as to why Great Britain, France, the United States, Germany, and other countries have provided military, technical, political, or financial assistance to Israel. Israel's friends may argue that the help has never been enough or never unconnected with unpleasant quid pro quo's. However, Israel has received more than the average country's share of outsiders' interest and support. Somewhere in the donors' environment has been a Christian attachment to the Holy Land.

Gentile affection is not only that of outsiders admiring a view. There is a noticeable element of possessiveness that hints at the possibility of intervention. The Archbishop of York expressed his sense of affinity in the middle of the nineteenth century:

> This country of Palestine belongs to you and me, it is essentially ours. . . . It was given to the father of Israel . . . that land has been given unto us. It is the land from which comes news of our redemption. It is the land to which we turn as the fountain of all our hopes; it is the land to which we look with as true a patriotism as we do to this dear old England.[36]

For some Christians, Israel is destined to serve their own religious agenda. They read the Book of Revelations to prophecy that the Jews' conquest of the Holy Land is a necessary prerequisite for the Second Coming of Christ. The end result for the Jews in this scenario involves an acceptance of Christ as the Messiah. However, such a view reflects an interpretation of biblical metaphors and post-biblical legend. It is not universally accepted among Christian scholars and clerics. Until the end of days when all this is supposed to occur, the Jews may be able to endure the attention and enjoy the support that they and others give to the land that Jews say was promised to them.

The country's security apparatus has prepared for a Christian threat during millennium celebrations in Jerusalem. It mobilized the intelligence gathering skills of the Mossad and the Shin Bet, sought the cooperation of intelligence agencies overseas to help in the identification of apocalyptic fanatics who might be planning to foment an end of the world catastrophe in the Holy Land.[37] The first announced arrests occurred in January 1999, when a number of American families living in a suburb of Jerusalem were taken into custody. According to Israeli officials, they were planning to commit suicide, or to provoke their killing by security forces in order to hasten the return by Jesus to the Holy City.[38]

It has been some time since a Christian power has appeared serious about realizing territorial claims in the Land of Israel. Muslim claims are now more belligerent, and have provided religious input to the nationalism of Palestinians and other Arabs. Israeli security officials worry about the seriousness of proclamations heard from Lebanon, Iran, Iraq, and Libya to liberate the Holy City or all of the Holy Land. Israel sent its air force to destroy an Iraqi nuclear installation in 1981 that President Saddam Hussein indicated was working on atomic weapons that would be directed against Israel.

In order to achieve goals that rank higher, the present cadre of Israeli officials, as well as those of Christian and some Muslim regimes, seem willing to compromise the aspirations their constituents feel for holy sites in Jerusalem and Israel. A guarantee of *access* to holy sites and regional peace compete as values with the *possession* of holy sites.

Each of the monotheistic religions has elements of absolutism that do not lend themselves to compromise. Yet peace by itself has religious value, as does the recognition of religious claims asserted by others. A willingness to share access to religious sites facilitates the pursuit of something that will meet the essential demands of different constituencies. The hope is that in politics as in religion, ideas about the Promised Land and Jerusalem will continue to illustrate how to reject absolutist interpretations of ambiguous doctrines, and to emphasize those religious and political themes that favor pragmatic accommodations.

Chapter 5

Conditions That Produced a Messiah, or Yet Another Jewish View of Jesus Christ

In a career of university teaching spanning thirty-five years I have known numerous students and colleagues with some of the traits described for Jesus: bright, creative, provocative, abrasive, and anti-establishmentarian in siding with the downtrodden and outcasts. Quite a few of these individuals have been Jewish. While none of my acquaintances has been crucified, some have provoked animosity. Not infrequently the Jews among the iconoclasts have brought forth anti-Semitism. The traits that seem to provoke those who cannot tolerate Jews include being different, radical, argumentative, opposed to the conventional, and prominent.[1] I recall a colleague at an American university who seemed to forget my own traits. The colleague spit out the epithet of "too ethnic" in reference to a Jewish faculty activist who was ceaseless and acerbic in demanding reform of the university and the larger society.

One cannot name individuals who resemble Jesus without risking a charge of gross exaggeration and even blasphemy. Who can be compared to the man revered by so many as Son of God? Any comparison is problematic. We have no biography of the real Jesus widely accepted among scholars as authentic. Much of the New Testament is hyperbole, written after his death in a situation of competition between the fragile Christian community and the Jewish establishment.[2]

It may be extreme, but it is suggestive analytically, to think of Jesus in the presence of Jewish students and faculty who rebel in their dress, language, ideas, and behavior. Those I have seen in the social sciences and humanities are almost always left of center in their concern for social justice. Americans with these traits were in the forefront of racial equality and withdrawal from Vietnam, as well as justice for the Palestinians. In visits to Australia I found the local variety concerned with aboriginal rights, nuclear disarmament, environmental pollution, Palestinians, and East Timor.

Hyperbole is the language of these critics. Israeli versions among academics and journalists criticize their country for having indecent disparities between rich and poor, when the more accurate description is that income differentials within Israel resemble those in other western democracies.[3] The movement labeled "post-Zionism" unites a number of intellectuals who emphasize uncomplimentary findings about the founding generation of national leaders, as well as more recent shortcomings.[4]

How Does This Chapter Advance the Theme of the Book?

What does the nature of Jesus and Jewish radicalism tell us about the similarities between religion and politics? For one thing, the very nature of Jesus' radicalism signals that Christianity got its start as a protest against a religious regime reinforced by the power of a ruling empire. For another thing, his story illustrates one of the periodic instances of Jewish radicalism. He typified a component in Jewish culture or religion that provokes speaking and acting against perceived injustice or other faults in the status quo.

Jesus was not the first, and by no means the last, Jewish radical. Amos preceded him by several centuries, with his proclamation that ritual correctness did not satisfy the Almighty who was concerned with justice and righteousness.

> Though ye offer me burnt offerings and your meat offerings, I will not accept them: neither will I regard the peace offerings of your fat beasts. Take thou away from me the noise of thy songs; for I will not hear the melody of thy viols. But let judgment run down as waters, and righteousness as a mighty stream.[5]

This sets a standard of criticism that is open ended. Actions can be proper in a formal sense, but not good enough.

Ideals of universal peace and comity appear in the Book of Isaiah: "nation shall not lift up sword against nation, neither shall they learn war any more."[6] The Book of Jonah is more profound than a fish tale. It describes God's mercy even for the arch-enemy Assyria. Micaiah and Jeremiah stood against kings and their courtiers. Job questioned the justice of the Almighty. Hosea married a harlot to make a point about the culture of his day. Nehemiah demanded justice for the poor and the indebted. The preacher of Ecclesiastes expressed existential values as opposed to authoritarian rules. Ecclesiastes also has some great one-liners useful against government and academics:

> If you witness in some province the oppression of the poor and the denial of right and justice, do not be surprised at what goes on, for every official has a higher one set over him, and the highest keeps watch over them all [7] . . . the use of books is endless, and much study is wearisome.[8]

Modern Jewish faultfinders have been prominent since the Enlightenment sent individuals out from their close communities and exposed them to the ideas and the injustices of the wider world. While we may have to overlook some complications in their status as Jews, prominent figures in the nineteenth century were Karl Marx and Benjamin Disraeli. Disraeli was a political conservative, but his literary portrayal of two nations (rich and poor) made him a world-class social critic.

An entire institution of the Jewish state fits the model of aggressive moralizing. The State Comptroller (equivalent to the U.S. General Accounting Office) is notable among its peers for having legal authority to criticize government units for failing to abide by the standard of "moral integrity," as well as the more conventional criteria of legality, economy, effectiveness, and efficiency. Reports of the State Comptroller have admonished the nation about inequalities in Jewish and Arab education, the patronage doled out by politicians to their supporters, and the donations given to separate parties by individual citizens. There is no Israeli law against contributing to more than one political party. Yet the State Comptroller found a higher moral ground.

> Contributions to a party are meant to express support for the ideology and the program of the party. The giving of contributions to a number of parties by one contributor, even to parties of different ideologies, arouses wonder concerning the purpose of the contributor.[9]

Intolerable Conditions That Produced a Messiah

Thomas Hobbes may have been thinking about ancient Judea when he wrote in *Leviathan* that life is likely to be "nasty, brutish and short." In both the Greek and Roman periods of ruling the Promised Land, there were numerous points of tension and outbreaks of mass violence. A bleak history of chronic insecurity in the face of foreign powers and bloody divisions among the Jews provided the background for messianic claims.

The Greeks came to dominate the Middle East with the conquests of Alexander the Great. Their rule was by no means all bad.[10] Greek language, styles of education, athletics, theater, and local government attracted many Jews, as did the abstract thought that was more typically Greek than Jewish.[11] Religious Jews derived their label for the wayward Jew (*epicouros*) from followers of the Greek Epicureans. Jews in the Greek Diaspora served in major administrative positions, as well as in numerous other occupations. They generally enjoyed autonomy "to live according to ancestral laws." This meant control over their own religious affairs, and exemptions from the rites to honor pagan deities. Jews also enjoyed an exemption from military service, insofar as it conflicted with their refusal to do work on the Sabbath or to participate in pagan ceremonies.

In the eyes of many non-Jews, the Jews wanted the best of two worlds (Jewish and Greek). Publicists attacked the Jews, and there were anti-Jewish riots in the Greek cities of Judea, Egypt, and Syria.[12] There was also bloodletting among the Jews. Hellenization set religious zealots against those who acted like Greeks. According to the first book of Maccabees, "some of the people built a gymnasium in Jerusalem, in the heathen fashion, and submitted to uncircumcision, and disowned the holy agreement . . . and became the slaves of wrongdoing."[13]

The revolt of the Maccabees was as much against Hellenized Jews as against Greeks and the Syrians who served as officials of the Greek regime throughout Palestine. Mattathias Maccabee saw a Jew who went to offer sacrifice at a Greek altar,

> and was filled with zeal, and his heart was stirred, and he was very properly roused to anger, and ran up and slaughtered him upon the altar. At the same time he killed the king's officer who was trying to compel them to sacrifice, and he tore down the altar.[14]

The Maccabees persisted in their rebellion and overcame the Greek forces in a series of encounters spread over twenty-five years. A half-century after the Maccabees' revolt, there was a civil war in the Jewish community that may have caused 50,000 deaths.[15] A social dimension to the conflict set wealthy, urbanized, and Hellenized Jews, who were close to the court, against poorer and more zealous Jews.[16] Two royal sons each sought Roman aid in securing his claim to the throne. Rome took advantage of the requests to strengthen their patron-client relationship with Judea. Eventually all signs of Judean independence passed when it became a province in the Roman Empire.

The Romans brought prosperity, cosmopolitan culture, and an appreciation of internal autonomy among many Jews. Other Jews felt that foreign rule was intolerable. Modern Israelis still quarrel about the quality of Jewish life under the Romans. Some political activists feel that the revolts against the Romans were justified, while others claim that they were the work of irresponsible extremists who brought catastrophe to the Jewish people.

Jews were disproportionately represented among the wealthy and the cultured in several of the Empire's major cities, as well as in high administrative ranks.[17] Rome viewed Judea as a buffer state on its eastern border, and valued the Jews for their extensive contacts throughout the Empire and in other regimes where the Romans had interests.[18] At their numerical high point, Jews may have comprised as much as 10 percent of the Empire's population.[19] The Romans continued the practice of the Persians and Greeks who preceded them in allowing internal autonomy in religious and social matters to Jewish communities, and permitting Diaspora Jews to send contributions to the Temple in Jerusalem.

Within Jerusalem itself, Roman officials brought sacrifices to the Temple to be offered by the Jewish priests.

The reign of Herod presents the immediate environment that gave rise to Jesus and the Christians, as well as other messianic figures and movements. Herod ruled as a Jewish king from 37 to 4 BCE, and represented the best and nearly the worst of Rome's ascendance over the Jews. His era was marked by prosperity and extensive building. He sought to turn Jerusalem into an international showcase. He rebuilt its walls and undertook a major reconstruction and enlargement of the Temple. He contributed to synagogues, libraries, and educational and charitable institutions for Jewish communities in the Diaspora.[20] Yet he was appointed by the Romans, and he was not really Jewish or a proper king in the eyes of some subjects. He was the son of a convert to Judaism who won his throne by political maneuvering in the imperial capital. He appealed to the Romans as a man who could be ruthless in controlling his people. He turned the office of high priest into his personal subordinate, and appointed and dismissed the incumbents at will. He was prone to periods of deep insecurity, and earned the label of barbarian for the mass killings that he ordered.

Like the Greeks, the Romans preferred to rule by accommodating local cultures, but it was not always possible. Concessions were never enough for Jewish zealots. And like other imperial rulers of ancient and modern times, neither the imperial rulers nor their soldiers were always wise or sensitive. There is one story about a period when a policy of accommodation was spoiled by low-ranking Roman soldiers who insulted the Jews by baring their bottoms in the vicinity of the Temple. The riots and repression that followed such incidents made the regimes anything but accommodating.[21]

The suffering of the Roman period that produced the protests of Jesus also gave rise to large scale Jewish rebellions. The two most prominent occurred in 66-73 CE, and 132-35. What is depressing to a contemporary Jewish perspective is not only the destruction of the Temple, Jerusalem, and much of the Judean population that resulted from the rebellions, but the civil wars among the Jews that coincided with them. Josephus provides the most harrowing descriptions for the revolt of 66-73. He may not be entirely trustworthy as to the details, insofar as he describes himself as both a proud Jew and a loyal Roman, and seeks to justify his change of sides during the revolt. He writes how one group of zealots ravaged a Jewish settlement at Ein Ged in order to gather provisions for their fortress on Massada. These are the same Jews who have come to be revered for their heroic stand, and their choice of suicide rather than to fall into Roman hands. Josephus sees them as fanatics, assassins, and bandits who murdered their own wives and children.[22]

Who Was the Real Jesus?

The Gospels tell us little about Jesus as a boy. We do not know if he was the bane of his playmates, parents, and teachers like precocious Jews of our time. It is not clear that he went to school or was literate.

Albert Schweitzer's doctoral dissertation was an early effort to identify the real Jesus by parsing the New Testament for what seemed likely to be historical fact as opposed to legend.[23] Haim Cohen, who was a justice of Israel's Supreme Court, is among those who have sought to comprehend the judicial reality amidst the traditional polemic about Jesus' trial and execution.[24] Amidst all the inquiries directed at the stories of Christ are some convoluted analyses concluding that he did not die on the cross, but was spirited away while still alive.[25]

A scholar at a papal university concludes that Jesus was not a poor boy as told by accepted legends, but was a well-educated son of an urban craftsman who enjoyed the ancient equivalent of a middle-class lifestyle.[26] The claim raises the tantalizing parallel between Jesus and a pattern that has repeated itself over and again among nineteenth- and twentieth-century Jewish radicals. Many have been children of middle-class or wealthy homes who seem to be rebelling as much against their family as against the larger social norms that they attack.

Why Jesus and Not Others?

How did Jesus come to be the center of a world faith while he was only one of the ancients who were acerbic critics of their regimes and messianic in promising a better world to come? Countless other rebellious moralists, Jews and non-Jews, have passed through life annoying their surroundings. Some have been persecuted, others have amassed something of a following, most have been ignored, and none have become a god.

This is part of larger questions, asked time and again, about the roots of religious experience: Why do so many people believe in the supernatural? And why do they believe one religious formulation rather than another?

Perhaps the ideas that Jesus actually promoted, as well as those added by early Christians, set him apart from a number of other potential figureheads who were circulating in the chaos of first-century Judea. It was a time ripe for messiahs and apocalyptic visions. A host of individuals and movements stood against the regime and local elites, claiming to have the key to a more perfect future. Josephus mentions the Essenes. Modern scholarship about the Dead Sea Scrolls finds evidence of numerous perspectives from within that community and others that placed themselves outside the establishment of Temple and priests.[27] John the Baptist qualifier inclusion among the iconoclasts, as well as Josephus himself on account of changing his loyalties from leadership of a Judean military unit against the Romans to becoming a Roman historian and polemicist. Akiba was a leading rabbi of the second century, whose name has been adopted by the youth movement of the religious Zionists in modern Israel. He is said to have declared that Simon bar Kosiba (Bar Kokhba), who led the rebellion of 1-35, was the messiah. The heroism of that rebellion and Akiba's death by having his skin ripped off his body by Roman torturers is viewed by some modern Israelis as points of national pride, but by others as the misery visited on those who hope for too much from their faith and politics.

We can make out Jesus to be a credible player in the morass of the first century without accepting the miracles attributed to him. His social ideas were within the normal range available from the Hebrew Bible. A messiah-sized ego could have been fed by followers. According to the Gospels, he was willing to provoke the establishment unto death by his flagrant behavior in the tense situation of Passover in Jerusalem, when the crowds were immense and the authorities nervous about disturbance. And he refused to recant when offered the opportunity by religious and secular authorities.[28]

> Some form of religiopolitical execution could surely have been expected. What he was saying and doing was as unacceptable in the first century as it would be in the twentieth—there, here, or anywhere. . . . What could not have been predicted and might not have been expected was that the end was not the end. Those who had originally experienced divine power through his vision and his example continued to do so after his death.[29]

What turned this rule-breaking Jew into a god (or Son of God) for about one-third of the world's population who call themselves Christians? The answers that are offered do not solve the mystery. Certainly they do not answer the equally provocative question of why one Jew's traits rendered him a god, while similar traits shown by countless Jews over the years have only provoked anti-Semitism.

Jesus belongs on a list of Jews that also includes Sabbatai Zevi and Jacob Frank. Unlike these medieval claimants to the role of messiah, however, Jesus did not choose Islam or any other alternative when he stood before the power holders whom he had annoyed by his iconoclasm and behavior. The death of Jesus contributed to his reincarnation as the Son of God.

The early success of Christ's fame among pagans got a boost when the Christians set themselves up as a sect that did not demand circumcision of male recruits. In a setting of male dominance, that policy probably decided the choice of entire families. The talents of those composing and editing the New Testament helped. They would not contest secular rule, but would render unto Caesar the things that were Caesar's.[30]

Three hundred years into Christian history the great leap forward came when Constantine added the sword of the state to the cross. The willingness of missionaries over the years to couple elements of Christianity and paganism helped with the common folk. We may thank these mixtures of traditions for the Christmas tree, the hobgoblins of Halloween, and practices surrounding local and national saints like Valentine and Patrick.

Why Do Others Become Prophets? Why Do People Believe the Unbelievable? Why Do They Believe What They Do?

Part of the religious mystery is why some individuals, as opposed to others, were granted status as a prophet of the Lord in the Hebrew Bible. The prophet's distinctive trait was to be accepted as speaking the words of the Lord and serving as an intermediary between the Almighty and his people. The Bible includes several stories of dispute between individuals who claimed to be prophets. Micaiah confronted 400 prophets in the court of Ahab who had given advice diametrically opposed to his own.[31] Amos sought to distance himself from prophets by asserting that he was neither a prophet nor the son of a prophet.[32] Jeremiah was characteristically uncharitable when he termed competing prophets "adulterers and hypocrites," and cursed them to suffer early and ignoble deaths.[33]

It was risky to assert one's status as a prophet. An unconvincing claimant could be condemned to death as a false prophet or ignored as insane. Some of those described in the Hebrew Bible as prophets of the Lord were persecuted or killed by the rulers they criticized. Micaiah was last seen being put in jail because of unwanted advice to Ahab.[34] Amos was sent out of the kingdom of Israel on account of his prophecies.[35] King Jehoiakim had Uriah killed for his prophecies.[36] Jeremiah was in and out of trouble during the regimes of Jehoiakim and Zedekiah. There is a rabbinical tale that King Manasseh had Isaiah sawn apart because of his prophecies.[37] Elijah fled to the desert in order to avoid the fate of other prophets killed on the orders of Queen Jezebel.[38] The test of true prophecy is never clearly specified. The compilers of the Bible accorded the status of prophet to some, and denied it to others.[39]

Neither do we have convincing explanations of why one or another sect emerges from the many that are created to grow and last long enough to become an established religion. We do not know why some continue to grow, like the Mormons, whereas others experience stability or decline, like Christian Science and the Shakers. For 200 years academics and publicists have proclaimed God's death. The rise of anti-clericalism in eighteenth-century France, twentieth-century Soviet Union, and elsewhere set powerful states against religion. What authoritarian governments could not do was expected to be done by the popular education of democracies.

God has not passed from the scene. Large majorities in most western democracies claim to believe in a deity. Even if the Lord exists only in human belief, active believers have shown their capacity to change the world in the name of the God they are following.

What is the essence of the religious experience? All that has been written has not gone significantly beyond the observation that it exists. According to Sartre, religious belief fills a "God-shaped hole in the human psyche."[40] Others have written that *Homo Sapiens* is *Homo Religiosus*: "creating gods is something that human beings have always done. When one religious idea ceases to work, it is simply replaced."[41]

Majorities in western countries say that they believe in God, and some are intense in their faith. The Roman Catholic Church has long investigated claims of miracles, and has certified a small minority of those claimed. Mormon scholars have traveled the migratory path identified in the Book of Mormon from Jerusalem eastward to the Americas looking for physical evidence that the migration really occurred. The parallel Jewish phenomena include women who pray for fertility at Rachel's tomb and political activists who cite murky passages of the Bible to justify their claims about the Land of Israel.

Religion continues as a thriving focus of popular observance and academic inquiry. Much of the research about religion by social scientists is set in the United States, and is concerned with describing and explaining the continued vitality of faith. The topic is especially fascinating in the context of official neutrality with respect to religion and traits of technological development that would seem to push the society toward secularism.[42]

Surveys find that over 90 percent of Americans profess a belief in God, almost 80 percent say that religion is important to them, more than 60 percent are likely to have attended a religious service within the past week, and about the same number say that they pray daily. Between one-third and two-thirds report that they have witnessed a miracle, felt the direct presence of God, or had one of their prayers answered.[43] Harold Bloom used the terms, "religion-soaked," and "religion-mad" for American society.[44] One commentary on the run-up to the 2000 presidential election found most of the candidates emphasizing their religious feelings. Skeptics asked if they were campaigning for the post of preacher or president, and surmised that it was easier to talk about amorphous personal feelings than controversial issues of public policy.[45] Violence in the name of religious belief is not only something that occurs in the Middle East and Northern Ireland but also appears at abortion clinics in the United States.

Jews remain a tribe, including humanists, agnostics, avowed atheists as well as the ultra-Orthodox, the moderately observant, and some fanatic members of non-Orthodox congregations. The residual unity of Jews in pluralist secular democracies is as much of a mystery as other questions concerned with religion. Jews have had more than their share of iconoclasts. They appear in science, the arts, and business, as well as religion. In all of these fields, rule breakers must figure on sharp opposition. Modern establishmentarians do not crucify rule breakers in universities, culture, and business, but they may deny them tenure or career advancement.

Fuzzy Boundaries between Judaism and Christianity

It is beyond the scope of this book to array the distinctions and overlaps between various modes of Christianity and Judaism. Both are clusters of doctrine and ritual, and are not defined with utmost clarity. Individuals can wander between the rituals of Reform Judaism and Unitarianism without noticing great difference. Some consider themselves both Jews and Unitarians. There is no religious police to intervene and defend the boundaries.

Prominent on the Jews' list of complaints against Christian clerics is that they have exaggerated the differences between Judaism and Christianity. Christians have identified a number of humanistic themes with Jesus, and neglect to emphasize the roots of these sentiments in the Hebrew Bible. They thereby further the message of the New Testament itself that Jesus represented a departure from the archaic morality of the Jews.

New Testament expressions in behalf of the poor and the miserable ("blessed be ye poor: for yours is the kingdom of God. Blessed are ye that hunger now: for ye shall be filled. Blessed are ye that weep now: for ye shall laugh.[46]) follow on the provisions in the Torah to care for the poor, widows, orphans and the foreigner, as well as the postures of Amos and Nehemiah against regimes that did not honor those provisions.

What are said to be Christian sentiments of justice ("He that is without sin among you, let him first cast a stone.[47]) have earlier roots in the Hebrew Bible's provisions against the giving of false witness, as well as a concern that courts seek truth. "You shall not be led into wrongdoing by the majority, nor, when you give evidence in a lawsuit, shall you side with the majority to pervert justice."[48]

The passage cited by Christians as indications of Jewish cruelty ("Eye for eye, tooth for tooth[49]) is seen by rabbis as limiting the extent of punishment to something fitting the crime.

The Book of Isaiah includes passages as sweepingly moral and humanitarian as anything in the New Testament: "with righteousness shall he judge the poor, and reprove with equity for the meek of the earth."[50]

As a precedent for New Testament sentiments in behalf of peace ("Blessed are the peacemakers: for they shall be called the children of God"[51]) the Hebrew Bible offers the visions of Isaiah when there will be peace among nations, the wolf will dwell with the lamb, and swords will be beaten into plowshares, Jerusalem will be for all peoples, and death will be no more.[52] Modern Israelis have been wont to adapt this passage to their own needs. When peace arrives, they say, they want to be the wolf rather than the lamb.

At about the time of Jesus' life, Jewish authorities were pursuing elaborate exegesis of the biblical text to limit the extent of capital punishment. A Sanhedrin that sentenced one person to death in a period of seventy years was said to be excessively cruel. Included in the Talmud are sentiments that God created only one human at first in order to teach us that when we sustain even a single life, we have sustained an entire world, and when we destroy as much as one single life, we have destroyed an entire world.[53]

Christian and Jewish scholars have approached one another's perspectives in recent years. It is now common for Christian scholars to conclude that the Gospels of the New Testament were written forty to sixty years after the death of Jesus, and that they reflect problems of Christian communities at those times.[54] According to one Christian scholar,

> in those early decades, almost every possible view of the relation between the two emerged. Christianity fulfilled Judaism; or else it superseded it; or it was built upon it; or it was the true Judaism; or it was a complete novelty . . . there is much to be said for the view that, despite their crucially distinct beliefs, the more mainstream Christians were precisely those who stuck closest to their Jewish roots, above all in the retention, albeit reinterpreted, of the Scriptures they came to call the Old Testament.[55]

Religious Jews have not given up hope that a true Messiah will appear. Among many, hope seems stronger than expectation. Perhaps they have learned from the disappointments. During the last years of his life, however, followers of Rabbi Menachem Mendel Schneerson, the Rebbe of the Lubavitcher movement of ultra-Orthodox Jews, were fervent in their messianism. The Lu-bavitcher, or Chabad movement, is centered in Brooklyn, but has a following in Israel. Billboards and bumper-stickers appeared across the country urging the people to prepare for the Messiah's appearance. When the rabbi died at the age of ninety-two without making the sought after proclamation about his status, some spokesmen for his movement offered a traditional explanation of the Messiah's delay: the Jewish people had not prepared themselves for the Messiah by ceasing their sins. Diehards expressed the sentiment that the rabbi would return to lead his people. Other religious Jews, and not a few secular Jews, snickered at this un-Jewish belief in an afterlife. To my knowledge, no one has reported seeing the rabbi on the streets of Brooklyn or the Holy Land.

Chapter 6

Modern Jewish Wars between Old and New Religious Movements: Ultra-Orthodox and the Orthodox versus the Conservative and Reform

Not all political disputes in Israel concern religion, but many of them do. When politicians and citizens argue, demonstrate, and legislate about Sabbath, marriage, divorce, food, and modesty, it is impossible to determine the boundaries between theology and ideology, religion and politics, beliefs and electoral tactics.

It is appropriate to begin this chapter with a warning and disclaimer. Liberal Jews may not find the details or the analysis to be what they desire. Some have accused me of having a hidden agenda of endorsing the Israeli status quo, and being insensitive to the feelings of non-Orthodox Jews in general, and feminists in particular. In fact, I have few strong feelings on such matters. I do have strong feelings in behalf of accurate description and the unfettered pursuit of explanation. What I describe below follows from several central features of Israeli politics and religion:

- almost all religious Israeli Jews are Orthodox or ultra-Orthodox;
- almost all non-religious Israeli Jews are primarily secular, and not particularly interested in, or supportive of, non-Orthodox Jewish religious movements;
- Orthodox Judaism raises several problems for feminists;
- there is in Israel a vocal opposition to the religious and sexist status quo, but to paraphrase a leading parliamentarian, until American Reform Jews send several hundred thousand immigrants to Israel, religiously progressive Jews are not likely to affect the country's decisions;
- a few hundred Reform Jews do immigrate each year, but they do not begin to make up for the much larger number of new Israelis born to ultra-Orthodox families.

Conflict between groups of Jews claiming to be orthodox and progressive (or their equivalents) has a long history. We have cited ancient disputes and violence between zealous Jews and those who would behave like the Gentiles from the periods of Ezra and Nehemiah, the Greeks and the Romans.

These episodes have relevance to present-day Israel, but more as a warning than as description. To date, history is not repeating itself in the conflicts between orthodox and progressive Jewries. In modern Israel there is considerable tension, lots of cursing, shoving, and throwing of stones and trash, but little by way of serious violence. The hope is that the assassination of Prime Minister Yitzhak Rabin was an anomaly. A book written before the assassination, and entitled *Political Assassinations by Jews,* concludes that after the creation of the Israeli state there have been few cases of political murder.[1] The absence of large-scale violence may owe something to the awareness by religious and secular leaders of the ancient civil wars. It is in this sense that the ancient chapters of Jewish history are more a warning of what may happen if passions are not restrained than a description of current reality.

Issues currently in dispute between orthodox and progressive religious Israeli Jews are conversions, marriage, divorce, and burial, the representation of Reform or Conservative Jews on official religious councils, the rituals to be permitted at the Western Wall, and the status of women.

The Attractions of Judaism and the Attractions of Assimilation

From ancient to modern times Judaic conceptions of God, the Chosen People, the Promised Land, and the Law (*halacha*) have proven powerful attractions to those born as Jews and to converts. Contrariwise, the demands of Judaism, the animosity of Gentles, and the attractions of being part of the dominant Gentile culture have proven to be powerful temptations in the direction of assimilation. Reform and then Conservative Judaism developed in German and American contexts. These progressive movements offer a form a Judaism as well as a me-dium of assimilation into the dominant culture. In their homelands and in Israel, they encountered strong resistance from Jews committed to orthodoxy. The line-up of forces in Israel, where non-Orthodox Judaisms have not developed in response to local conditions but have come from outside the country, has been overwhelming in favor of institutionalized orthodoxy. Israeli Jews who do not identify with the Orthodox tend to be secular, and indifferent to the appeals of non-Orthodox.[2]

The majority or near majority of Israeli Jews who are secular parallel those among the ancients who adapted to the cultures of Greece and Rome. Some secular Israelis are actively anti-religious even while they are explicit in asserting their status as Jews. Secular politicians occasionally side with progressive religious movements in common disputes against an Orthodox or ultra-Orthodox campaign to apply Jewish religious law more thoroughly against the non-Orthodox population. However, most Israeli politicians who are prominent in struggles against the Orthodox and ultra-Orthodox are non-religious, rather than members of progressive congregations.

Secular Israelis have managed to hold their own against the vocal minority (so far less than 25 percent) of Knesset members who have represented Orthodox and ultra-Orthodox political parties. Progressive religious Israelis do about as poorly as expected in a democracy where they have only a small number of vocal activists in the population, and no party to represent them in the national parliament. What power the non-Orthodox religious movements enjoy in Israel derives from their status in the Diaspora, particularly the United States. The financial contributions of American Reform and Conservative Jews have been crucial in setting up their synagogues, schools, and other institutions in Israel. Their influence in the Diaspora guarantees access for prominent Reform and Conservative rabbis to the Israeli prime minister and other ranking politicians. Those Israeli politicians, however, depend more directly on the weight of ultra-Orthodox and Orthodox parties in the Knesset.

Perhaps the strongest deterrent to a development of non-Orthodox religious Judaisms in Israel lies in the nature of those Judaisms. They developed in the Diaspora, where they provide a degree of religion acceptable to assimilating Jews, as well as a focus of Jewish education, identity, and social life. Israeli Jews have little need for those services. Their Jewish identity is without dispute. Even "secular" education provides a great deal of Bible study and other facets of Jewish history and culture. Almost all of the national holidays are religious in origin and are celebrated widely. The social life and marriage partners of Israeli Jews are almost entirely Jewish. Israelis in need of marriage, divorce, or burial can obtain whatever incidence of religious ceremony they desire from the Orthodox establishment. Those who wish to avoid Orthodox rituals can marry or divorce overseas in ways that the state will recognize.

This chapter focuses on the conflict in Israel between Orthodox and ultra-Orthodox Judaism, and that part of the progressive front represented by reli-gious, but non-Orthodox Jews. The principal representatives of non-Orthodox Judaism are rabbis affiliated with the Conservative and Reform movements. Their power base is outside of Israel, mostly in the United States. They are concerned to legitimize their movement in Israel, and to make a statement in favor of pluralism in Judaism. Some part of the disputes to be described are outright organizational self-interest: my kind of rabbi against your kind of rabbi. However, mixed in the stew of religious conflict are topics dealing with peace, the Land of Israel, Jewish relations with Muslims and Christians, and the rights of women.

Surveys of American religions find that the Jews are least likely to attend religious services regularly, and most likely to express doubts about the existence of God.[3] The respondents to those surveys may not include the intense individuals who come to Israel and promote American-based, non-Orthodox Judaism. It is puzzling that such committed activists supporting a watered-down Judaism can emerge from a Jewish culture that exhibits a generalized indifference to religiosity. Yet those who have read this far should be immune to surprise about any combination of behaviors or ideas among those who claim to be religious.[4]

The following sections survey the main issues of conflict that pit various groups of Orthodox and non-Orthodox religious Jews against one another in Israel. They identify core and peripheral issues; describe the tactics of the major combatants; judge the direction of movement, or who is winning; and assess the prospects for accommodation as opposed to continued or even escalating conflict. Many who write about the conflict between Orthodox and other Jewish religious movements are active in one camp or another, and there is much distortion in their portrayal of issues. I do not identify with any of the protagonists. My concern is to describe and explain what happens, rather than promote one or another interest.

Agenda of Conflict

The conflict between Orthodox and ultra-Orthodox on the one hand and progressive congregations on the other hand has not split the Jewish community into hermetically sealed camps. The ethnic component in Judaism limits the extent to which the Orthodox and ultra-Orthodox can accuse the progressives of not being Jewish. Orthodox and ultra-Orthodox rabbis claim a monopoly of legitimacy within the framework of interpreting religious law. The Conservative movement claims to operate within its views of the law, and individual Reform rabbis differ from one another in their postures toward the law. We have already seen that individual Orthodox rabbis are viewed by their nominal colleagues as falling outside the acceptable realm of orthodoxy. On particular issues of relevance to Judaic doctrine, the lineup of rabbis is profoundly mixed. While some Orthodox rabbis are intense in their commitment to Jewish control of the biblical Land of Israel, other Orthodox rabbis are willing to relinquish some of the Land of Israel in return for peace, and many ultra-Orthodox rabbis seem more interested in other religious issues. Rabbis affiliated with Conservative, Reform, or smaller progressive movements differ in their concerns for land and peace. The lack of simple alignments confuses analysis, but it also prevents an all-encompassing *us* versus *them* and thereby moderates tensions between the various religious movements.

Individual disputes can be grouped into clusters concerned with conversion to Judaism, marriage, divorce, and burial, the practice of Reform or Conservative rituals at the Western Wall, and the representation of non-Orthodox Jews on local religious councils. In practice, particular cases may straddle two or three of these categories. A conversion that is not accepted by the Orthodox Rabbinate would prevent marriage to a Jew in Israel, or burial in a Jewish cemetery.

For some participants, the status of women is a distinct issue of prime importance. It appears prominently in disputes about rights of partners in divorce proceedings, the rituals permitted at the Western Wall, and the representation of non-Orthodox Jews on local religious councils.

We can describe a conflict as being on either of two levels: an individual case or a matter of general principle. The actual dispute may involve a person demanding to be registered as a Jew by the Ministry of Interior. At the same time, it can be viewed as part of a larger conflict about a principle, such as the right of non-Orthodox rabbis to perform conversions. Individuals seek to resolve their dispute in a particular forum, most often the local office of a government ministry or the courts. Organizations adopting the case wish to arouse public support for a more general campaign. Israel's courts present the most fertile field for non-Orthodox organizations. Due to the power of Orthodox and ultra-Orthodox parties, the Knesset has not proven to be a hospitable forum for changing the status quo.

A judicial decision about one individual might not transfer to other cases that seem be of the same type. Administrators hostile to a ruling can begrudgingly apply it to the case at hand, but not to other cases that are similar. As a result of the weakness of non-Orthodox Judaisms in the Knesset and the bureaucracy, it is not easy to summarize where the country stands on the general lines of argument. Individuals win some claims that fit into the categories of demands made by non-Orthodox Judaism, but the lack of carryover to general policy requires separate struggles by other claimants.

Conversion

The issue of conversion to Judaism involves the acceptance or not of conversions performed by non-Orthodox rabbis. The issue has increased in temper during recent years. One occurrence that renders the issue important is the migration of close to one million people from the former Soviet Union and Ethiopia since the late 1980s. A substantial number of non-Jewish spouses and other relatives have come with Jewish migrants. Some of them have shown an interest in conversion, either out of conviction or to facilitate their life in Israel, looking ahead perhaps to their needs for marriage, divorce, or burial. A less sudden occurrence, but one that has been building for some time, is the phenomenon of mixed marriages in the Jewish communities of North and South America.

Marriage is a separate issue of conflict between Orthodox and other Jews, and will be treated below. However, it is associated with conversion when the non-Jewish partner is willing to become Jewish. Mixed marriages and quickie conversions that occur in the Diaspora figure in Israeli disputes. Some mixed couples migrate to Israel from North America, and the partners converted by a non-Orthodox rabbi want to be registered as Jews. Beyond these cases, Israeli Orthodox and ultra-Orthodox campaigns against Conservative and Reform Judaism feature stories of rabbis in the Diaspora performing a Jewish marriage ceremony involving a non-Jewish partner; performing a marriage ceremony along with a Christian priest or minister, perhaps in a church; or a rabbi performing an easy conversion to Judaism for someone wanting to marry a Jew.

The issues of conversion that sets Orthodox and other communities against one another are the extent of study and commitment demanded of a convert. The conventional Orthodox practice is to discourage conversion, and then to demand a long period of study and a convincing commitment to live a religious life as a Jew. The typical Orthodox charge against non-Orthodox rabbis is that they perform superficial conversions, often as a fig-leaf for a mixed marriage that an Orthodox rabbi would not perform in any case.

As in other cases of dispute between Orthodox and non-Orthodox perspectives, an important element in the issue is the collective status of Orthodox and non-Orthodox rabbis. The practices of particular rabbis get lost in the noise. Individual rabbis in both the Conservative and Reform movements claim to discourage potential converts and then perform only serious conversions. There are also visionary Orthodox rabbis who seem motivated by an intense commitment to produce more Jews. One Orthodox rabbi made the news by arranging the migration to Israel of Peruvian Indians he perceived to have a special affinity for Judaism.[5]

The Supreme Court found a flaw in the procedure that had provided Orthodox rabbis a monopoly of conversions to Judaism performed in Israel. The Court did not recognize conversions by non-Orthodox rabbis, and indicated that the Knesset should consider a revision of existing legislation.[6] This provoked another round of the hyperbole that marks the language used by Orthodox and non-Orthodox rabbis about one another. When combined with convoluted proposals and bureaucratic manipulations, it makes one question the spirituality that is expected to coexist with religion.

According to non-Orthodox activists, proposals in the Israeli Knesset to affirm the sole right of Orthodox rabbis to perform conversions within Israel are said to delegitimize the Judaism practiced by the majority of American Jews.[7] At one point a group of eight Conservative and Reform rabbis chained themselves to the entrance of the Interior Ministry in Jerusalem, "because our communities are being held hostage." The police came but did not take action, and the protesters unchained themselves and left after about an hour.[8] Individual members of North American Reform congregations, who should have no doubt about their status as Jews, have expressed their fear that they would not be recognized as Jews in Israel.

A number of court cases have ordered Interior Ministry officials to register as Jews individuals converted abroad by non-Orthodox rabbis. Bureaucrats opposed to registering doubtful cases as Jews have pursued no end of detailed checking in search of justifications for their inaction. Individuals converted by non-Orthodox rabbis within Israel have managed to be registered as Jews by the Israeli Interior Ministry after traveling abroad and repeating their conversion overseas. Others in the same situation have been refused registration as Jews on the ground that their trip abroad was meant to disguise the fact that they had been converted illegally in Israel by a non-Orthodox rabbi.

Some actions defy understanding. Individuals who have been converted in Israel by an Orthodox rabbi have received documents indicating that their conversion is not valid outside of Israel.[9]

A former chief Ashkenazi rabbi said that a conversion should be valid only if the convert had lived for three years in the community which converted him.[10] This opinion may have no legal status, but can be cited by a clerk opposed to registering an individual claimant as a Jew. If the claimant does not appeal, then the clerk's decision remains authoritative.

One proposal offered by a Orthodox Member of Knesset affiliated with a secular political party was convoluted to the extent that it defied clear explanation. He proposed that non-Orthodox converts be identified as such in the Interior Ministry's population registry, but not in their identity cards. Perhaps this was a way to allow Orthodox Jews to check on the status of someone who might marry into their family, without making a problematic status so blatant as to be indicated in a card that must be shown on demand on numerous occasions (e.g., cashing a check, being stopped for a traffic violation, registering at a university, or making an application for service in a government office). The formula was approved by a committee of Conservative and Reform rabbis, together with representatives of Israel's governing coalition. The arrangement fell through, however, for lack of recognition by Orthodox and ultra-Orthodox rabbis.[11]

While some Orthodox and non-Orthodox rabbis seem only to shout slogans at one another, others express the reasons that render conversion a matter of serious dispute. According to an Orthodox rabbi who retired from an American congregation:

> Parents who are embarrassed at their child marrying a non-Jew can have him or her quickly and painlessly converted often without the requirement of a minimal knowledge of, or commitment to, Judaism. The primary interest in such conversions is usually not Moses, but Melanie or Michael. . . . When would-be converts came to see me, trying to weed out the frivolous from the serious I would ask: "Why do you want to become Jewish?" More often than not the question would stump them. I often found myself having to explain to their dismay that Jews do not believe in Jesus or celebrate Christmas. . . . Whether one does or doesn't recognize the rabbinic credentials of the rabbis involved is beside the point. What is at stake is the wholesale and corner-cutting acceptance of converts who have no interest in being Jews.[12]

The best argument for non-Orthodox conversions addresses the non-Jewish spouses and children in mixed marriages who are brought into the Jewish community. Many develop close attachments to their congregations, to Jewish traditions and rituals. Some migrate to Israel. Perhaps they would not find acceptance in an Orthodox congregation, but the Judaism they pass onto their children is richer than that found in many homes that are formally Jewish but ignorant of traditions and entirely non-observant.

The case of one family brought together a number of issues: the authenticity of conversion by a Conservative rabbi, the power of bureaucrats in the Interior Ministry, the concern of Israeli officials not to provoke anti-Jewish feelings among African Americans, and the problems raised by a group of self-styled Jews, the "Black Hebrews." The Black Hebrews are a community of African Americans who made their own way to Judaism and Israel. Opponents describe them as a cult led by a dictatorial charismatic figure who has claimed to be the leader of "true Jews" as opposed to white impostor Jews. If they had their way, Interior Ministry officials might have deported the community more than twenty years ago. But the political power of African Americans in the United States and the delicacy of African-American-Jewish relations provided an umbrella over the Black Hebrews. Nevertheless, it took some years for individual members of the community to be recognized as Israeli residents entitled to schooling for their children and other benefits. Among those who have suffered are African-American tourists to Israel. Individuals with no connection to the Black Hebrews have been held up at the airport by authorities who suspect them of posing as tourists with the intention of joining the cult once in Israel and then resisting all efforts to deport them.

Newspaper reports expressed confusion as to which members of the family of Eliezer Israel received official recognition of their conversion by Conservative rabbis in the United States, and what their status would be in Israel. The family had initiated immigration proceedings in 1996, but their case did not proceed smoothly. Interior Ministry officials indicated that they suspected the family of being Black Hebrews because they came from Chicago, as did a number of the Black Hebrews. They also questioned the completeness of their conversion to Judaism. When they appeared at the Ben Gurion airport, authorities detained them and sent for higher officials from the Interior Ministry. One official queried the family members and found much to be lacking in a teenager's understanding of the Sabbath. The official concluded that the family would join the Black Hebrews.

Meanwhile, Conservative activists in the United States pressured Israel's prime minister to intervene, indicating that the family had been active in their Jewish community for several years. The Interior Ministry recognized the family head as an Israeli citizen due to documents he had previously acquired, but granted only tourist status to his wife, children, and grandchildren. The ostensible limit on their stay was thirty days, but the case seemed likely to drag on for longer.[13]

Efforts to organize cooperation between Orthodox and progressive rabbis on the matter of conversion alternatively have kindled hope of a solution, and revealed mistrust and stubbornness. One proposal would have rabbis from all movements involved in the training of converts, but would leave it to the Orthodox Rabbinate to perform the actual ceremony of conversion (and presumably decide when a candidate was ready for conversion). A crisis in the committee organized to deal with the problem erupted over charges by Orthodox rabbis that Reform and Conservative rabbis would not agree to cease independent conversions in Israel outside the cooperative framework being proposed. An Orthodox representative on the committee accused Reform and Conservative members of pursuing their own interests, while Reform and Conservative members of the committee accused Orthodox members of publicizing distorted information.[14] One of the factors preventing agreement was the refusal of Orthodox rabbis to participate in formal meetings with Conservative and Reform rabbis. The Knesset passed a resolution endorsing the conclusions of this committee, which falls short of turning the recommendations of the committee into law. Ultra-Orthodox members of the Knesset opposed this resolution, which one of them termed a cause of schism that would wreck the Jewish people.[15]

With the fate of the committee *in extremis* a Jerusalem Reform congregation announced that it would proceed to mixed prayers at the Western Wall, which was one of the actions that Reform Jews had suspended in order to give the committee an opportunity to reach agreement on conversion. Reform and Conservative leaders also indicated that they would move ahead with asking the Supreme Court to end the Orthodox monopoly on conversion, which was another action suspended while the committee deliberated.[16] Heads of Reform congregations in the United States indicated that they would boycott fund drives of the United Jewish Appeal, and contribute only to Reform congregations in Israel.

A decision by a district court ratcheted the issue of non-Orthodox conversions at least temporarily to the top of Israel's agenda. The judge found no reason in law to reject conversions performed in Israel by non-Orthodox rabbis, and ordered the Interior Ministry to register as a Jew a woman born in Romania to a Jewish father and a Gentile mother, who had immigrated and undergone a non-Orthodox conversion. The decision was greeted with applause by anti-Orthodox activists, and various expressions of sorrow and scorn by religious politicians and prominent Orthodox rabbis. Chief Ashkenazi Rabbi Israel Lau warned that untold thousands of pseudo Jews in the former Soviet Union would seize the opportunity for an easy conversion as a route to immigration. The ultra-Orthodox SHAS Interior Minister indicated that he would hold off the registration ordered by the court pending his appeal to the Supreme Court.[17]

Conservative and Reform communities do not always stand together in their disputes with the Orthodox. When leading Orthodox rabbis proposed six conditions for continued discussions about acceptable conversions to Judaism the Conservative movement accepted the conditions, while the Reform movement rejected them. The conditions were: that a Jew is someone born to a Jewish mother and not a Jewish father; that mixed marriages are not to be accepted; that there must be no marriage ceremonies between members of the same sex; that a previously married individual may not be married again without having received a divorce according to Jewish law; that a conversion must not be granted to someone who does not accept religious commandments; and that the basis of the faith is a complete Torah that was received from God and cannot be changed by humans.

In response to the Conservative announcement that it was accepting these conditions, a leading Reform rabbi said that the conditions were only a tactic to delay discussions, and that the Orthodox Rabbinate would never hold serious discussions with representatives of progressive Judaism.[18] At about the same time the rabbi who chairs the Council of Torah Sages of a prominent ultra-Orthodox movement reinforced the pessimistic forecast of the Reform rabbi. The ultra-Orthodox rabbi told the Prime Minister and a group of visiting American Orthodox rabbis that the entrance of Reform Judaism to Israel would bring about destruction of a land already made rotten by individuals who do not understand that it is impossible to compromise on the laws of the Torah.[19]

Marriage

Issues associated with marriage are perhaps the most complicated of those setting Orthodox Israelis against the non-Orthodox. There are religious laws of long standing indicating who can be married to whom. A man's status as a *kohen* (priest) is important here, as well as a woman's status as a divorcée or a convert, and either partner's misfortune to be labeled as a bastard or as a non-Jew. A man with the surname of Cohen or someone with another surname who is known to be a *kohen* cannot be married to a divorcée in Israel, and a bastard cannot be married to a Jew. The status of a bastard differs from Christian traditions that designate a bastard as the child of a couple not married to one another. The child of unmarried parents may not be a bastard in Judaism. Jewish law bestows the status of bastard on the child of a couple who *could not* be married to one another by virtue of one or another prohibition of religious law. Men have more freedom than women in this corner of Judaism. The child of a married man and an unmarried woman is not a bastard. But the child of a man and a woman married to someone else is destined for life as a religious outcast, and the child's descendants inherit the stigma. Yet there are provisions that provide room for interpretation, and inclinations among rabbinical judges to find a reason for not deciding that a person is a bastard.

Israeli law gives to Orthodox and ultra-Orthodox rabbis a monopoly of control over the marriage of Jews in Israel. There are enough complexities in both religious and secular laws to occupy an army of experts. As in the case of conversion, Israel's secular courts have expanded the rights of Jews who marry outside of the recognized Rabbinate, but administrative officials have at times refused to apply those rulings to similar cases.

Evasions of the religious rules are easy for someone who is not bound by conscience or family pressure to accept Orthodox rituals. Individuals who cannot be married in Israel, or who prefer not to bow to Orthodox procedures, can marry overseas, perhaps by mail, and have Israel's Interior Ministry register them as married. And individuals who wish to thumb their noses at the whole business can live together as a couple, taking advantage of Jewish and secular laws that recognize such unions and grant the partners and their children status and rights with respect to support and inheritance. For some purposes, however, the informal arrangement of living together may not provide the couple with the same rights as individuals who are officially married. Certain mortgages, employee privileges, and tax concessions may be available only to individuals who are recorded as married in their identity cards.

Non-Orthodox organizations do what they can to keep the marriage issue before the public. When a *kohen* and a divorced woman were refused a marriage license by the Israeli Rabbinate, the Reform Union of American Hebrew Congregations arranged their ceremony to coincide with the group's biennial convention in Atlanta, in order to "bring home to Reform Jews in the United States the problems some Jews have in marrying in Israel." The organization of American Reform Zionists set out to raise $2 million in a campaign built around the issue of marriages not allowed in Israel.[20]

What Israelis call a "Cyprus marriage" (which may be performed in any number of countries as well as Cyprus) may be had for the cost of travel, plus a waiting period required by the locale and the fees associated with a civil marriage. For what was estimated in 1991 as a cost of between $800 and $1,500, an Israeli couple could arrange through a lawyer to be married in Paraguay, without leaving Israel. Both Cyprus and Paraguayan marriages are recognized by secular authorities in Israel, although clerks opposed to the process may raise questions and cause a couple to begin a lawsuit before the marriage is actually registered. Reform Jewish activists call the procedures insulting and a nuisance. They have cited the costs involved as pricey but not prohibitive.[21]

Some Israelis object to the aesthetics of the Orthodox ceremony. They describe the traditional marriage contract as "buying a wife," say that the Orthodox rabbi performing the ceremony "mumbles words that they do not understand," and claim that Orthodox rabbis will only accept witnesses who observe Sabbath according to Orthodox demands.

One way out of these problems is to marry abroad. Another way is to comply with Israeli legal requirements quietly by a brief ceremony in the study of an Orthodox rabbi, and to arrange a public ceremony (without legal standing) for family and friends with a non-Orthodox rabbi who will accept whatever witnesses are provided, compose a marriage document agreeable to the couple, and include in the ceremony whatever clearly spoken words are desired by the couple. Yet another way is to make arrangements with one of the numerous Orthodox rabbis with a reputation for accommodating the style desired by a couple, speaking clearly, and not examining the Sabbath behavior of the individuals who come forward as witnesses. Some Orthodox rabbis are known for not insisting on seeing a certificate from a ritual bath (mikvah) testifying to the bride's immersion prior to the ceremony.

According to one of the organizations active in the anti-Orthodox camp (the Council for Freedom of Science, Religion and Culture in Israel), perhaps 20 percent of Jewish couples marrying in recent years have evaded the official Rabbinate's procedures. For 1994 the Rabbinate recorded 21,000 marriages, while the Central Bureau of Statistics reported over 26,000 marriages involving Jews. An activist with another anti-Orthodox organization (the Israel Religious Action Committee) estimates that more Israelis are avoiding the entire set of marriage options and simply living together.[22]

An Orthodox rabbi expressed concern about the looming problem of Israelis without religion who could not marry. He wondered why the issue had not caused a scandal, which may reflect the large number of relevant individuals who had found satisfactory ways around the formal impediments. His suggestion was to create a status that would provide individuals without religion (and thereby unable to marry according to Jewish, Christian, or Muslim procedures) a way of creating a family union and to benefit from all the privileges that banks, tax authorities, and employers grant to married couples. He gave to the proposal the temporary label of "sub-marriage," and indicated that he was searching for a more attractive term that would distinguish the proposal from a proper marriage but still provide it with respectability.[23]

A Reform rabbi was reported to have performed a "marriage" between two gay women in the middle of 1997. The incident set off denunciations from an organization of Conservative congregations and a denial by a Reform organization. According to a spokesperson for the Conservative movement, the ceremony had crossed a "red line" in terms of religious law, and it was a mistake to carry out such a marriage at a time of delicate negotiations involving legislation about non-Orthodox conversions to Judaism. "We see no way, according to *halacha* (religious law), to make homosexual marriage a *halachic* norm, even though we recognized the rights of the gay community for civil rights." The Council of Progressive Rabbis, the central body of Reform rabbis, denied the ceremony had been a marriage. The Council called it a "bonding ceremony" intended to make the relationship public. The Council indicated that it had begun discussions about homosexual marriages, and decided that for the time being no such ceremonies should be performed.

Meanwhile, a Knesset member of an ultra-Orthodox political party saw the incident as confirming what he already knew: that the wedding between two women is proof that the Reform movement had rejected the Torah and is only interested in destroying Judaism.[24]

Divorce

The way out of marriage bears some resemblance to the way into marriage for those Israelis who object to the Orthodox Rabbinate. Israeli law provides a monopoly for Orthodox rabbinical courts to handle cases of divorce. The problems for secular and non-Orthodox Israelis include Orthodox rules of procedure that provide substantial advantages to the man in a case of dispute. Somewhat less prominent in public discussion, but still troublesome for individuals, are reli-gious rituals associated with divorce, and rabbinical judges who demand another period for reconciliation even when both partners want an immediate divorce.

Israel's secular courts have ruled in favor of divorces granted by civil authorities overseas, and they have issued rulings concerned with financial settlements and child custody. Where religious and secular courts have ruled differently on the same points, the state's bureaucrats have at times followed the ruling of religious courts. In these cases, however, the route remains open to secular courts, and anti-Orthodox movements exist to assist the plaintiffs.

A newspaper article that appeared on St. Valentine's Day in 1994 reported comments pertaining to divorce by representatives of the Working Women's Association (Na'amat), Israel's Women's Network, and the Israel Religious Action Center. They attacked a statement of the chief rabbis that the civil courts are "non-Jewish," and that the rulings of secular courts should not be followed. They accused the rabbinical courts of ignoring the laws giving women equality, and with setting themselves up as an independent legal authority, outside the High Court's jurisdiction.[25]

Burial

From one perspective, Israeli burial arrangements are progressive in comparison with other countries. National Insurance pays for a plot and internment. The family of a deceased makes its own arrangements for a memorial stone, and pays a fee to the burial society if it wants a choice site for a grave, or to reserve grave sites for other family members alongside the deceased.

Problems focus on the virtual monopoly of Orthodox organizations for the burial of Israel's Jews. The picture resembles that of marriage, insofar as the incidence of troublesome cases has increased with immigrations from the former Soviet Union and Ethiopia.

One problem concerns deceased Israelis who are not Jews, or whose claims to Judaism do not satisfy the Orthodox burial societies that deal with civilians or the Orthodox rabbis who control military burials. Some of these cases have provoked widespread dismay and anger: recent immigrants killed as soldiers, who thought themselves Jewish, whose families suffered as "Jews" while in the Soviet Union, but who could not be buried in the Jewish section of an Israeli military cemetery; deceased civilians about whom someone "whispered" to the Rabbinate that they were not really Jewish, and where the Rabbinate insisted on what may become a lengthy investigation; a deceased whose family considered itself Jewish, but who cannot convince the Rabbinate, and whose claim to Judaism keeps the family from turning to a Christian cemetery, or prevents a Christian cemetery from accepting them; a non-Jewish deceased with no connection to a Christian or a Muslim community.

An Israeli who died in December 1997 left behind a record of being born as a Muslim, marrying a Jewish woman, converting to Judaism, then returning to Islam and marrying a Muslim woman. Each of his families quarreled over the body. A compromise seemed acceptable: he would be buried in a Muslim cemetery close to the boundary of a Jewish cemetery, with internment ceremonies of both faiths. During the day when this was supposed to have been put into practice, the police had to intervene in order to break up a fight between the Jewish and Muslim families.

As in the case of marriage and divorce, Orthodox burial has rituals that disturb some Jews. They or their family members want their last journey or final resting place to be something of their own design. Israeli practice is to clean and wrap a body in a shroud and to bury without a coffin. Jewish law prohibits cremation, and will not allow the burial among Jews in a Jewish cemetery of non-Jewish relatives of a Jew. As a result, a non-Jew and a Jew who had lived together as man and wife cannot be buried alongside one another in a Jewish cemetery. Some local Orthodox burial societies do not permit non-Hebrew dates or script on gravestones.

Kibbutzim have provided space in their cemeteries for cases where the deceased or family cannot qualify for a religious burial or does not want a reli-gious burial. The privilege can be expensive at U.S. $5,000 per plot, as opposed to no charge for a plot in a cemetery managed by an Orthodox burial society. The limited space of the kibbutzim cemeteries has led to legislation establishing public secular cemeteries. In 1996 the Knesset enacted a law requiring the establishment of secular cemeteries no farther than fifty kilometers from each settlement. The opposition of Orthodox burial societies delayed the selection and preparation of public secular cemeteries. In June 1998, the Ministry of Religions responded to a citizen's suit by indicating that it had appointed a committee to locate a site for the first such cemetery.[26] Shortly thereafter, the management of a secular cemetery in Beer Sheva announced its impending opening.

Non-Orthodox Rites at the Western Wall

The issue of religious freedom is perhaps most stark in the case of non-Orthodox Jewish movements that want to perform their rituals at the Western Wall. In practice, this is likely to mean prayers involving men and women together, with or without women carrying the Torah and reading from it, perhaps with the women wearing *kipah* (skullcap) and *tallit* (prayer shawl). Other problems affecting individuals directly (marriage, divorce, burial) have room for alternative procedures, however unpleasant. Yet there is only one Western Wall viewed as a remnant of the Temple destroyed by the Romans. Efforts have been made to arrange non-Orthodox rituals at what is called the "little wall," outside the plaza known to world Jewry since it was cleared in 1967. The efforts have so far not succeeded in attracting either the support of the non-Orthodox or the tolerance of the Orthodox.

The problem arises when Orthodox Jews claim that it is a violation of religious law or custom for men and women to pray together, for women to carry the Torah or read from it, or to wrap themselves in a prayer shawl. The Orthodox claim a prior right to pray at the Western Wall, and assert that the sight of women violating law or custom disturbs their prayers.

As in other issues considered here, there is something of a muddle in decisions of Israel's Supreme Court and actual practice. The court has ruled that women should receive police protection for their prayers at the Western Wall on condition that they refrain from reading from the Torah and wearing prayer shawls. On one occasion, police had been stationed near the Wall but did not intervene to protect Reform women from verbal abuse, spitting, and shoving.[27] In a later episode, the Supreme Court heard a case brought by Reform Jewish women who demanded to pray as they wish (i.e., without restrictions pertaining to reading the Torah or wearing prayer shawls). Against their petition were Orthodox Jews who did not want their own prayers disturbed by the presence of women doing what they viewed as unacceptable. The Court decided that it was not possible to respond positively to the Reform women.[28]

During the holiday of Shavuot in 1998 the police escort assigned to protect a group of Conservative Jews allowed to pray in a designated corner of the plaza had to employ force in order to protect the Conservative contingent from some of the many ultra-Orthodox gathered at the wall. On another occasion, during an ordinary weekday when there were few ultra-Orthodox Jews at prayer, the police assigned to protect a group of Reform Jews had little to do.[29] At yet another time, a group of Reform Jews managed to pray in the plaza before the Wall, but had to remain within barriers set up by the police and had their service disturbed by the shouts of ultra-Orthodox protesters.[30]

The same committee that was assigned to deal with the problem of conversions toured the area of the Western Wall in order to find a location where Reform and Conservative Jews might conduct mixed prayers without disturbing the Orthodox and ultra-Orthodox. A newspaper report of the tour described a condition of numerous interests with conflicting demands and antipathies. The situation resembles the problems of Christians at their holy sites: too many denominations, a history of conflict between them, and sites that are too small to provide satisfaction for everyone.

Reform Conservative rabbis remain insulted at the need to segregate their followers from the area of the Wall that has come to be known since 1967 as Judaism's central holy place, but they may be satisfied with a site off to the side alongside an extension of the Wall. When the Orthodox chair of the committee indicated that this portion of the Wall was no less sacred than the better known segment, one of the non-Orthodox rabbis quipped that the Orthodox Rabbinate could take for itself that portion, and the non-Orthodox would go to the section vacated by the Orthodox Rabbinate. The section offered was also problematic from the perspective of the Antiquities Authority, who indicated that they would not surrender its right to continue archeological excavations there. And a group of non-Orthodox women, who had been demonstrating periodically at the Wall for some time, were opposed to any compromise. They wanted the right to recite their own prayers in the well-known section of the Wall, including women wearing prayer shawls and reading from the Torah.[31]

The Appointment of Non-Orthodox Members to Local Religious Councils

The appointment of non-Orthodox members to local religious councils is a case of organizational competition with material payoffs. The councils distribute public funds for religious institutions. Membership for non-Orthodox representatives means financial allocations for non-Orthodox synagogues, schools, and social services. Appointments to the councils are made partly by the municipal councils to members of local political parties in proportion to their parties' seats on the municipal council.

Non-Orthodox claimants have won judgments in Israel's Supreme Court that one's identity among the competing streams of Judaism should not disqualify an appointment to a local religious council. Representatives of the left-wing Meretz party on the Jerusalem city council assured themselves maximum publicity by naming a female Reform rabbi as one of its delegates to the religious council. The high court ordered her enrolled as a member of the religious council, but did not order the Orthodox members of the religious council to address her as rabbi, or to accept her demands with respect to budget allocations.[32] In January 1999, the Knesset enacted legislation authored by religious parties that required members of religious councils to accept the authority of the Orthodox Rabbinate on matters of religious law. Ultra-Orthodox spokesmen indicated that this would keep non-Orthodox Jews off the councils. After the law was enacted, however, Reform and Conservative activists said they could accept the new law as a condition for sitting on the councils. Then skeptics asked if Orthodox and ultra-Orthodox rabbis would sit with non-Orthodox members of religious councils, or whether ultra-Orthodox rabbis would pledge to honor the rulings on religious law of the official Rabbinate.[33] Those asking the question knew the answer. Ultra-Orthodox activists would not elevate decisions of the state's Rabbinate over decisions of rabbis affiliated with their own congregations.

Where Things Stand: Who's Winning?

The issues considered above do not exhaust the agenda of issues that deal with religion and politics in Israel. Also prominent are disputes about Sabbath observance (e.g., regulations concerned with the opening of businesses, public modes of transportation, and the closure of roads in religious neighborhoods); availability of non-kosher food; the justice of military exemptions granted to students in religious academies, and their implications for secular Israelis who must accept conscription; the weight of financial allocations to Orthodox and ultra-Orthodox institutions; ultra-Orthodox demands for modesty in public places that ban advertising posters showing women in short sleeves; and ultra-Orthodox protests about the continuation of construction projects that uncover ancient Jewish graves. For the most part, these issues produce conflicts between Israelis who define themselves as religious (i.e., Orthodox or ultra-Orthodox) and secular. Conservative and Reform Jews may join secular Israelis in these disputes, but the interests of Conservative or Reform Judaism per se, are not as central as in those issues identified above.

We have seen that there is little room for courtesy in the religious disputes of Israel. An ultra-Orthodox Member of Knesset was not holding out much promise of cooperation when he said that, "Letting a Reform rabbi sit on the Tel Aviv religious council is the equivalent of letting a terrorist into the General Staff headquarters. The Reform are terrorists, not rabbis." When this same individual was present at a meeting with Reform and Conservative representatives, he called them "clowns" and "liars."[34] A group of Reform rabbis made their own contribution to the holiday spirit just before Passover in 1995 by proclaiming that the custom of symbolically selling products that Jews cannot eat on Passover to an Arab, and then buying them back after the holiday is a "bluff, swindle, and hypocrisy" by the Orthodox Rabbinate.[35]

Non-Orthodox Jewish institutions and programs improved their standing during the Rabin-Peres governments of 1992-96. For part of the government's term, no Orthodox or ultra-Orthodox party was formally part of the ruling coalition. Representatives of the overtly secular Meretz Party served as ministers of education and culture, and a secular member of the Labor Party served for a while as minister of religions. During this period the Ministry of Education and Culture added instruction in Conservative and Reform Judaism to religious programs in Jewish secular schools. The minister of religions opened to public scrutiny the Rabbinate's list of Jews forbidden to marry in Israel. He demanded that individuals placed on the list on account of one or another provision of religious law be given an opportunity to appeal their designation, and he proposed public funding for travel overseas in order to obtain a secular marriage. With the change in government that occurred after the elections of 1996, the Ministry of Education and Culture passed to a member of the Orthodox NRP, and the Ministry of Religions was to be headed in rotation by a member of the Orthodox NRP and the ultra-Orthodox SHAS. With these changes, the Ministry of Education and Culture renewed its stress on traditional Jewish values in teaching programs on citizenship. Nothing was heard from the Ministry of Religions about public support for Jews traveling abroad for civil marriages.

Explaining the Weakness of Non-Orthodox Judaisms in Israel

The weakness of non-Orthodox religious Jews begins with their limited numbers in Israel. Surveys of Jewish religiosity in Israel carried out by Israeli social scientists tend not even to ask about Reform and Conservative affiliation. The categories that are well known, and questioned by survey research, are Orthodox, ultra-Orthodox, traditional, and secular. Israelis who consider themselves traditional are mostly Sephardi who see themselves as adhering to many, but not all, of the commandments. When Israelis hear of "Conservative Judaism," they may think of something that is conservative (i.e., Orthodox) rather than progressive.[36]

One survey of Israeli Jews found 10 percent of the population within each of the "ultra-Orthodox" and "Orthodox" categories, 29 percent "traditional," and 51 percent secular.[37] Thus, a large majority of Israelis are non-Orthodox. The size of the "secular" camp varies with the issue at hand and the position of "traditional" Jews. With respect to using automobiles, cook-outs in public parks, and football (i.e., soccer) on the Sabbath, many traditional Jews stand with the secular. With respect to marriage, divorce, or kosher food, traditional Jews may go along with the Orthodox.[38]

Whether they consider themselves traditional or secular, the overwhelming majority of non-Orthodox Israelis show little interest in the religious doctrines raised by Reform and Conservative Jews. Orthodox and ultra-Orthodox traditions have no provision for female rabbis. Women who call themselves rabbis are unusual, as are women who wear religious garments associated with men (*kipah* and *tallit*). Issues of gay and lesbian congregations, rabbis, or marriages are mostly unknown in Israel, except as they provide material for Orthodox and ultra-Orthodox denunciations of other Judaisms.

A prominent indication of progressive Judaism's weakness is the lack of Knesset representation. Against religious parties that in one form or another have represented Orthodox or ultra-Orthodox movements since Israel's Independence and count twenty-seven Members of the Knesset elected in 1999, there is no party in the Knesset that represents Reform or Conservative Judaism.

Left-wing, secular Israeli politicians would appear to be the most receptive to Reform and Conservative demands. However, some of these have made a point of criticizing the activists of liberal Judaism for being out of touch with political realities in Israel. Former Interior Minister Haim Ramon and former Health Minister Efraim Sneh (both members of the Labor party) have wanted the help of Jews well connected in America with the peace process. They have come away from meetings with leaders of liberal Judaism saying that those people are interested only in their own religious agenda.[39]

According to Ramon, there are only two important Jewish communities in Israel as defined by their attitudes toward religion: Orthodox and secular. For him, others are insignificant. To change that, he said, would require the Reform movement to send several hundred thousand of its members to Israel as immigrants. Reacting to the American flavor of Reform Judaism, Ramon said, "I don't tell you what to do in the U.S.; don't tell me what to do here."[40]

Additional indications of the non-religious character of non-Orthodox Israelis surfaced soon after the massive demonstration and counter-demonstration of ultra-Orthodox and secular Israelis that we described in chapter 3. Newspaper advertisements in behalf of the Reform and Conservative movements indicated the affiliation of Amos Oz and a number of other prominent intellectuals. Some said that they were formally joining a non-Orthodox congregation in protest against the demands of the ultra-Orthodox. Soon after, however, the liberal newspaper *Ha'aretz* published a skeptical review of what the advertisement claimed. According to the *Ha'aretz* report, a number of those claiming to affiliate with one or another liberal movement were, at best, casual in their religious observances. Some indicated that they were committed to a secular lifestyle, but would take a formal act in support of the non-Orthodox as a protest against the ultra-Orthodox. The article indicated that the Reform and Conservative movements together have about 25,000 members in Israel, or about one-half of one percent of the Jewish population. The author of the article reported claims by a Reform spokesman of greatly heightened interest as a result of the newspaper advertisements, but further inquiries led him to express skepticism about the number of inquiries that were claimed, or the staying power of those who indicated that they would join non-Orthodox congregations.[41]

While Reform and Conservative rabbis often join one another in condemning the monopolies enjoyed by Orthodox rabbis, the differences between Reform and Conservative movements serve to weaken their collective political clout. Conservative leaders have distanced themselves from the Reform on what Conservatives are likely to describe as speedy, superficial, or non-*halachic* conversions, and the casual approach of Reform rabbis to mixed marriages.

One confrontation in the Yad Vashem Holocaust Memorial raised doubts both about the sensitivities of Reform demonstrators and about the attitudes of those playing the role of Orthodox protesters against them. The fracas between two sets of extremists suggested a planned and ritualized confrontation, with each knowing in advance the likely presence of the other.

The event began with a Reform rabbi leading gay and lesbian Jews in a commemoration ceremony in Yad Vashem's Hall of Remembrance. It included an adaptation of the traditional memorial prayer that included reference to "our lesbian sisters and gay brothers." Their ceremony was interrupted by a demonstration led by Orthodox-Nationalist Avigdor Eskin, who came to prominence some years later when he was arrested for planning to throw a pig's head among Muslims gathered for prayer on the Temple Mount/Haram Esh Sharif during the Muslim Holy Month of Ramadan. After the police intervened in the Yad Vashem episode, the Reform rabbi began again only to be stopped by an elderly man who screamed wildly, snatched the rabbi's notes, and dashed them to the floor.[42]

Scenarios

The conflict between Orthodox and non-Orthodox Judaisms appears likely to continue more or less at its present level for the indefinite future. It shows no signs of heating up to the temper of the ancient conflicts described in Maccabees or Josephus. The limited extent of conflict, and the lack of resolution in favor of non-Orthodox Judaisms derives in large part from the meager representation of non-Orthodox Judaisms in Israel. There is a sizable majority of non-Orthodox Israeli Jews, but they are not religious. Few of them seem interested in quarrels between various groups of rabbis about doctrine and ritual.

The limited nature of the conflict may reflect the lessons learned from ancient civil wars. Israeli political and religious elites know their history, and have shown themselves concerned to pull back from the abyss of violence when religious or anti-religious demonstrators threaten to move beyond a tolerable level of intensity. The Americans who come to Israel in behalf of liberal Judaism are marginal to these conflicts, and they, too, seem disinclined to violence. They have more often received blows than delivered them when doing what Israeli Orthodox and ultra-Orthodox view as unacceptable, such as insisting on men and women praying together at the Western Wall.

Orthodox and ultra-Orthodox political parties are well represented in the Knesset. Even if a prime minister manages to put together a government without their participation, ultra-Orthodox and Orthodox parties are unlikely to be left out of the political calculus. Secular Israelis will remain alert to the prospect of subsequent electoral victories by Orthodox and ultra-Orthodox parties, and their importance in future coalitions. Non-Orthodox religious Jews can co-operate with secular Israelis in publicizing Orthodox excesses. The non-Orthodox can count on a continuation of modest allocations from Israeli public resources for religious schools and synagogues. What is doubtful is an increase of Israeli resources to non-Orthodox religious institutions to a size sufficient to arouse Israel's Orthodox and ultra-Orthodox parties. Orthodox and ultra-Orthodox power in Israel dwarfs that of non-Orthodox religious congregations, and Orthodox and ultra-Orthodox rabbis are intense in their opposition to non-Orthodox Judaism.

Secular Israelis have little need for the functions provided by non-Orthodox Judaism. Their Jewish social life, culture, and identity come from the dominant society. Israelis in need of marriage, divorce, or burial can obtain service from an Orthodox rabbi without regular attendance at an Orthodox synagogue. The state recognizes alternative means of marriage and divorce for those who wish to avoid the Orthodox establishment. The slogans about religious intolerance in Israel that Reform and Conservative rabbis purvey to their overseas congregations are inaccurate. Israel tolerates a plurality of religious and non-religious traditions, even if it does not assure them equal standing in law or equal financial support. Individual Orthodox rabbis and their congregations differ in their attitudes and practices with respect to non-Orthodox Jews. There is more variety in Israeli Orthodoxy than non-Orthodox activists are willing to admit.

The low-level conflict between Jewish religious perspectives in Israel resembles the conflicts about religion that occur in numerous other western democracies. Many individuals remain religious, despite 200 years of insistence by the enlightened that sooner or later the religious will cease believing the unbelievable. A variety of religious beliefs and practices compete with one another for adherents, and compete against the non-religious on issues like abortion, euthanasia, divorce, religious ceremony in public spaces, and the content of public education. Since World War II, and owing perhaps to the Holocaust, religious tolerance is now more apparent than is repression in western societies. There seems to be a general standoff, or a tied score in the continued competition of religiosity versus anti-religiosity, or dominant versus minority religions.[43] Israelis can hardly expect to be different.

The results of these disputes are not free of pain. As in other issues of spirituality, there is no neutral judgment of the hurt suffered by those denied what they want, or who feel the insults of insensitivity. Non-Orthodox Jews from North America or Western Europe have learned to insist on their rights as Jews in non-Jewish societies. Their experiences as a minority in the Diaspora may prepare them for a status as Jewish outsiders in the Jewish state.

Chapter 7

Representing Judaism in Israel: Religious Political Parties

We have already seen that religion is a persistent topic of political dispute in Israel. The rabbis who head the various movements and congregations view politics as serious business. Even the ultra-Orthodox who are doubtful about the religious authenticity of this Jewish state (as opposed to that of David and Solomon) employ political activity in order to enhance the Judaic character of the regime, and add to the funding of their organizations.

This chapter examines certain features of how Israel's religious Jews practice their politics. The starting point is the literature developed elsewhere about interest groups and political parties. It considers the principal questions asked about interests: the source of their influence, strategies and tactics, and their success in shaping public policy. It distinguishes the Israeli phenomenon from one prominent theme in the international literature: that interest groups pursue sectoral interests, and differ from political parties in not seeking electoral victory and control of government.[1] Israeli religious parties mix the traits generally assigned to interest groups and political parties.

Representing the Religious Interests of Israel's Jews

Giovanni Satori wrote some years ago, "Israel is very definitely a case by itself to be understood as such."[2] Satori was correct, at least with respect to the nature of Israel's religious political parties. Unlike the conventional conception of political parties, they do not campaign in order to capture the government and determine the full range of national policies. They differ from the Christian Democratic parties of Europe in failing to develop programs for important segments of national interests. None of the Israeli religious parties has a prominent concern with national economic policy, a social policy for the nation's poor, or— except for the concern of one religious party with maintaining control over the Land of Israel— a foreign policy.

Despite these missing ingredients of "political parties" as conceived in the literature of political science, the concerns of Israel's religious parties do more than what is usually associated with interest groups. Unlike interest groups, they do not limit themselves to pursuing narrow interests from outside the government. They aspire to membership in the governing coalition even if they do not expect to gain the major policymaking positions reserved to a dominant party in the coalition (prime minister, minister of defense, foreign minister, or minister of finance). One or another religious party has been affiliated with every coalition since Israel's creation, at least until the election of 1999. When the ultra-Orthodox SHAS party left the Rabin government part way through its term and the government was formally without a religious partner, the ultra-Orthodox United Torah Judaism party lent the government support "from the outside." This meant that the party received some consideration in legislation for its commitment to support the government on certain issues. This book is being prepared for the press immediately after the election of 1999. It is too early to see clearly the coalition being assembled by the newly elected prime minister, Ehud Barak.

Religious Parties

Despite organizational splits, consolidations, and name changes, the total Orthodox and ultra-Orthodox party sector remained stable for many years. The number of their seats in Israeli Knessets ranged between thirteen and eighteen (out of 120) from 1949 through the election of 1992. Their number increased to twenty-three as a result of the 1996 election, and increased again to twenty-seven as a result of the 1999 election. Table 7.1 provides the record of religious parties' representation in Israel's Knesset since the first national election.

The ultra-Orthodox parties represented in the Knesset are SHAS and United Torah Judaism. The National Religious Party (NRP) is an Orthodox party that has been represented in each Knesset since the first national election of 1949.

SHAS (an acronym for a Hebrew name that translates as the Sephardi Torah Observants) is a relatively new player in the ultra-Orthodox sector long dominated by Agudat Israel. Sephardi Jews trace their background to Spain, North Africa, the Balkans, and Asia. SHAS emerged as a protest against what its founders felt was the anti-Sephardi discrimination by Ashkenazi (European) leaders of the ultra-Orthodox party Agudat Israel. SHAS also appealed to Sephardi voters who had supported the NRP. In the first national election in which it campaigned (1984), SHAS won four seats in the Knesset, Agudat Israel's number dropped from four to two and the NRP's from six to four.

Table 7.1

Religious Parties' Representation in the Knessets of Israel

Years	Number of Religious Party Seats
1949-51	16
1951-55	15
1955-59	17
1959-61	18
1961-65	18
1965-69	17
1969-73	18
1973-77	15
1977-81	17
1981-84	13
1984-88	14
1988-92	18
1992-96	16
1996-99	23
1999-	27

Sources: *Statistical Abstract of Israel 1996* (Jerusalem: Central Bureau of Statistics, 1996), Tables 20.3, 20.4, *Ha'aretz,* May 19, 1999. Hebrew.

SHAS attracts voters materially with a school system from pre-kindergarten through high school and religious academies. It has used its swing position in coalition politics to acquire government money for its schools, with its leaders justifying their tactics as making up for years of deprivation at the hands of the Ashkenazim who dominate the Israeli establishment. The parliamentary leader of SHAS Ariyeh Deri was the subject of a prolonged police investigation concerned with charges that, as interior minister, he provided special allocations for municipalities to use in supporting programs sponsored by SHAS. The investigation began in 1990 and reached the stage of an indictment for bribery and other crimes only at the end of 1993. During the period of campaigning for the 1999 elections, a Jerusalem district court found him guilty, and sentenced him to four years in prison. SHAS responded by charging official discrimination against religious and Sephardi Jews, and made Deri a centerpiece of its electoral campaign.

SHAS's patronage tactics resemble those used in the past by other Israeli parties. By one view, it is the party's bad luck to come on the scene after a change in the informal rules of the game. Techniques of patronage in allocating public resources that had been routine are now grounds for prosecution and incarceration. By another view expressed by SHAS supporters, the change in norms has been directed against SHAS, with the persecution of party leaders reflecting jealousy of the movement's success.

A newspaper report in April, 1998 indicated that SHAS was making an effort to recruit children from non-religious homes to its schools. One claim charged that 150 students enrolled, another that 500 did, and a third that 1,000 were enrolled. SHAS schools offer more hours of daily instruction and shorter vacations the public schools, plus hot meals and transportation. Each of these features appeal to the population targeted by SHAS: traditional Jews from North African backgrounds, who tend to be middle or lower income, and may not be fully observant but whose attitude toward religion is positive. SHAS sees such students as potential recruits with both religious and political payoffs. Their enrollments serve to determine the financial allocations received from municipalities and national government ministries. In the long term, the party expects that the graduates of its schools will be ultra-Orthodox and SHAS voters. Suspicious officials indicated that claims of enrollment would have to be checked carefully.[3] Israel's State Comptroller has found that SHAS and other ultra-Orthodox movements have padded their enrollments for the sake of per-student financial allotments from the government.[4]

SHAS's 1999 election campaign paid off. The party increased its Knesset representation from ten to seventeen. Its leaders claimed that the voters had justified their charge that the justice ministry and court had persecuted Ariyeh Deri. The leaders of other parties asserted that they would not sit in a coalition with SHAS, or narrowed their comments to say that they would not deal with the party as long as it was led by a convicted felon. As Barak was setting out to create his coalition, he seemed motivated by a desire to include as wide a spectrum as possible of Israeli parties to provide backing in expected negotiations with Palestinians and Syrians. Among the problems he faced was, on the one hand, the weight represented by SHAS, which had become the third-largest party in the Knesset, and, on the other, the problems associated with a party that had affirmed as its leader an individual already convicted of bribery, and the subject of one and possibly two pending indictments.

SHAS's success illustrates a theme of this book: the difficulty of separating issues of religion, party politics, and other issues like ethnicity. The party's 1999 campaign dealt explicitly with the animosity felt from secular, Ashkenazi, and upper-income Israelis. Its commercials appealed to voters' feelings of remaining outsiders despite several decades' residence in Israel, as well as the party's defense of Judaism. It is not yet possible to determine the weight of social class or ethnicity in its appeal to voters as opposed to the defense of religion. Each was explicit or implicit in the party's campaign. Whatever its appeals, the party won a greater percentage of the vote than ever before by an Israeli religious party.

SHAS's willingness to compete for resources in state forums has served to bring other ultra-Orthodox congregations into a closer relationship with government institutions. Traditionally the ultra-Orthodox, represented by Agudat Israel and a variety of independent congregations, distanced themselves from the Zionist state. Moreover, SHAS's success in garnering votes has served to shake up the organization of Agudat Israel. Agudat Israel is now a component of United Torah Judaism. Its parliamentary leaders have accepted policymaking positions in the ministries of housing, welfare, and labor, and the important Knesset post as chair of the finance committee. In these positions, they have a say in resource allocations and personnel appointments that puts their party into the patronage game.

United Torah Judaism is a tense coalition between ultra-Orthodox communities whose animosities go back to European conflicts between Hasidim and their opponents (*Mitnagdim*). The Lubavitcher (Chabad) ultra-Orthodox congregations are something of an out-group in the world of the ultra-Orthodox, and United Torah Judaism has had only partial success in attracting their support.

The National Religious Party served in every governing coalition from the founding of Israel until the Rabin government that was created after the election of 1992. NRP is the party of religious Zionists: Orthodox Jews who support the Israeli state. NRP's founding rabbis saw the country's emergence as a sign of the messianic age. In their view the role of religious Jews is to seek redemption by building a Jewish state in the land given to Jews by the Almighty.

The Six-Day War of 1967 created immediate opportunities and eventually problems for the NRP. On the one hand, stunning victories gave control of the West Bank and all of Jerusalem to Israel. The heart of the biblical Land of Israel was in Jewish hands for the first time in two millennia. This seemed further proof that the Lord was on the side of Israel. Individuals associated with the NRP created Gush Emunim (the bloc of the faithful), and took as their cause the promotion of Jewish settlement throughout the newly occupied territories. Their program began modestly under Labor governments that served until 1977, and then thrived under Likud governments from 1977 to 1992.

The problems for Gush Emunim and the NRP developed along with the prospects for Israeli-Arab peace. Jewish settlements established by earlier governments had become stumbling blocks on the road to peace. The NRP responded to the peace initiatives of the 1990s by moving to the right and taking a posture in support of continued settlement and opposition to territorial compromise. This initially added to the political isolation of the party that followed events that had served to weaken it among the electorate. For some years, the Orthodoxy that provided the basis of the NRP had been losing individuals to a resurgence of ultra-Orthodoxy. And when SHAS developed as a Sephardi religious alternative, numerous Sephardim who had voted NRP left the Ashkenazi-dominated party. NRP's share of the vote fell from 10 to 5 percent between the elections of 1969 and 1992, while that of ultra-Orthodox parties (including SHAS) increased from 6 to 8 percent.

The election of 1996 improved the status of the entire religious bloc. SHAS won ten seats, NRP nine, and United Torah Judaism four. All of them joined the coalition government of Benjamin Netanyahu. As indicated above, SHAS did especially well in the election of 1999. It increased its seat from ten to seventeen. United Torah Judaism increased its representation from four to five. NRP had trouble separating its appeal from that of a more overtly nationalist party concerned with the Land of Israel, and declined from nine to five seats.

Anti-Religious Parties

It is appropriate that this is a short section. "Anti-religion" sells among some of Israel's intelligentsia and its emerging yuppie class. It is politically correct in university faculties of social science and humanities, but does not do well in the Knesset. Political arithmetic is against an overtly anti-religious posture. The left-of-center Meretz Party (nine members in the Knesset elected in 1996 and ten in that of 1999) is the most consistently anti-religious of Israeli parties. However, efforts to minimize the power of religion in Israel are not its only concerns. It has also staked out a position of strong support for concessions to Palestinians in the peace process, and for the rights of non-Jewish minorities within Israel.

The parliamentary leader of Meretz, Yosi Sarid, is a symbol of all that is evil in the eyes of the ultra-Orthodox. SHAS's newspaper for children has run a serial about a corrupt member of Knesset who plots to kill two ultra-Orthodox children. The name of the character in the series is Yosef Zacor ("zacor" means remember, while "sarid" means remnant) and is portrayed with a Sarid-like bald head and round eye glasses. Sarid has threatened to sue the newspaper and a SHAS official charges him with attempted censorship.[5]

Another party staked out a limited anti-religious platform in the election of 1999. A former newspaper editor and television personality, Tomy Lapid, teamed with a sitting member of the Meretz delegation to create a breakaway movement called Shinui (Change). Lapid campaigned on a stridently anti-ultra-Orthodox platform, focusing on the charges of corruption against Ariyeh Deri and the resources that Lapid said were squeezed from the national treasury by the political power of SHAS and United Torah Judaism. Complicating the appeal, however, was Lapid's assertion that he was not anti-religious, and certainly not anti-Jewish. His media appearances over a period of several years recalled some elements of Ronald Reagan's pre-political career as a television personality. Both identified with strongly nationalistic folk themes. While Reagan built an identity associated with rugged individualism, Lapid played on his own history as a Hungarian Jew who had suffered persecution, and his pride in Israel's development. His party won six seats in the Knesset, and Lapid signaled his openness to sitting in a coalition with the NRP, but not with SHAS.

Members from both of the major parties (right-of-center Likud and left-of-center Labor), as well as the right-of-center Tsomet party and the Russian immigrants' party led by Natan Sharansky have spoken out against the demands of religious parties. (Tsomet was a nationalistic party that rose to prominence on the strength of its founder, a former commanding general of the Israeli Defense Forces. It won two seats in the election of 1988, eight seats in 1992, two seats in 1996, and failed to win the minimum required in the election of 1999.)

The pressures of coalition politics have led Labor, Likud, Tsomet, and the Russian immigrants' party to moderate the anti-religious postures of their parliamentarians, or to impose on them party discipline in behalf of religious interests on specific votes. Even Meretz came under pressure from Prime Minister Yitzhak Rabin. After repeated complaints from religious parties about the "scandalous" anti-religious comments of then-Meretz leader and minister of education and culture Shulamit Aloni, Rabin took away the education portfolio and demoted her to minister of culture.

The Issues

Israel's character as a Jewish state emerges more in the preoccupation of political activists with Jewish issues than with any consensus about religion or what is good for the Jews. The religious parties would expand the range of issues governed by religious law. This involves Sabbath observance, *kashrut*, the treatment of ancient graves, the enforcement of decency standards with respect to women's dress and the content of print electronic media, medical practices of abortion, post-mortems, and organ transplants, and the definition of who is a Jew. They would increase financial allocations to religious schools and other institutions, and housing for religious families. Religious parties also want to minimize the status of progressive Judaism in Israel. They oppose the appointment of Reform and Conservative members to the local religious councils that allocate public funds. They oppose granting Reform and Conservative rabbis a role in marriages, divorce, or conversions to Judaism that occur in Israel. The NRP, more clearly than other religious parties, stands opposed to substantial further withdrawals from those portions of the Land of Israel captured in the war of 1967.

The justifications that the religious parties use in behalf of their demands are no less sweeping than the range of demands. To them, God's laws are revealed in the Torah and more than two thousand years of rabbinical commentaries. One argument in behalf of exempting tens of thousands of men from military service is the claim that their studies in religious academies protect the nation in ways even more effective than those of the soldiers. Ultra-Orthodox young men are fulfilling God's commandment to study Torah, and thereby assuring God's protection. During the Iraqi scud missile attacks on Israel during the Gulf War of 1991, a student praying at the Western Wall told an interviewer that, "prayer is all that is left. . . . Prayer always helps, doesn't it? What assurance do you have that your gas mask will help?"[6]

Tactics

The campaigning techniques of the religious parties add to their image as real parties concerned with maximizing their parliamentary representation, even if they do not aspire to leadership of an Israeli government. Their capacity for getting out the vote is legendary. Their elementary building blocks are the religious academies and the homogeneously religious neighborhoods where many of their voters live. In the Knesset election of 1988, ultra-Orthodox parties won more than 70 percent of the vote in their Jerusalem neighborhoods. In contrast, the secular Likud Party was not able to gather more than 50 percent of the vote in the socially homogeneous working-class neighborhoods that provided the core of its support in the city, and the Labor Party could not get more than 40 percent of the vote in the middle- and upper-income neighborhoods that were the base of its support.[7]

The parties' concern for patronage is another of the elements that renders them more like political parties than interest groups. All three Orthodox and ultra-Orthodox parties that won seats in the Knesset election of 1996 proceeded to negotiate their membership in the governing coalition assembled by prime minister-elect Benjamin Netanyahu. Key demands were positions as ministers and deputy-ministers, and chairs of Knesset committees. The ultra-Orthodox United Torah Judaism affirmed its traditional posture that it would not seek a ministerial post so as not to dirty its hands with too close an identification with the Zionist state and its violations of Sabbath and other religious laws. However, it bargained hard for the post as deputy minister of construction and housing, and saw to it that there would be no appointment of a minister of construction and housing. Subsequently, the ultra-Orthodox deputy minister concerned himself with appointing party loyalists to key positions, and the construction of housing for ultra-Orthodox families.

In her 1998 Annual Report, the State Comptroller indicated that the state was discriminating in favor of the ultra-Orthodox in several programs. She criticized religious academies that falsify their enrollment figures in order to increase their allocations from the government, and criticized the ministry of religions for not auditing its reports. She criticized the ministry of construction and housing for favoring housing for ultra-Orthodox families.[8] A few days later, the ultra-Orthodox deputy minister of construction and housing said that the State Comptroller's remarks about his ministry at her press conference bordered on incitement, and that her office's analysis of his activities was amateurish.[9]

One of the crises of coalition negotiations after the 1996 elections concerned the choice of a minister of religions. The ministry is a honey pot of Israeli patronage, charged with allocating funding for religious academies, synagogues, and ritual baths, as well as appointing numerous community rabbis and other religious functionaries. The initial crisis was settled by an agreement between the ultra-Orthodox SHAS and the Orthodox NRP to accept a division of appointment, with each party naming the minister who would serve for two of the four year expected life of the new government. Then a crisis erupted over which party would name the minister for the first two years. Both feared that if the rival got the first appointment, its minister would effectively sew up personnel appointments and other patronage opportunities, and reduce significantly the value of the ministry for the second appointee.

Reckoning the Success of the Religious against the Anti-Religious, and of Various Competitors among the Religious Movements

It is no simple task to reckon the success of religious movements whose promises to their adherents are, in large measure, spiritual and otherworldly. Questions such as which competing movement is the most chosen from among the Chosen People must wait for the end of days, or the coming of a Messiah that all movements will recognize as such.

It is difficult even to measure the success of religious movements by focusing on their programmatic demands for material benefits or other concrete enactments in the here and now. It is in the nature of religious movements, like secular parties and interest groups, to highlight their successes and minimize their failures. Who is to measure the relative success of ultra-Orthodox activists in closing 200 meters of a Jerusalem road during the hours of prayer on Sabbath and religious holidays, against the failure of religious activists to close bars, discotecheques, and cinemas in the Holy City during Sabbath? Some ultra-Orthodox activists celebrated their partial victory on the road closing as a major success, even though they had demanded its closure during all of the Sabbath and religious holidays. Some called the failure to close bars, discotecheques, and cinemas a minor issue, insofar as the places open on the Sabbath are not in religious neighborhoods, even though they had earlier demanded their closure throughout Jerusalem.

Intemperate accusations rather than systematic analysis appear in Israeli discussions about the achievements of religious and anti-religious politicians. Both religious and secular politicians accuse one another of being anti-Semitic. Religious figures say that secular Israelis are ignorant of Judaism, are "goyim who speak Hebrew," and threaten the end of the Jewish people by their aspirations to mimic other nations. Anti-religious politicians term the religious "parasites" for their evasion of military service by studying in publicly supported re-ligious academies. The anti-religious cite the untold numbers of "students" who violate the terms of their public stipends by working in the untaxed informal or underground economy, who claim to be studying in order to evade the army.

Ultra-Orthodox and Orthodox activists seem to have accomplished the most in their demands for financial allocations to schools and other institutions affili-ated with their congregations, as well as for the construction of new neighbor-hoods for their growing families. Orthodox and ultra-Orthodox political parties were well situated in the Knesset and the governing coalition that emerged from the 1996 election. They comprised 19 percent of Knesset membership, but more than a third of the coalition that supported the government of Prime Minister Benjamin Netanyahu.[10] For this reason only, they could expect to do well in the allocation of resources. Although the religious parties increased their representa-tion in the Knesset elected in 1999, speculation was that they would pay a price for campaigning against the victorious prime minister, Ehud Barak. While it is not yet clear which parties he will include in his coalition, his range of possible partners from the center or left of the political spectrum is such that none of the religious parties has the power to make or break his government. The situation was different for Prime Minister Netanyahu. His natural partners were parties from the center or right of the political spectrum, and there the religious parties could make or break his coalition if he did not give them what they demanded.

It is not feasible to make a systematic and convincing reckoning of policy successes by religious politicians. Material assistance to religious and secular institutions comes from a variety of government and quasi-government organi-zations, as well as donations raised from Israeli citizens and overseas. Fund raising, government budgeting, and programming are competitive, and do not lend themselves to candor. Government ministries that provide funds, as well as organizations that receive them, do not clarify the flows in ways that indicate who gets how much. There are discounts in utility charges, other service fees, and taxes given to heads of large families, who, for all intents and purposes, might be counted as additional support for the religious sector. However, the same discounts also benefit many in the Arab sector, as well as large families that are neither Arab nor religious Jews.

The overall record of the ultra-Orthodox and Orthodox movements has been mixed. Moreover, both its victories and those of its rivals have been narrowly specific. Episodes dealing with Sabbath observance, modesty, the treatment of graves uncovered in development projects, or the status of non-Orthodox rabbis burst onto the national agenda, cause intense demonstration by religious and anti-religious activists, and then find a detailed treatment. The general principle behind the episode is not adopted as public policy. Similar episodes erupt again, cause their own commotion, and may end with a different outcome. At times an issue simply disappears from the public agenda without resolution.

Secular Israelis can skirt around the Orthodox Rabbinate's monopoly of marriages and divorces involving Israel's Jews. Couples who cannot qualify for an Israeli marriage or divorce, or who do not want to participate in Orthodox rituals, can marry or divorce abroad in civil procedures, and have their documents recognized by Israeli secular courts and the ministry of interior. Laws the sale of non-kosher food or the opening of Jewish shops on the Sabbath are enforced sporadically.

The picture is one of muddled stand-off between the ultra-Orthodox and Orthodox on the one hand and the secular or anti-religious on the other. The picture is hardly clearer in the case of demands made by non-Orthodox Jewish movements. We saw in chapter 6 that non-Orthodox claimants have won specific victories in Israeli courts, but there have been problems in applying the precedents to subsequent cases that appear to be similar.

Another Look at Religion and Politics, after the Election of 1999

The outcome of the 1999 election and post-election maneuvers toward a governing coalition provide yet another opportunity to assess who wins and looses in the politics of religion or the religion of politics. Among the issues that came to the surface in negotiations toward a coalition were the legitimacy of SHAS as a coalition partner, which party would get to control the interior ministry, and the drafting of ultra-religious men into the military.

None of the issues were straightforward. The status of SHAS depended on the status of Ariyeh Deri, its leading figure who had been convicted of serious crimes in a district court and was awaiting appeal to the Supreme Court. The elected prime minister refused to consider SHAS as a coalition partner if Deri continued as its leader, but he could not lightly dismiss a potential partner with seventeen seats in the Knesset, especially one that was likely to cooperate with his efforts to reach agreements with the Palestinians and the Syrians. Deri resigned his seat in the Knesset and his position as head of the party. This allowed Barak to begin serious negotiations with SHAS, even while Meretz cautioned that it was testing the seriousness of Deri's separation from the SHAS leadership and Shinui continued to insist that it would not sit in a government with SHAS. This put Barak in the quandary of wanting to include a seventeen-member party in his coalition that might threaten the staying away of two parties with a combined membership of sixteen! The issue became more murky at one point when SHAS leaders insisted that they must be allowed to consult with Deri, even though he did not occupy any formal position in the party, and when the rabbi who was the party's spiritual leader insisted that he had declared Deri innocent and that it was evil persons who were continuing to persecute him. For Meretz and Shinui, these actions and statements indicated that Deri would continue to lead SHAS even though he had ostensibly resigned his leadership positions.

Both SHAS and Natan Sharansky's party of Russian immigrants demanded the interior ministry. Among the ministry's responsibilities is the designation of whether or not an immigrant is a Jew, and the distribution of resources to local authorities. SHAS had held the ministry through the administrations of several prime ministers, and had a reputation of applying religious criteria to the registration of immigrants. For that reason alone Sharansky wanted the ministry for his party. Numerous immigrants felt themselves mistreated and mislabeled, with implications for the ease with which they could marry or be buried.

The ministry's control of local authority budgets was no less important. Charges against Ariyeh Deri focused on his misuse of ministerial powers to direct funds to the schools and other social services associated with SHAS. Sharansky wanted more of those funds for programs to serve recent immigrants. When Prime Minister Barak indicated that he would name Sharansky as Interior Minister, the SHAS leadership proclaimed that it was insulted, and went into yet another huddle to decide if it would accept the terms being offered for joining the government.

The issue of drafting ultra-Orthodox young men into the military was no simpler. With the immigration of a million people in the most recent decade and the hoped-for end of the military threat from the Palestinians and other neighbors, Israel no longer seemed in need of additional military personnel. Moreover, the physical and intellectual preparation of ultra-Orthodox teenagers was such that their training would require substantial investment and little foreseeable payoff for the military. Thus the issue of their being drafted boiled down to one of an ideology focused on the equality of enduring military service rather than an equality of exposure to serious danger. Senior military personnel expressed doubt that it would be worth the effort to recruit and train the ultra-Orthodox. Various proposals were made to recruit them for limited training, prepare them for reserve service as guards and other low-quality duty, and provide generous exemptions to young men who were intensely committed to religious studies.

The status of SHAS and the drafting of the ultra-Orthodox, as well as other recurring problems of state and religion, seemed likely to remain matters of contention. When Ehud Barak finally presented his new government, it included ministers of SHAS and the NRP, as well as the occasionally anti-religious Meretz. Some static could be expected from the ministry of education, that would have a Meretz Minister and NRP Deputy Minister, as well as from the sharing of power between SHAS and NRP in the ministry of religions. Barak assigned the ministry of health to SHAS toward the end of coalition negotiations. It seemed to be a political decision of secondary importance by a secular prime minister who needed SHAS in his government in order to support his primary concerns for negotiations with Palestinians and Syrians. The appointment raised the prospect that, with an ultra-Orthodox party in control, the ministry would be less friendly toward the sensitive issues of abortion and organ transplants. Initial speculation was that the new minister would work to create an ultra-Orthodox health maintenance organization, and lessen the resources available to the sorely pressed existing organizations. United Torah Judaism signed on as a partner to the coalition, even though it did not receive any ministerial appointments. Shinui continued with its anti-ultra-Orthodox posture, and remained in the parliamentary opposition.

Even with SHAS in the coalition, its spiritual and political leaders seemed likely to be ambivalent with respect to the legitimacy of the country's legal system. Being persecuted by the secular Ashkenazi elite was part of SHAS's appeal to its voters, and Deri's conviction on criminal charges added to that appeal. The formulations that Barak and SHAS found that would allow them to work together would not erase suspicion in the minds of SHAS supporters about the secular legal system, or the doubts among secular Israelis about the corruption of SHAS. Adjustments in the recruitment of ultra-Orthodox would not make them fully contributing members of the military nor eliminate the feelings among secular critics that they were dodging their obligations.

With the start of the new administration, there were numerous complaints by coalition partners and opponents that the election did not resolve the country's problems or their personal aspirations. None were declaring victory amidst feelings of unresolved injustices.

Like Other Countries in the Big Picture, but Distinctive in Details

The outcome of religious struggles in Israeli politics resembles parallel confrontations in other western democracies. Issues touching on religion are often on the political agenda, but neither religious nor secular activists can overcome the other. Elsewhere the issues may be divorce, abortion, religious ceremonies in public places, or religious content in elementary and secondary education. Conditions favor the side that supports the status quo. Changes are likely to be piecemeal. Dramatic changes like the United States Supreme Court decision in *Roe v. Wade* that removed sweeping bans against abortion stand outside this generalization. However, the continued dispute and numerous subsequent changes in both pro- and anti-abortion directions support the generalization. Religious and anti-religious sentiments can motivate policymakers as was large segments of democratic societies, but these actors have only limited ability to transform their agenda into public policy. More typical than the sweeping decision of *Roe v. Wade* was the signing by 153 members of the U.S. House of Representatives as co-sponsors of a proposed constitutional amendment to permit prayers in the public schools. Commentators noted the intensity and persistence of those who put the item on the agenda, alongside their failure to persuade the requisite number of their colleagues to endorse the measure.[11]

Israel's religious parties show traits generally associated with both political parties and interest groups. Unable to fit neatly into one or another of the categories used by political scientists in analyzing other countries, the religious political parties of Israel reflect distinctive traits of Israel's culture. Although Israel is homogeneous in the sense that 79 percent of its residents are Jews, the nature of Judaism renders that population divided on the dimension of religiosity. Issues are fought out mostly between an ultra-Orthodox and Orthodox segment on the one hand, and a secular segment on the other hand. A third segment of progressive religious Jews draws on an overseas power base. It has won favorable rulings from Israeli courts, but has trouble turning those decisions into general policy against the disinterest of secular Israelis who are generally unmoved by the religious demands of the non-Orthodox, and against the intense opposition of the Orthodox and ultra-Orthodox who are well placed in the Knesset and key bureaucracies.

Chapter 8

Ambiguities in Religion Resemble Those in Politics: One That Makes Promises for the World to Come and Another That Makes Promises for the Government to Come

We have seen in previous chapters that religion and politics both have large audiences in modern states. Congregations and political parties compete for adherents. For many adherents, both religion and party are inherited traits, passed from one generation to another. Some believers may shop around for a church or a preacher just as voters occasionally depart from party loyalties. Periodic election campaigns encourage defections in ways not unlike revival meetings of proselytizing preachers. Both faith and politics have their "stay at homes," or individuals who overlook the competition or direct curses at all the options. Mass defections from a faith or party are rare, and tend to attract considerable attention when they occur.

Doctrine is important in both political and religious competitions, but the ideas are loosely formulated and selectively quoted. Individuals who affiliate with a religious congregation or a political party may be uninformed about doctrinal details, and perhaps uninterested. Both religions and political parties tend to accept a loose view of principles and tolerate abstentions from prayer services and elections, at least in western democracies. This is an admirable trait, insofar as both religion and politics have shown their capacity to excite the masses to violence. We live better with a bit of faith and political loyalty, rather than with a lot of either.

Religion and politics depend on faith and the promise of what is to come. Yet neither has achieved the paradise that they offer. Sectarians and party activists try to recruit affiliates to their own cluster, and to elicit more activity from affiliates. There are sophisticated theoreticians, crafty leaders, and simple believers in both realms. The behaviors suitable to politics and religion are interchangeable and the fields overlap. For some, politics is their religion. Pursuing the "art of the possible" competes with the spiritual values of religion for its moral worth. Religion is the offering of many engaged in politics, ranging from the Christian Right in the United States to ultra-Orthodox in Israel, along with Protestants and Catholics in Northern Ireland, Islamic Fundamentalists throughout the Middle East, and other varieties in countries that are more and less democratic.

The focus of this chapter is the ambiguity of religion. Like intellectual leaders in politics, those in religion are not precise in their doctrines. And critics of religious and political figures need be no more precise than those they censure for failing to deliver on their commitments. There is more vagueness and contradiction than exactness in classic texts as well as the most recent commentaries, sermons, or campaign rhetoric. There are proof texts for wide ranges of theologians, preachers, candidates, and officeholders who manage to exist within the generous boundaries of religious and political movements. Doctrines that promise much in the distant future are safe against protests that they are wrong. Themes of organizational theory that explain behaviors as reflecting the pursuit of institutional self-interest are often more successful in explaining the actions of religious and political figures than the doctrines that they proclaim.

Ambiguity is inherent in religion and politics. Both employ fuzzy doctrines that may help in recruiting support, and prevent clear judgments failure. Imprecise promises exceed tangible accomplishments. Religious Jews anticipate the Messiah, but they have a history of rejecting those who claim to be the Messiah. Governments never have enough resources to deliver on all of the campaign promises.

Ambiguous Monotheism

The monotheistic religions assert their revealed truths, but their histories are replete with argument. Did the miracles described in the Bible really happen, or are they "stories for children" meant to convey great ideas to individuals of limited capacity?

Among the ambiguities in the Hebrew Bible that also relate to ancient politics are passages about kingship. The Book of Deuteronomy calls on the Israelites to appoint as king the man chosen by God.[1] Then no king of Judah or Israel escapes the wrath of biblical critics. It was Samuel against Saul, Nathan against David, Elijah and Micaiah against Ahab, Elisha against Jehoram, and Jeremiah against Jehoiakim and Zedekiah.

A simple reading of Ecclesiastes finds expressions of emptiness, futility, and meaninglessness that challenge precepts of absolutism that appear elsewhere in the Bible. Death is the end of us all, the wise as well as the foolish.[2] The book professes change as opposed to constancy, and urges judgment about the situation as opposed to a faith in absolutes. "Everything has its season . . . a time to be born and a time to die; a time to plant and a time to uproot; a time to kill and a time to heal . . . a time to love and a time to hate; a time for war and a time for peace."[3]

The Ten Commandments are at the heart of biblical law, but they are not without their ambiguities. The original Hebrew of the sixth commandment is לֹא תִּרְצָח (lo tirtzach).[4] Modern Hebrew speakers are likely to translate it as *Do not murder.* Thus it appears in the translation by the Jewish Theological Seminary of America, as well as the New English Bible. The meaning, perhaps, is premeditated intentional killing. However, the same passage is translated as *Do not kill* in the King James Version and the Revised Standard Version. This suggests a more sweeping prohibition that may bar self-defense and support pacifism. The word רְצַח (retzach) now usually associated with murder appears in other episodes when the intention appears to be *to kill* rather than *to murder*, as in the case of individuals who kill without prior intention, and can seek protection from vengeful relatives of the deceased in a city of refuge.[5] The Bible also uses the word usually translated as kill in modern Hebrew (הֶרֶג : hereg) when the intention appears to be murder, as in the story of Cain and Abel.[6]

Further complicating the Bible's reputation for absolute truth are its uses of metaphor, allegory, and symbolism. What is said about the biblical interpretations of the apostle Paul can apply to many other readings by Jews and Christians. "We cannot be sure that if Paul had interpreted the same passage twice he would have interpreted it in the same way."[7]

A well-known Christian interpretation of murky biblical language is that the story about the suffering servant in the Book of Isaiah predicts the life of Jesus. Traditional Jewish commentators view the suffering servant as a symbol for the Israelite nation, or as Isaiah's view of himself.[8]

Integral to the development of Judaism are the decisions in cases brought before rabbis. By tradition, the rabbis explicate the Oral Torah in a process that began with Moses. More than two millennia of decisions, as well as commentaries on them, provide for numerous ways of viewing current cases and previous decisions—or precedents—that appear to be relevant. Among the accusations said about Judaism is "hair splitting," or the definition of fine distinctions that allows, or prevents, one case from being used as a basis of deciding another. What to anti-Semites may be excessive argument about insignificant issues is to religious Jews the way of discerning God's intentions.

Richard Lamm of the Orthodox Yeshiva University considered the various streams of rabbinical commentary that shed light on the issue of homosexuality. He found themes that counsel empathy for the homosexual and a willingness to include homosexuals within a religious community rather than to banish them. Yet he found nothing in the Jewish tradition to endorse or encourage homosexuality. He could not condone congregations established for homosexual Jews, and he could not recommend repealing secular laws against homosexual practices. Given Judaic concerns for compassion as well as modern political realities, however, he would urge police and judges not to enforce existing laws against homo-sexual practices.[9]

A lack of clarity in religious expression is not only something from the Bible and its commentaries. A number of distinguished rabbis in modern Israel are inclined to express themselves in parables that depend for their comprehension on the insight or imagination of their followers. The spiritual leader of the ultra-Orthodox Sephardim said in the midst of one political controversy, "the head of the flock is a blind man who stumbles and falls." This caused something of a problem for the rabbis' followers in the government coalition, but they were quick to assert that the rabbi was not referring to the prime minister.[10]

The plurality of doctrines even within the same religious tradition assures continued dispute as to what is the religious position in terms of specific worldly controversies. One case in point is environmentalism. Recent concern might be traced to the appearance of Rachel Carson's *Silent Spring* in 1962 and a subsequent surge of legislation, administrative, and judicial actions in many countries. Those who would search scripture for environmental guidance find more problems than solutions. The first chapter of Genesis is perhaps the most problematic. It assigns to humans "dominion over the fish of the sea, and over the fowl of the air, and over the cattle, and over all the earth," and enjoins them to be "fruitful and multiply." The chapter indicates that humans should "replenish the earth" as well as "subdue it."[11] The authors were not prepared for our debates, and did not specify what limits, if any, should be set on efforts to be fruitful and multiply, or how much effort we should devote to replenishing the earth. Holy Scripture shows no sensitivity to the needs of limiting human reproduction. Its interpreters among Roman Catholics or Orthodox Jews stand prominently against the prime commandment of environmentalists to limit births.

Ambiguity May Assist or Retard
Political or Religious Purposes

The problems of ambiguity in politics are well known. Participants do not know exactly where they stand. There are no fixed boundaries or guidelines to behavior that can be described as legitimate, reasonable, or acceptable. At the very least, ambiguity produces the stress of not knowing one's own limits or those of one's adversaries.

The situation is similar in religion. Individuals who consider themselves faithful find themselves banished from their congregations for articulating postures anathema to a spiritual leader. Today the punishment may be only emotional— loss of face among fellow members of the congregation. In the past, and even today in non-democratic theocracies, the fate of heretics and apostates has been more severe.

The other sides of ambiguity consist of the opportunities for preachers and politicians to choose and blur their doctrines for the sake of recruiting more souls and voters and to justify a pragmatic choice of action on the basis of one or another proof text.

The Fuzziness Surrounding Religion and Politics in the Jewish State

Israel offers a tantalizing canvas on which to examine the ambiguities of religion and politics. Politics is intense and elicits wide interest and participation.[12] Politicians cope with problems that are too difficult to solve in a forthright manner, and ambiguity often appears as one of their coping mechanisms.

Religion as well as national borders are prominent among the unsolved problems of Israel. Israel declared itself a *Jewish state* in 1948 when other democracies were well on their way to secularization. The ambiguity in the nature of Judaism supports numerous contentious postures among religious and secular Israelis about Judaism and their Jewishness. Is Judaism simply what Jews believe and do, or does it require the acceptance of certain doctrines? If there are mandatory doctrines, what are they?

Lacking a unifying central authority since ancient times, Judaism has been free to evolve without fracturing into distinct faiths. Moreover, dispersion exposed Jews to the influences of many cultures. The gathering in Palestine/Israel during the last century has brought a diversity that continues to evolve.

Israeli intellectuals have claimed leadership of the Jewish world. However, Diaspora Jews are ambivalent with respect to their acceptance of Israeli leadership on matters of faith or politics.[13] Non-Orthodox Jews are dominant in several Diaspora communities, especially the United States, and they express protection of the non-Orthodox religious minority in Israel. This pits Jews with little direct support in the Israeli electorate against Orthodox and ultra-Orthodox parties that are well situated in the Knesset. Israeli prime ministers welcome overseas financial donations to their own campaigns as well as to Israeli institutions, and the political assistance that non-Orthodox Diaspora Jews can wield with their own governments. Israeli prime ministers are less welcoming of Diaspora involvement in Israeli politics. When Diaspora leaders say what they want the Israeli government to do, the responses are likely to be vague commitments implemented in partial or ambiguous fashion.

The ambiguity in the treatment of religious disputes among Jews is apparent when both religious and anti-religious activists claim losses in what seems like an ongoing tug-of-war. Both can also claim gains, but they tend to avoid boasting in order to play the part of the downtrodden at the next encounter. On some occasions, each can claim *both* victory and defeat, as when authorities enact measures that seem to favor one side, but implement them only partially and sporadically.

Ambiguities are assured insofar as religious versus secular religious disputes focus on particular cases, and avoid any effort to resolve once and for all time the general issues that are at stake. The individual cases find a solution or disappear from the public agenda without resolution, and the same underlying conflict returns again at another time or another site. There is no clear indication whether religious or secular are winning, or what is general policy with respect to Sabbath activities, rules of modesty, or the status of non-Orthodox Judaism.

We saw in chapter 4 that both Israelis and Palestinians have perceived the utility of ambiguity in treating the sensitive issue of Jerusalem. A lack of clear resolution allows those who are peaceably inclined to live close to one another. However, ambiguity also allows, or even provokes, others to exploit opportunities to advance their interests even while they threaten others.

The cumbersome nature of Israeli politics and the lack of final resolution of dispute warn that ambiguity is no magic potent. While neither religious nor anti-religious activists have been able to dominate, neither is satisfied. Some Jews suffer because the state does not enforce religious law strictly enough. Others suffer because the state is too Jewish. The intensity of hatred appears on the faces and in the screams of religious and anti-religious Israelis when they demonstrate against one another. Still others suffer because they cannot tolerate a situation where there are no clear outcomes to the chronic disputes. The last snicker may go to the observer who concludes that the results of ambiguity in religion as well as in politics are ambiguous. Ambiguity prevails. It is not ideal. Yet ambiguity may keep Israel from even more destructive conflict among its Jews.

The workability of ambiguity and other forms of coping requires a mutual willingness to profit from them. All sides must be willing to take some chances, and to make some concessions in order to convince their partners and adversaries that the results are worth the risks. Individuals of different perspective will reach contrasting conclusions as to the balance between losses and gains, or whether the losses that are suffered are worth the gains that are achieved.

Ambiguity is worth the costs so long as the participants continue with their partial losses and gains, and do not throw over the process and seek a more clear, complete, and final solution to the problem. The preacher saw the problem a long time ago. "To everything there is a season, a time for every purpose under heaven." Ecclesiastes mentions birth and death, planting and harvesting, killing and healing, breaking down and building up, weeping and laughing, mourning and dancing, casting away stones and gathering them up, embracing and refraining, tearing and sewing, silence and speech, love and hate, war and peach. Why not ambiguity and clarity?[14]

Likewise in Utah

No two religious groups seem more different than the Mormons and Jews, yet the Mormons' homeland of Utah resembles Israel in the ambiguity that surrounds the political accomplishments of religious activists.[15]

Mormons not only set themselves apart from Jews by their acceptance of Jesus as the Messiah, but the Mormons go beyond other Christians in elaborating Jesus' resurrections (including an appearance in the Americas) as well as his relationships with God and other figures. One Mormon version of the Book of Genesis, said to be a correct translation by Joseph Smith, begins with a conversation between God and Moses about Jesus.[16] Proselytizing is central to Mormon practice. The church conducts sophisticated programs of recruiting and training missionaries, and sending them out to enlist new souls. Judaism has discouraged converts since Roman times. Mormons claim continuing revelations to the prophet who rules their hierarchical church. Jews say that there has been no prophet since Malachi (perhaps sixth century BCE). The Hebrew prophets were critics of the elites rather than rulers.

Mormons continue to employ church tribunals to banish those who speak or act against official doctrines. According to one recent prophet, the church allows members to think what they will, but not to express doctrines contrary to those accepted by the church.[17] A statement issued by church-owned Brigham Young University illustrates the ambiguity of religious expression, as well as conveying the threat of a church that aspires to discipline.

> For the most part, there exists at BYU the standard responsible freedom and vitality that the best universities have attempted to protect and foster. . . . The only point of closure is that the University will not freely tolerate an advocacy of its destruction through attacking the foundation of the religion that sustains it. . . . [BYU] administrators are advised not to publish in *Dialogue, a Journal of Mormon Thought*, or to participate in *Sunstone's* symposia where they may be viewed as attacking the General Authorities of the University's sustaining Church or the foundations of its faith.[18]

Several persons have fallen outside of these boundaries. Spokesmen for the university attributed the denial of tenure to a Mormon instructor in 1988 to his views that Joseph Smith drafted the *Book of Mormon* in the nineteenth century, rather than having translated it from ancient plates; that prophets of the Hebrew Bible spoke mainly to people of their time and were not concerned primarily with predicting events far into the future; and that the Bible was created by humans and can be examined with the tools of the critical historian.[19]

The decision did not pass without inner turmoil and faculty grumbling. Characteristically, these expressions were quiet, and without dramatic gestures of protest. Justifications given for the dismissal reflect the view that the university has a pastoral mission that is more important than its academic mission. It was said that personnel who received their salaries from the tithing of church members should not be allowed to criticize basic doctrines of the church. And that church members send their children to BYU in order to have their faith strengthened, and not destroyed by contrary interpretations or self-doubt.

These justifications are troubling for individuals who put a priority on free expression, or who would strengthen religious commitments via the free exchange of ideas even at the risk of losing a few souls. In connection with the instructor's dismissal, one of his faculty colleagues said that a Mormon instructor could not be comfortable at the university unless he believed in angels. Another said that the instructor can thank his naivete rather than his religious beliefs for his dismissal. "He could have behaved like 40 percent of the faculty and lots of other Mormons, and kept his doubts to himself. He made a mistake by trying to reform the university. He should have known that he could not have overcome the orthodox members of the faculty. He provided them with an irresistible target." Five years later, the former BYU instructor, then teaching at Brandeis University, was found to be continuing with the expression of improper doctrine and was excommunicated from the church.

Utah is the center of a religious community with some eleven million members world-wide. An estimated 67 percent of the state's population and more than 90 percent of the people in some localities affiliate with the Church of Jesus Christ of Latter-day Saints (LDS).[20]

Along with what appear to be unifying doctrines and strict discipline, Utah Mormons exhibit some of the pluralism apparent among Israeli Jews. Moreover, the diversity of the population, along with the imposing legal and cultural influences of the United States, makes Utah no more of a theocracy than Israel.

Individual Mormons vary in the extent to which they take part in church activities, adhere to its precepts, or identify with the attitudes that prevail among the members. Roughly one-third of the readers of *Dialogue*, a journal that describes itself as Mormon but non-official, responded to a questionnaire in a way to suggest that they do not accept basic doctrines.[21] Some Mormons distinguish between doctrinal requirements of the church, which they must accept under penalty of being denied access to a Temple and its sacraments, and the advice of church leaders, which they can ignore without penalty (e.g., to avoid excessive debt or overeating). Individuals also describe matters of political conscience where the church should not assert itself.

Church doctrine is sufficiently ambiguous to provide the current leadership substantial discretion on contemporary issues. This ambiguity also permits church members to differ among themselves and to disagree with church leaders. Some say that the doctrine is clear, but that its application to specific issues is open to dispute.

Like the religious establishment of Israel, the LDS Church has a mixed record in trying to legislate issues of doctrine. Liquor and gambling illustrate the points. The church has to curtail or limit both activities. Yet Utahns can buy alcohol in state liquor stores and purchase drinks in many restaurants. The church has been successful in resisting on-track betting and casinos. But there are limousine services from Salt Lake to the casinos of State Line, Nevada, and Utahns make day trips to horse racing in Wyoming.

Utah's neighboring state of Nevada also shows Mormon flexibility and pragmatism. Mormons are the state's second-largest religious denomination.[22] They are politically active and have made their peace with legalized sin. While some Mormons assert that their co-religionists live pristine lives that are isolated from Nevada's tourist industry, others admit that this is impossible in a state with few economic options. Active church members serve the casinos as dealers, corporate officers, accountants, and attorneys. One Mormon has been chair of the Nevada Gaming Commission.[23]

All is not moderate among the Mormons. Members of schisms that describe themselves as the true Mormons insist that polygamy is the Lord's way. A newspaper report in 1998 estimated that 40,000 Utahns (two percent of the population) lived in polygamous households.[24] The Mormon Church has banned the practice since the 1890s. Utah authorities generally do not enforce laws against polygamy while living together without marriage and other voluntary sexual practices have become widespread throughout the United States. However, there are problems with the abuse of women whose participation in polygamous relationships is not voluntary. Families have moved from polygamy to economic crimes and other violations, and into violence against law enforcement officials and errant family members.

Mormons and Judaism

There is no exact and objective manner to array the doctrines and practices of Jews and Mormons. Judaism differs from the LDS Church in being overtly pluralistic without an authoritative center. Liberal rabbis and Jewish humanists range far from Orthodox doctrines and practice, and this diversity suggests that Judaism is more open to diversity than Mormonism. The Jewish posture that Malachi was the last prophet stands prominently against the Mormon doctrine of latter-day sainthood and a contemporary prophet who is ruler of the church. Jewish traditions of acerbic criticism and intellectual creativity appearing in the biblical books of the prophets, Job and Ecclesiastes, as well as the wide-ranging creativity of modern Jewish intellectuals contrast with Mormon trials for heresy. The biting humor that Jewish writers have directed at biblical figures, as in Joseph Heller's *God Knows* or Stefan Heym's *The King David Report*,[25] contrast with the piety that marks Mormon fiction about biblical characters.[26]

With all of these differences, individual rabbis and other learned Jews exhibit a number of the behaviors associated with Mormons. Local rabbinical courts in modern Israel declare individuals to be dangerous on account of aberrant expressions or behaviors, and warn other Jews from having any contact with them. In response to a road accident that killed schoolchildren on a class outing, a rabbi who later became minister of interior said that the tragedy was due to the practice in their town of opening places of entertainment on the Sabbath. Another rabbi, the spiritual leader of the ultra-Orthodox Sephardi movement, has proclaimed that early death and a designation as non-Jews are appropriate punishments for Jews who violate the Sabbath.[27]

Jews who smile at Mormons' stories of being helped by angels should not overlook their own co-religionists who ask for favors at the tombs of revered figures or visit rabbis with reputations for working miracles. Individual rabbis of all traditions—from the ultra-Orthodox to the Reform—express their belief that the Lord provided the written and oral Torah to Moses on Mount Sinai, and accept the doctrine that contemporary rabbis give expression to the oral Torah when they interpret religious law. Jews who wonder at the bizarre rituals of the Mormons, like the baptism of individuals long dead, might wonder at the practice of Israeli burial societies of circumcising those Jews whose bodies they find to be uncircumcised.[28] Alongside the worldly sarcasm of writers like Heller and Heym there are pious Jewish tales that create wholly admirable characters out of the complex figures described in the Hebrew Bible.[29]

What Israel and Utah Tell Us about the Nature of Religion

Similarities in detail among communities as distinct as Judaism and Mormonism illustrate the mysteries at the heart of religious practice. Despite the looming difference on the status of Christ, contrasts on the dimension of doctrinal pluralism, and all the lesser points that separate Jews and Mormons, individual Jews as well as Mormons act as pre-Enlightenment zealots. They express a continuing belief in miracles, call down the punishment of heaven on those who articulate improper doctrines, and in extreme cases seek to do the Lord's work by employing violence.

Both the religious Jews of Israel and the Mormons of Utah make persistent efforts to expand their influence through the power of the state, and both fail to overcome their opponents. In Israel and Utah, religious issues are often on the public agenda. Critics of both polities term them theocracies, but they fall short of Saudi Arabia, Iran, Afghanistan, Pakistan, or Sudan. If those countries are theocracies, then Utah and Israel are something else. While religious authorities in Utah and Israel have substantial power over their adherents, those who do not adhere can follow their own consciences on matters of marriage and divorce, abortion, Sabbath observance, liquor, gambling, and other issues that the religious would regulate.

Jacob Neusner's insight into the plurality of Judaisms helps to clarify this picture. In several writings he claims to identify *eight* or *ten* varieties of Judaisms, depending on one's reading of his text.[30] Mormons have had much less time to develop variations of doctrine and interpretation, and the posture of the official LDS hierarchy toward dissidents is meant to discourage creativity. However, articles in *Dialogue* and *Sunstone* show efforts to differentiate rituals and interpretations of doctrine, and to stretch the range of what is tolerated. For more than a century the Reorganized Church of Jesus Christ of Latter-day Saints, with its center in Independence, Missouri, has provided an institutionalized alternative to the Salt Lake Church. Residents of Utah and other western states can also find numerous local varieties of Mormonism, typically with their own self-styled prophet and polygamous households.

There is a common explanation of both phenomena considered here: the plurality of practice within the same religious communities and the modesty of political power shown by religious activists in Israel and Utah. These phenomena suggest that the importance of religion is considerable, but limited. This chapter has shown this to be the case in two locales of heightened religious consciousness. If religion is limited in Israel and Utah, it is not likely to be more powerful in other democratic polities that are more overtly secular.

Religion is important enough to assure its presence on the agendas of western democracies, but religious leaders are neither capable of dominating their congregations on matters of doctrine nor capable of dominating their polities on matters of public policy. Religious loyalty has proved able to resist two centuries of secularization. Yet while religious leaders in Israel, Utah, and other democratic polities speak out against secular norms, they seem to have accommodated themselves to the strength of values that are not their own. Perhaps they are led by a sense of realism, or a recognition of the potential costs of seeking to impose on their communities what the true believers see as their monopoly of the truth.

Chapter 9

If Conditions Resemble Those That Produced a Messiah, Why Are Religion and Politics Relatively Moderate?

We have seen the intensity of the ultra-religious and the ultra-anti-religious in Israel and elsewhere. In Israel and most other western democracies, there is also a lack of widespread destructive violence focused on issues of religion. Modern democracies, including Israel, have proved themselves willing and able to contain religious excesses. This poses the central question of this chapter: If conditions in Israel are chronically tense, comparable in some respects as they were at the time of Jesus, why is it that contemporary religious and political conflicts are moderate?

Modern Israel like ancient Judea is small in size and population, set upon by hostile neighbors having at their disposal great wealth, large armies, and vast armaments. The modern country is also beset with a sharply divided population, between cosmopolitans willing to adopt the culture of foreign powers and zealots concerned to guard against foreign influences.

The differences between the two periods help to explain why the chronic tensions about religion in Israel have not spilled over into domestic violence or messianic fervor.

Surrounded by hostility, modern Israel has been able nevertheless to best its neighbors in a series of wars and, by so doing, may have convinced them to desist from the military option. It has helped that Israelis are better educated than their neighbors and that the national economy is more advanced. Israel's wealth and technological sophistication provide it with advantages on the battlefield as well as in international markets. Israel has sought the help of foreign powers, but has been fortunate in that those assisting have been sensitive to Israel's concerns for independence. It is better to exist in an age dominated by the United States than one by that of Rome.

The study of history deserves some credit. Both Israel and the great powers have learned the dangers in pushing their points too sharply. They accommodate ambiguities in their relationships. Two centuries since the Enlightenment have not destroyed religion, but they have educated enough of the elites and masses to look with some skepticism at the claims of religious leaders that their particular faith poses a monopoly on truth. Religious as well as secular leaders know the consequences of ancient civil wars, and they have sought to cool tempers of their followers when tensions seem to be getting dangerous. The religious Jews of Israel have been made wary of messianic claims by Jesus Christ, Sabbatai Zevi, and Jacob Frank. It is a wonder that the Lubavitcher looked to their Rebbe as a likely messiah. It is not surprising that other religious Jews ridiculed them.

Religion generally, at least in western democracies, has evolved toward moderation. Such a conclusion seems at odds with explosions at abortion clinics, excitement about the teaching of evolution, the millions of American families that have taken their children out of public school in order to provide them with religious instruction in home teaching, the limping toward peace in Northern Ireland, and the assassination of Yitzhak Rabin.

Many of the home schoolers, like the members of new religious movements, may be going along with fashions. Some are teaching their children at home out of frustration with the poor quality of public school instruction, without reference to religion. We will have to see how this movement develops for a number of years before we judge its holding power. We have seen that even nominally religious Utah, like nominally religious Israel, applies its religion with a moderate degree of intensity against secular opponents. Mormonism is perhaps only marginally less strong in Utah than is Judaism in Israel. The differences may be due mostly to the weight of the United States Constitution, the overwhelming majority of non-Mormons in the country as a whole, and the easy penetration of Utah by non-Mormons. Newcomers are attracted by the natural beauty, economic opportunities, and lifestyle created by the two-thirds of the population that is Mormon. Some or the outsiders or their children become Mormons. However, not all Mormons are loyal followers of their church in matters of doctrine or politics.

Israel provides its own variety of believers, doubters, and fence-sitters. Most intense are religious Zionists committed to maintaining Jewish control of as much as possible of the Land of Israel, and perhaps 10 percent of the population that is ultra-Orthodox. Doubters are most likely to appear among the 50 percent of the population who identify as secular. The fence-sitters are the "traditional" Jews, mostly of North African origin, who observe some of the religious commandments some of the time, but not when they wish to travel on the Sabbath for a football game or to cook steak at a family picnic.

Political scientists propound the doctrine that democracies do not go to war against one another. The religious parallel is that Christian nations today fight one another less than they did in the past. Memorable is the passage in Tolstoy's *War and Peace* in which he describes how millions of Christian men professing the love of their fellows prayed to the same God asking him to aid them in slaying other Christians who were intoning similar prayers. The end of Christian war is not yet at hand. Peace among Protestants and Catholics in Ireland is shaky. Orthodox Serbs and Roman Catholic Croats recently killed one another in the Balkans. Nonetheless Christians may be farther along the road to peace than Muslims, whose recent record is bloodier: Turks against Kurds, Iraq's invasions of Iran and then Kuwait, as well as Muslim Afghans doing what they can to kill one another.

These residual cases of strife that are at least partly religious in their origins contrast with the relatively peaceful tension among the Jews of Israel. Assuming that the killing of Yitzhak Rabin by a religious nationalist was an anomaly, we should ask why the lack of serious violence.

In general terms, moderation apparent in modern democracies affects both religion and politics. To be sure, the condition is not complete. However, the larger picture is one of temperance in dispute rather than one of violence. The situation is common to both politics and religion in countries that are reasonably well-to-do and democratic.

Explanations of the situation include a realization of the costs associated with extremism that may reflect lessons learned from the destruction of World Wars I and II and the Holocaust; a general decline of religious fervor since the Enlightenment; material benefits in western democracies accruing from post-World War II prosperity; and the relatively benign international influence of *pax Americana*. We have not seen an end of ideology or theology, but we have seen a decline in the extremism and intensity of both.

Substantial migration affecting Western Europe, North America, and Australia may makes its own contribution to the moderation of religious dispute. While the introduction of many foreigners to existing populations does provoke animosity, the result is a dilution of prior majorities and the addition of representatives of the newer communities to each country's political elites. Hate crimes occur, but they are not respectable and not encouraged by the leaders of major parties. The rules of democratic countries recognize the legitimacy of different perspectives, and provide for the peaceful settling of disputes. They discourage incitement, and punish those who violate the rules.

There are also more precise explanations suitable to the details of each country. The emphasis in this book has been on Israel, and we have indicated a number of traits that may affect a moderation of religious dispute.

Differences among religious Jews help to diffuse and moderate conflict. The agenda of religious Zionists affiliated with Gush Emunim is not that of the Lubavitcher ultra-Orthodox. Both are mystical in their anticipation of salvation, but the concern of one with land settlement leads in a different direction from the concern of the other with the possible resurrection of a dead rabbi.

Included in the development of a religion whose practitioners have been literate for perhaps 2,500 years is a great diversity of writings that have explored the lives of its heroes. Quarrels between Jews who are cosmopolitan and those who are zealous in their adherence to religious law have a history of at least two millennia. The culture provides for the cynic and the clown as well as the pious. Irreverent portrayals of the biblical David by the American Jewish novelist Joseph Heller and the German Jewish writer Stefan Heym stand against the continued propagation of pious Jewish myths. Readers can choose between David as an over-sexed bumbler who ends his life as a cold, impotent, and senile old man who cannot take advantage of the young virgin employed to warm his bed, or the heroic king who always submitted his decisions on religious questions to learned men to make sure that they were in accordance with God's law.[1]

Hints of self-deprecating humor appear in the Hebrew Bible. Toward the end of the Book of Job, after the miserable man has spilled his soul in lament for his sufferings and begged God for an explanation of his plight, it was God's turn to answer. To say the least, the divine performance is disappointing. There was a great wind and much noise, but the words were beside the point. God asserted his status and put man in his lower place. It is God who will ask questions, and man who will answer.[2] The questions attributed to God are tendentious and bombastic: Who are you to speak to me as you do? Where were you when I created the earth? Did you proclaim the rules that govern the heavens? Did you determine the laws of nature? Do you know where the darkness dwells? Do you know when the mountain goats are born? Can you pass a cord through the whale's nose?

To the pious, God's speech is a forthright proclamation of his power. A skeptic might wonder if an author meant it to be a ridicule of the Lord by emphasizing his loud evasion of Job's problems. A further indication of ridicule by understatement appears in Job's response. In contrast to the overstatement by the Lord, Job says, "What can I say . . . I already spoke, and will not speak again."[3] Saadia Gaon, in his commentary of the tenth century, noted that Job's response to God is ambiguous. Saadia wrote that Job either indicated his acquiescence in God's power or his feeling of being overborne by a God who had the upper hand in a dispute that could not be judged by a neutral arbitrator.[4]

Jokes about the Almighty are part of the discourse in modern Israel. The following explanations of God's failure to receive tenure circulate among the country's university academics. Item 2 reflects the practice to award recognition only to those scholars who succeed in reaching audiences outside of Israel, in some language other than Hebrew.

Why God Never Received Tenure at the University?

Because He had only one major publication.

And it was in Hebrew.

And it had no references.

And it wasn't published in a refereed journal.

And some even doubt He wrote it himself.

It may be true that He created the world but what has He published/done since ?

His cooperative efforts have been quite limited.

The scientific community has had a very rough time trying to repeat His re-sults.

It is not easy to decide if cynicism, subtle humor, theater for the sake of con-stituents, or serious dispute occurs in Knesset discussions about religion. Some of the rabbis who represented religious parties in the Knesset during 1990 ex-pressed rage and others laughed when, in opposition to their proposal to strengthen the laws against pornography, a secular member read from the *Song of Songs*: "thy neck shall be as a tower of ivory. . . thy breasts shall be as clusters of the vine.[5] A left-wing Knesset Member provoked an outburst from religious parliamentarians when she referred to the love between David and Jonathan in support of homosexual rights.[6] Foreign Minister Shimon Peres set off a shouting match when he said he could not defend all that King David had done, especially with respect to Bathsheba. Religious members of the Knesset asserted that this was an unacceptable insult of the author of Psalms. One ultra-Orthodox parlia-mentarian went to the Knesset clinic with what he claimed was a heart attack.[7] Calmer observers noted that God's prophet Nathan considered David a sinner, and that rabbis have pondered the different implications of David's activities over the centuries.[8]

Less difficult to interpret are the anti-religious barbs that appear regularly in a Jerusalem weekly newspaper.

A piece about the municipality's Internet web site asked if it would be turned off on the Sabbath and religious holidays, if it would be turned off during those days only during times of prayers (as in the case of the arrangement for the closing of a Jerusalem street), or if it would be operated by Arabs and thus be free of the laws governing Sabbath and holiday work by Jews.[9]

Other items with more bite than humor include:

- One that described a festive bar mitzvah celebrated by a prominent ul-tra-Orthodox family on the Memorial Day for members of Israel's security forces. The point was that ultra-Orthodox parties have a long history of not honoring the institutions of the Israeli state, and taking advantage of exemp-tions from military service. Once again the ultra-Orthodox had been found celebrating on a day of mourning for secular Israelis whose sons had been killed during service in the armed forces. The celebrants responded that a bar mitzvah is a sacred duty that takes precedence over mourning, even in the case of a death in the immediate family. The newspaper conveyed the message that the celebration could have been more modest out of respect for dead soldiers.[10]

- A story of a soldier required to serve on guard duty at a settlement in the territories for more than twenty-four consecutive hours before he was relieved. The message of the story was the human costs paid by Israelis in order to maintain and protect the settlements of religious Zionists.[11]

- Reports about a messy bankruptcy of Carmel Carpets, the family business of a parliamentarian representing United Torah Judaism. Initial articles dealt with the failure of the business to pay final salaries to low-wage workers in the depressed town where it had a factory. Later stories reported charges that members of the politician's family engaged in fraudulent activities to siphon money from the firm, perhaps as much as one billion Israeli shekels (US $333 million).[12]

There is no doubt about the importance of Jewish symbols in the political discourse of Israel. Yet they do not reflect the dominance of religious interests. Quite the contrary, they show religious activists struggling on a competitive field against secular opponents, with both seeking to advance their perspectives. Shouts of protest and ridicule reflect a stand-off and continuing tension, rather than the clear dominance of one side or the other.

So What? Implications for an Activist

This book is more empirical than normative. That is, it conditions and draws implications, rather than sets out to indicate what should be done.

This is how I see my work. However, when dealing with an issue as sensitive as religion, a writer looses control of his implications for readers who are religious or anti-religious, Orthodox or progressive in their Judaism, Christian or Muslim, or something else. While I do not intend to insult any of these traditions, some offense may be perceived. It is risky to reduce religious faith to something like political activism, and that is what I have intended.

Surely some will see this as blasphemy or foolishness. I may be read as implying that the heroes of the great religions are nothing more than candidates for public office. This would be an error of reading that I must correct. While individual preachers and rabbis may be no more inspiring or learned than a municipal council member, it is the rare politician who can match the likes of the widely revered prophets. The great prophets provided themes that have been central to more than a few political campaigns: justice and righteousness, with a special concern for those in society who are weak. The awareness of timing that appears in Ecclesiastes is political. National leaders must sense when it is the season for silence or speech, embracing or refraining, breaking down or building up, peace or war.[13]

For the politically active religious or secular Israeli, there seems no end to struggle and frustration. The marginal success of the religious or the secular has increased or declined with the weight of parties that are assertively religious or secular in the governing coalition. There is no sign on the horizon that Israel will alter its status as a "Jewish state" or that its voters will select a Knesset majority from a single party intent on sweeping legislation in the religious or anti-religious direction.

The Israelis for whom a fulsome religious or secular life is vital will continue to suffer, perhaps more than their equivalents in other democracies where religion is currently not so prominent on the agenda of disputes. A few secular families will take a stand and not circumcise their sons, and thereby risk embarrassment for them years later in the locker room or the army barracks. Others will pay the fee for a secular burial in a kibbutz cemetery. Larger numbers will forego the rites of bar mitzvah or a religious wedding. Intensely religious Jews will scream *Shabbos* as cars drive near their neighborhoods on the Sabbath, and screen potential marriage partners for a relative who stained an entire family by serving in the Israeli army or attending university. The majorities of secular and religious Jews will avoid these extremities. They will spend most of their time with their own kind. A number of secular Jews will explain their emigration as their inability to suffer religious dictates. Some ultra-religious Jews will make their home in New York, and avoid coming to the Holy Land until the true messiah finally arrives.

Israeli Jews as well as members of other religious communities elsewhere may ask if religious or political leaders provide the most reliable guidance. A dispassioned review of history and current affairs indicates that the answer is "neither." The personal failings of Bill Clinton have their equivalent in stories of television evangelists. Catholic priests and teachers at Jewish religious academies have been found wanting in their treatment of boys who come to them for instruction. The Jewish sages of long ago restricted the sin of adultery to relations between a man and a woman married to someone else. Modern women may chafe at the differential freedoms recognized for men and women, but the religious laws of Judaism and the secular laws of Israel provide certain protections to the unmarried partners of married men and their children. Is this greater wisdom, or simply the existence of a tradition that differs from that which prevails in Christian societies? Were Clinton an Israeli Jew, it might have lessened his problems.

The politician's pursuit of consensus and conflict minimization is no less commendable than the dictates of the commandments found in the Torah. To be sure, much of politics deals with the mundane, and some of it is corrupt. Perhaps the same can be said about the activities of religious leaders. Most of them carry out routine work, some of them are corrupt, and some are profound in providing counsel and guidance. Are political campaigns all that much different from revival meetings? Do the deliberations of thoughtful policymakers about the details of a government program differ significantly from arguments in the Talmud or the exegesis of Saint Thomas? There is no obvious solution to the trade-off between individual freedom and collective norms. Likewise, biblical prohibitions against killing and commandments to battle for communal defense require some thought as to when each is appropriate.

Israeli politicians continue to debate issues associated with religion, although some of them may prefer peace and quiet on this front. Policy changes have occurred, and will continue. The Supreme Court currently appears inclined to favor secular interests, while the Knesset and the ruling coalition that governed in the 1996-99 period supported religious interests. The details of the government will change as a result of elections in May 1999, and the composition of the Supreme Court will change with deaths and resignations. I cannot specify the details to come. I have reported the success of the religious parties in the 1999 elections, but it is too early to indicate the composition of Prime Minister Ehud Barak's government, and too early by far to judge the changes, if any, in government policies with respect to religion. It is one of the admirable Jewish traditions that Malachi was the last prophet recognized as speaking for the Lord, and he finished his work about 2,500 years ago.

Neither religion nor politics can claim a monopoly of virtue or an absence of evil. Political demagogues have their religious equivalents in self-serving individuals who say that they are prophets of the Lord or the messiah. The history of both religion and politics teaches the value of deliberate thought and doubt in the face of claims that are far reaching. The continued pursuit of knowledge and intellectual self-confidence are useful in defense against being swept up in momentary passions that are either religious or political, or that cross the boundaries between the two realms. If there is a prescription in this book, it differs in detail but not in principle from that of Ecclesiastes. Like the preacher, I am getting old. Yet I am not tired of study.[14] The more I learn, the more I appreciate further learning, and the skepticism that it supports.

Notes

Chapter One

1. Samuel Hellman, *Defenders of the Faith: Inside Ultra-Orthodox Jewry* (New York: Schocken Books, 1992), chapter 14.

2. Tamar El-Or, *Educated and Ignorant: On Ultra-Orthodox Women and Their World* (Tel Aviv: Am Oved, 1992), Hebrew.

3. Joshua 10:40. Citations and quotations from the Hebrew Bible come from a variety of translations, and some have been translated by the author.

4. Judges 3:5-6.

5. Judges 2:20-21.

6. The arrangement of books in the Bible used by Jews differs from that in what Christians call the Old Testament. The terminology used here is "Hebrew Bible" to denote the order and content traditional among Jews. Translations come from various sources, including the author's own.

7. Stuart A. Cohen, *The Three Crowns: Structures of Communal Politics in Early Rabbinic Jewry* (Cambridge: Cambridge University Press, 1990).

8. I Samuel 15:2-3.

9. Yehoshafat Harkabi, *The Bar Kokhba Syndrome: Risk and Realism in International Relations*, translated by Max D. Ticktin, edited by David Altshuler (Chappaqua, N.Y.: Rossel Books, 1983); and his *Israel's Fateful Hour*, translated by Lenn Schramm (New York: Harper and Row, 1988).

10. Norman Rich, *Why the Crimean War? A Cautionary Tale* (Hanover, N.H.: University Press of New England, 1985); Brison D. Gooch, ed., *The Origins of the Crimean War* (Lexington, Mass.: D.C. Heath and Co., 1969).

11. *Jerusalem Post*, December 9, 1994, p. 2.

12. *Kal Ha'ir*, June 5, 1998, p. 51f. Hebrew.

13. *Jerusalem Post*, May 26, 1995, p. 11.

14. *Jerusalem Post*, December 31, 1993, p. 1b; *Jerusalem Post*, April 5, 1996, p. 7.

15. *Jerusalem Post*, May 18, 1990, p. 7.

16. Bryan S. Turner, *Religion and Social Theory* (London: Sage Publications, 1991), p. xxi.

17. "Common Era" (CE) and "Before the Common Era" (BCE) are ways to express secular dating without using the explicitly Christian terms of AD and BC.

18. For analyses that parallel some of the points emphasized in this book, see Sabrina Petra Ramet and Donald W. Treadgold, eds., *Render unto Ceasar: The Religious Sphere in World Politics* (Washington, D.C.: American University Press, 1995); Talal Asad, *Genealogies of Religion: Discipline and Reasons of Power in Christianity and Islam* (Baltimore: Johns Hopkins University Press, 1993); and Clifford Geertz, "Religion as a Cultural System," in his *The Interpretation of Cultures* (New York: Basic Books, 1973).

19. Anthony Storr, *Feet of Clay: A Study of Gurus* (New York: Free Press, 1997), especially chapter ix.

20. Michael Walzer, *Exodus and Revolution* (New York: Basic Books, 1985); also see Turner, *Religion and Social Theory*.

21. Max Charlesworth, *Religious Inventions* (Cambridge: Cambridge University Press, 1997), pp. 24-25.

22. Josephus, *The Jewish War*, translated by G. A. Williamson (New York: Penguin Books, 1970); Norman Golb, *Who Wrote the Dead Sea Scrolls? The Search for the Secret of Qumran* (New York: Scribners, 1995).

23. See, for example, Acts 5:37; II Peter 2:1.

24. James A. Beckford and Thomas Luckmann, eds., *The Changing Face of Religion* (London: Sage Publications, 1989).

25. Theodore Caplow, et al. *All Faithful People: Change and Continuity in Middletown's Religion* (Minneapolis: University of Minnesota Press, 1983); and Wade Clark Roof and William McKinney, *American Mainline Religion: Its Changing Shape and Future* (New Brunswick, N.J.: Rutgers University Press, 1987).

26. R. Laurence Moore, *Religious Outsiders and the Making of Americans* (New York: Oxford University Press, 1986).

27. Moore, *Religious Outsiders,* postscript.

28. Charlesworth, *Religious Inventions,* pp. 3-4.

29. See, for example, Turner, *Religion and Social Theory,* Appendix.

30. *The Condition of Jewish Belief: A Symposium Compiled by the Editors of Commentary Magazine* (New York: Macmillan, 1966), p. 181.

31. On religiosity in the United States, see David C. Leege and Lyman A. Kellstedt, eds., *Rediscovering the Religious Factor in American Politics* (Armonk, N.Y.: M.E. Sharpe, 1993); Stephen D. Johnson and Joseph B. Tamney, eds., *The Political Role of Religion in the United States* (Boulder, Colo.: Westview Press, 1986); Robert Wuthnow, *The Restructuring of American Religion* (Princeton: Princeton University Press, 1988); R. Laurence Moore, *Selling God: American Religion in the Marketplace of Culture* (New York: Oxford University Press, 1994); Michael J. Lacey, ed., *Religion and Twentieth-Century American Intellectual Life* (New York: Cambridge University Press, 1989); and Kenneth D. Wald, *Religion and Politics in the United States* (Washington, D.C.: CQ Press, 1992); John C. Green, James L. Guth, Corwin E. Smidt, and Lyman Kellstedt, eds., *Religion and the Culture Wars: Dispatches from the Front* (Lanham, Md.: Rowman & Littlefield Publishers Inc., 1996); and N. J. Demerath III and Rhys H. Williams, *A Bridging of Faiths: Religion and Politics in a New England City* (Princeton: Princeton University Press, 1992).

32. *The Economist*, April 11-17, 1998, Internet edition.

33. Thomas F. O'Dea, *The Mormons* (Chicago: University of Chicago Press, 1957),

pp. 183-84.

34. Leonard J. Arrington and Davis Bitton, *The Mormon Experience: A History of the Latter-day Saints* (New York: Vintage Books, 1979), chapter 14.

35. Peter Beinart, "Battle for the 'Burbs,'" *New Republic,* Internet edition, October 19, 1998.

36. Anton Wessels, *Europe: Was It Ever Really Christian? The Interaction between Gospel and Culture* (London: SCM Press, 1994); Ellen Badone, ed., *Religious Orthodoxy and Popular Faith in European Society* (Princeton: Princeton University Press, 1990).

37. See, for example, John Dart, *The Jesus of Heresy and History: The Discovery and Meaning of the Nag Hammudi Gnostic Library* (San Francisco: Harper and Row, 1988), especially chapter 18.

38. Baruch Halpern, *The First Historians: The Hebrew Bible and History* (San Francisco: Harper and Row, 1988), chapter 11.

39. Genesis 18:23-33.

40. Exodus 32:10-14.

41. Exodus 13:17: "And it came to pass, when Pharaoh had let the people go, that God led them not through the way of the land of the Philistines, although that was near; for God said, Lest peradventure the people repent when they see war, and they return to Egypt."

42. Job 38-41.

43. John L. McKenzie, S.J., *The Two-Edged Sword: An Interpretation of the Old Testament* (Garden City, N.Y.: Image Books, 1966), p. 104; and Mordecai Zar-Kavod, "Introduction to Kohelet," in *The Five Scrolls* (Jerusalem: Mossad Harav Kook, 1973), Hebrew, p. 26. For the development of concept of God, both before and after the biblical period, for Jews as well as non-Jews, see Karen Armstrong, *A History of God: The 4,000-Year Quest of Judaism, Christianity and Islam* (New York: Ballantine Books, 1993).

44. Brad H. Young, *Jesus and His Jewish Parables: Rediscovering the Roots of Jesus' Teaching* (New York: Paulist Press, 1989), p. 130.

45. Dart, *The Jesus of Heresy and History,* chapter 18.

46. Michael Kazen, "The Politics of Devotion," *The Nation,* April 6, 1998, Internet edition.

47. Tim Chappell, "Rationally Deciding What to Believe," *Religious Studies,* March 1997 vol. 33 no. 1 pp. 105-9.

Chapter Two

1. Chris C. Park, *Sacred Worlds: An Introduction to Geography and Religion* (London: Routledge, 1994), Chapter 1.

2. Michael H. Ducey, *Sunday Morning: Aspects of Urban Ritual* (New York: The Free Press, 1977).

3.*Plays, Pleasant and Unpleasant* (1898). Cited by Park, p. 128.

4. Barry A. Kosmin and Seymour P. Lachman, *One Nation Under God: Religion in Contemporary American Society* (New York: Crown Trade Paperbacks, 1993), p. 25.

5. David M. Wulff, *Psychology of Religion: Classic and Contemporary Views* (New

York: John Wiley & Sons, 1991), p. 629.

6. Jon Butler, *Awash in a Sea of Faith: Christianizing the American People* (Cambridge: Harvard University Press, 1990), p. 1.

7. Ecclesiastes 1:9.

8. Harold Kushner, *When Bad Things Happen to Good People* (New York: Avon Books, 1981).

9. Marvin H. Pope, *Job*, The Anchor Bible (Garden City, N.Y.: Doubleday, 1973); and Amos Chacham, "Introduction," in *The Book of Job* (Jerusalem: Mossad Harav Kook, 1984), Hebrew.

10. Thomas W. Murphy, "Guatemalan Hot/Cold Medicine and Mormon Words of Wisdom: Intercultural Negotiation of Meaning," *Journal for the Scientific Study of Religion* 36, 2 (June 1997): 297-308.

11. David Yamane, "Secularization on Trial: In Defense of a Neo-secularization Paradigm," *Journal for the Scientific Study of Religion* 36, 1 (March, 1997): 109-22.

12. N. J. Demerath III and Rhys H. Williams, *A Bridging of Faiths: Religion and Politics in a New England City* (Princeton: Princeton University Press, 1992).

13. Robert S. Lynd and Helen M. Lynd, *Middletown: A Study in American Culture* (New York: Harcourt, Brace and Company, 1929.

14. Theodore Caplow, et al., *All Faithful People: Change and Continuity in Middletown's Religion* (Minneapolis: University of Minnesota Press, 1983).

15. Langdon Gilkey, *Society and the Sacred: Toward a Theory of Culture in Decline* (New York: Crossroad, 1981).

16. Raymong Firth, *Religion: A Humanist Interpretation* (London: Routledge, 1996), pp. 213-14.

17. Ducey, *Sunday Morning.*

18. Ducey, *Sunday Morning,* chapter 9.

19. See, for example, Carol Meyers, "David as Temple Builder," in Patrick D. Miller, Jr., Paul D. Hanson, and S. Dean McBride, eds., *Ancient Israelite Religion* (Philadelphia: Fortress Press, 1987), pp. 357-76; and Nehama Leibowitz, *Studies in Bamidbar (Numbers)*, translated and adapted by Aryeh Newman (Jerusalem: The World Zionist Organization, 1980), pp. 21-22.

20. *Ha'aretz*, October 11, 1995, p.5. Hebrew.

21. Wulff, *Psychology of Religion,* p. 242.

22. For example, Rodney Stark, "German and German American Religiousness: Approximating a Crucial Experiment," *Journal for the Scientific Study of Religion* 36, 2 (June 1997): 182-93.

23. For example, Joseph E. Faulkner, ed., *Religion's Influence in Contemporary Society: Readings in the Sociology of Religion* (Columbus, Ohio: Charles E. Merrill Publishing Co., 1972), especially Section II; and N. J. Demerath, III, et al. eds., *Sacred Companies: Organizational Aspects of Religion, and Religious Aspects of Organizations* (Oxford: Oxford University Press, 1998).

24. Elisabeth Arweck and Peter B. Clarke, *New Religious Movements in Western Europe: An Annotated Bibliography* (Westport, Conn.: Greenwood Press, 1997).

25. Max Charlesworth, *Religious Inventions* (Cambridge: Cambridge University

Press, 1997), p. 21.

26. See, for example, Morton Smith, *Palestinian Parties and Politics That Shaped the Old Testament* (London: SCM Press, 1987); John Bright, *Covenant and Promise: The Prophetic Understanding of the Future in Pre-Exilic Israel* (Philadelphia: The Westminster Press, 1976); Joseph Blenkinsopp, *A History of Prophecy in Israel: From the Settlement in the Land to the Hellenistic Period* (Philadelphia: The Westminster Press, 1983); Northrop Frye, *The Great Code: The Bible and Literature* (San Diego: Harcourt Brace Jovanovich, 1983); Richard Elliott Friedman, *Who Wrote the Bible?* (New York: Harper and Row, 1987); and Giovanni Garbini, *History and Ideology in Ancient Israel* (New York: Crossroad Publishing Company, 1988).

27. See the introductions in the multivolume *The Bible With Commentaries* (Jerusalem: Mossad Harav Kook, from 1971), Hebrew.

28. R. B. Y. Scott, *Anchor Bible: Proverbs and Ecclesiastes* (New York: Anchor Books, 1965) p. 196.

29. Meir Sternberg, *The Poetics of Biblical Narrative: Ideological Literature and the Drama of Reading* (Bloomington: Indiana University Press, 1987), pp. 64, 67.

30. Michael Fishbane, "Sin and Judgement in the Prophecies of Ezekiel," in James Luther Mays and Paul J. Achtemeier, eds., *Interpreting the Prophets* (Philadelphia: Fortress Press, 1987), pp. 170-87.

31. Marcia Falk, *The Song of Songs: A New Translation and Interpretation* (San Francisco: Harper, 1990).

32. Bernhard W. Anderson, *The Living World of the Old Testament* (Essex, England: Longman, 1988), pp. 608-10.

33. Adin Steinsaltz, *Biblical Images: Men and Women of the Book* (New York: Basic Books, 1984), chapter 25.

34. Steven A. Moss, "Who Killed Goliath?" *The Jewish Bible Quarterly* XVIII, 1 (Fall 1989): pp. 37-40.

35. J. Maxwell Miller and John H. Hayes, *A History of Ancient Israel and Judah* (Philadelphia: The Westminster Press, 1986), p. 87.

36. Yehuda Kil, *The Book of Samuel* (Jerusalem: Mossad Harav Kook, 1981), p. 112. Hebrew.

37. Paul D. Hanson, *Old Testament Apocalyptic* (Nashville: Abingdon Press, 1987).

38. John Goldingay, "The Stories in Daniel: A Narrative Politics," *Journal for the Study of the Old Testament* 37 (February 1987): 99-116.

39. Hugh J. Schonfield, *The Passover Plot* (London: Corgi Books, 1967), p. 74. Schonfield's book is not innocent of serious scholarship, even while its main argument ought to be viewed as fanciful speculation.

40. For a view that the book was composed by Isaiah and his students or listeners, see Amos Chacham, *The Book of Isaiah* (Jerusalem: Mossad Harav Kook, 1984).

41. Chacham, *The Book of Isaiah*, pp. 13-17.

42. Edwin M. Good, *Irony in the Old Testament* (Philadelphia: The Westminster Press, 1965), chapter 5.

43. *The New English Bible* (New York: Oxford University Press, 1970), Isaiah, 53:5.

44. Chacham, *The Book of Isaiah*, pp. 567 ff. Hebrew.

45. Kil, *Chronicles*, Introduction.

46. Stefan Heym, *The King David Report: A Novel* (New York: G.P. Putnam's Sons, 1973).

47. Robert Davidson, *The Courage to Doubt: Exploring An Old Testament Theme* (London: SCM Press, 1983), p 13; Roger Tomes, "The Psalms," in Stephen Bigger, ed., *Creating the Old Testament: The Emergence of the Hebrew Bible* (Oxford: Basil Blackwell, 1989), pp. 251-67; James A. Sanders, "Isaiah in Luke," in James Luther Mays and Paul J. Achtemeier, eds., *Interpreting the Prophets* (Philadelphia: Fortress Press, 1987), pp. 75-85; Thomas M. Raitt, "Jeremiah in the Lectionary," in Mays and Achtemeier, pp. 143-56. Passages about the suffering servant in the Book of Isaiah, for example, offered answers for Christians concerned to explain the Jews' rejection of Jesus.

48. "Book of Moses," *The Pearl of Great Price* (Salt Lake City: The Church of Jesus Christ of Latter-Day Saints, 1982).

49. Stephen Bigger, "A Muslim Perspective," and "Moses," in Bigger, *Creating the Old Testament*, ed., pp. 43-37; 117-34.

50. Matthew 3:7.

51. Matthew 15:14.

52. Matthew 23:1.

53. Luke 23.

54. Matthew 28:11.

55. I Corinthians 9:9. For a commentary on the competition between early Christians and the Jewish establishment, see John L. McKenzie, S.J., *The Two-Edged Sword: An Interpretation of the Old Testament* (Garden City, N.Y.: Image Books, 1966)

56. See, for example, Tryggve N. D. Mettinger, *Solomonic State Officials: A Study of the Civil Government Officials of the Israelite Monarchy* (Lund: CWK Gleerup, 1971); and Joseph Blenkinsopp *Gibeon and Israel: The Role of Gibeon and the Gibeonites in the Political and Religious History of Early Israel* (Cambridge: Cambridge University Press 1972).

57. Stephen Prickett, *Words and the Word: Language, Poetics, and Biblical Interpretation* (Cambridge: Cambridge University Press, 1986).

58. Demerath and Williams, *Bridging of Faith*, p. 306.

Chapter Three

1. The data come from *Statistical Abstract of Israel 1996* (Jerusalem: Central Bureau of Statistics, 1996), Table 22.14.

2. H. Mark Roelofs, "Hebraic-Biblical Political Thinking," *Polity* XX, 4 (Summer 1988): 572-97; and Roelofs, "Liberation Theology: The Recovery of Biblical Radicalism," *American Political Science Review* 82, 2 (June 1988): 549-66.

3. Ecclesiastes 3:1-8.

4. Mordechai Zar-Kavod, "Ecclesiastes," in *The Five Scrolls* (Jerusalem: Mossad Harav Kook, 1973). Hebrew.

5 . *Jerusalem Post*, January 7, 1994, p. 4B. For a discussion of nuances among categories of Israeli Jews, see , pp. 1-42; Eliezer Don-Yehiya, "Does Place Make a Difference? Jewish Orthodoxy in Israel and the Diaspora," in Chaim I. Waxman, ed., *Israel as*

a Religious Reality (Northvale, N.J.: Jason Aronson Inc, 1994), pp. 43-74.

6. Karen Armstrong, *A History of God: The 4,000-Year Quest of Judaism, Christianity and Islam* (New York: Ballantine Books, 1993), p. 90.

7. Numbers 14:22.

8. Numbers 20.

9. Genesis 12:1.

10. Exodus 2.

11. Exodus 3:11.

12. Exodus 5:1.

13. I Samuel 25:2-44.

14. I Samuel 27:6.

15. I Samuel 28:1-2.

16. I Samuel 29:1-5.

17. Ecclesiastes 2:13; 7:16.

18. Ecclesiastes 3:11.

19. Ecclesiastes 8:13.

20. Ecclesiastes 12:13-14.

21. Ecclesiastes 7:16-17; i:14-17; 9:2-6.

22. Ecclesiastes 11:9-10.

23. Ecclesiastes 12:12.

24. See, for example, Richard Tarnas, *The Passion of the Western Mind: Understanding the Ideas That Have Shaped Our World View* (New York: Ballantine Books, 1991); Michel Foucault, *Discipline and Punish: The Birth of the Prison*, translated by Alan Sheridan (New York: Vintage Books, 1979); and Henry J. Aaron, Thomas E. Mann, Timothy Taylor, eds., *Values and Public Policy* (Washington D.C.: Brookings Institution, 1994).

25. Ezra Mendelsohn, *On Modern Jewish Politics* (New York: Oxford University Press, 1993); Jonathan Frankel, *Prophecy and Politics: Socialism, Nationalism, and the Russian Jews, 1862-1917* (Cambridge: Cambridge University Press, 1981); Zvi Gitelman, ed., *The Quest for Utopia: Jewish Political Ideas and Institutions through the Ages* (Armonk, N.Y.: M.E. Sharpe, Inc, 1992); and Eli Lederhandler, *The Road to Modern Jewish Politics: Political Tradition and Political Reconstruction in the Jewish Community of Tsarist Russia* (New York: Oxford University Press, 1989).

26. *Ha'aretz*, April 28, 1998. p. 7. Hebrew.

27. *Ha'aretz*, May 17, 1999. p. 7. Hebrew

28. *Kal Ha'ir*, April 29, 1998, p. 41. Hebrew.

29. *Kal Ha'ir*, July 24, 1998, p. 29. Hebrew.

30. *Kal Ha'ir*, April 29, 1998, p. 23; August 14, 1998, p. 27. Hebrew.

31. Quotes in *Haaretz*, July 5, 1998, p. 5. Hebrew.

32. Irene R. Prusher, "Israel's Social Unifier, or Just a Political Survivor?" *Christian Science Monitor*, June 2, 1998. Internet edition.

33. *Ha'aretz*, April 6, 1998, p. 6. Hebrew.

34. *Kal Ha'ir*, May 8, 1998, p. 20. Hebrew.

35. Morning News, Israel Radio, May 11, 1998.

36. Raphael Pinhasi on Channel 2, May 12, 1998.

37. *Ha'aretz*, September 18, 1998, pp. 1, 2, 12; September 23, 1998, p. 8. Hebrew.

38. *Ha'aretz*, February 11, 12, 14, 15 1999. Numerous articles. Hebrew.

39. Charles S. Liebman and Elihu Katz, *The Jewishness of Israelis: Resonses to the Guttman Report* (Albany: State University of New York Press, 1997).

40. Charles S. Liebman and Eliezer Don-Yehiya, *Civil Religion in Israel: Traditinal Judaism and Political Culture* (Berkeley: University of California Press, 1984).

41. A. B. Yehoshua, "The Golah as a Neurotic Solution," *Forum: On the Jewish People, Zionism and Israel* (Spring/Summer, 1979): 17-36.

42. Isaiah 49:6.

43. *Jerusalem Post,* February 8, 1993, p. 2.

44. For example, Walter Martin, *The Kingdom of the Cults* (Minneapolis: Bethany House Publishers, 1997).

45. Robert A. Campbell and James E. Curtis, "Religious Involvement Across Societies: Analysis for Alternative Measures in National Surveys," *Journal for the Scientific Study of Religion* 33, 3 (1994): 215-29.

46. Martin Marty, "The Spirit's Holy Errand: The Search for a Spiritual Style in Secular America," *Daedalus* 12 (1996): 160-71.

Chapter Four

1. Genesis 15:5-14.

2. See Joshua 10:40 and 23:9-13, and Judges 2:20-21.

3. Jeremiah, chapters 42-43.

4. Jeremiah, 29:3-7.

5. See, for example, Jeremiah 44:11-12.

6. D. S. Russell, *The Jews from Alexander to Herod* (Oxford: Oxford University Press, 1967), chapter vii.

7. Chaim Potok, *Wanderings* (New York: Ballantine Books, 1978), p. 263.

8. Samuel Sandmel, *Judaism and Christian Beginnings* (New York: Oxford University Press, 1978), p. 17.

9. Numbers 34:2-13

10. Numbers 13:17-29.

11. William G. Dever and W. Malcolm Clark, "The Patriarchal Traditions," in John H. Hayes and J. Maxwell Miller, eds., *Israelite and Judaean History* (London: SCM Press Ltd., 1977), pp. 70-148.

12. Yohanan Aharoni, *The Land of the Bible: A Historical Geography*, Translated by A. F. Rainey (Philadelphia: Westminister Press, 1979), p. 6.

13. Joseph Heller, *God Knows* (New York: Dell Publishing Company, 1984), p. 256.

14. *Jerusalem Post,* November 25, 1994, p. 6.

15. I Kings 4.

16. A. Leo Oppenheim, *Ancient Mesopotamia: Portrait of a Dead Civilization* (Chicago: University of Chicago Press, 1977), p. 163.

17. Samuel Sandmel, *Judaism and Christian Beginnings* (New York: Oxford University Press, 1978), p. 3.

18. Isaiah, 1:7-8; 2:2-4.

19. Jeremiah 9:10.

20. Jeremiah 19:8-9.

21. Lamentations 1:1.

22. Foreign Broadcast Information Service: FBIS-NES-93-217, p. 47.

23. *Kal Ha'ir*, February 23, 1996, p. 23; May 22, 1998, p. 39. Hebrew.

24. *Jerusalem Post*, May 22, 1996, p. 5.

25. Yehoshafat Harkabi, *The Bar Kokhba Syndrom: Risk and Realism in International Relations*, Translated by Max D. Ticktin, edited by David Altshuler (Chappaqua, N.Y.: Rossel Books, 1983).

26. Harkabi, *Bar Kokhba,* p. 83.

27. Harkabi, *Bar Kokhba,* pp. 172-76.

28. Harkabi, *Bar Kokhba,* pp. 113-14.

29. Yeshayahu Leibowitz, *On Just about Everything: Talks with Michael Shashur* (Jerusalem: Keter Publishing House, Ltd, 1988), Hebrew, p. 24.

30. I Kings 12:4.

31. I Kings 12:14.

32. I Kings 12:16.

33. *The Economist* April 25-May 1, 1998. Internet edition.

34. Robert T. Handy, ed., *The Holy Land in American Protestant Life 1800-1948* (New York: Arno Press, 1981), p. xiv.

35. Handy, *The Holy Land,* p. xviii.

36. Quoted in Neil Asher Silberman, *Digging for God and Country: Exploration, Archeology, and the Secret Struggle for the Holy Land 1799-1917* (New York: Anchor Books, 1990), p. 86.

37. *Kal Ha'ir*, October 2, 1998, p. 23. Hebrew.

38. *New York Times*, January 4, 1999. Internet edition.

Chapter Five

1. Leonard Dinnerstein, *Anti-Semitism in America* (New York: Oxford University Press, 1994).

2. See, for example, Daniel J. Harrington, S.J., "The Jewishness of Jesus: Facing Some Problems," *The Catholic Biblical Quarterly* 49, 1 (January 1987): 1-13; E. P. Sanders, *Jesus and Judaism* (Philadelphia: Fortress Press, 1985); Donald A. Hagner, *The Jewish Reclamation of Jesus: An Analysis and Critique of the Modern Jewish Study of Jesus* (Grand Rapids, Mich.: Zondervan Publishing House, 1984); Brad H. Young, *Jesus and His Jewish Parables: Rediscovering the Roots of Jesus' Teaching* (New York: Paulist Press, 1989); and John Dart, *The Jesus of Heresy and History: The Discovery and Meaning of the Nag Hammadi Gnostic Library* (San Francisco: Harper and Row, 1988).

3. Ira Sharkansky, "Israeli Income Equality," *Israel Studies*, 1, 1 (Spring, 1996): 306-14.

4. See, for example, Michael Shalev, *Labour and the Political Economy in Israel* (New York: Oxford University Press, 1992); and Baruch Kimmerling, ed., *The Israeli*

State and Society: Boundaries and Frontiers (Albany, State University of New York Press, 1989); Sammy Smooha, *Arabs and Jews in Israel: Conflicting and Shared Attitudes in a Divided Society* (Boulder, Colo.: Westview Press, 1989); Benny Morris, *1948 and After: Israel and the Palestinians* (Oxford: Clarendon Press, 1994); and Avi Shlaim, *Collusion Across the Jordan: King Abdullah, The Zionist Movement, and the Partition of Palestine* (New York: Columbia University Press, 1988). For a post-post-Zionist criticism of this movement, see Efraim Karsh, *Fabricating Israeli History: The New Historians* (London: Frank Cass, 1997).

5. Amos 5:22-24.

6. Isaiah 2:4.

7. Ecclesiastes 5:8. See Robert Davidson, *The Courage to Doubt: Exploring an Old Testament Theme* (London: SCM Press, 1983), pp. 191-192.

8. Ecclesiastes 12:12.

9. *Report on the Results of Expenditure Audit of Political Groups for the Period of the Election to the 13th Knesset: 1.1.92 to 31.7.92* (Jerusalem: State Comptroller, 1993). Hebrew.

10. D. S. Russell, *The Jews from Alexander to Herod* (Oxford: Oxford University Press, 1967), chapter ii.

11. Victor Tcherikover, *Hellenistic Civilization and the Jews*, translated by S. Applebaum (New York: Atheneum, 1959).

12. Tcherikover, *Hellenistic Civilization*, part ii, chapters 2-4.

13. *The Apocrypha: An American Translation*, by Edgard J. Goodspeed (New York: Vintage Books, 1959), I Maccabees, 1:13-15.

14. I Maccabees, 2:24-25.

15. Peter Schafer, "The Hellenistic and Maccabaean Periods," in John H. Hayes and J. Maxwell Miller, *Israelite and Judaean History* (London: SCM Press Ltd., 1977), pp. 605-77.

16. Tcherikover, *Hellenistic Civilization*, p. 258.

17. Max I. Dimont, *Jews, God and History* (New York: Signet Books,1964, chapter 9; Michael Grant, *The History of Ancient Israel* (London: Weidenfeld and Nicolson, 1984), chapter 19.

18. Russell, *Jews from Alexander to Herod,* chapters vi, vii.

19. Paul Johnson, *A History of the Jews* (New York: Harper, 1987), p. 112.

20. Johnson, *A History of the Jews,* pp. 110-18.

21. Gerd Theissen, *Sociology of Early Palestinian Christianity* (Philadelphia: Fortress Press, 1978).

22. Josephus, *The Jewish War*, translated by G. A. Williamson (New York:Penguin Books, 1959), pp. 263-65, 380f.

23. An English translation has been published as *The Psychiatric Study of Jesus: Exposition and Criticism* (Boston: Beacon Press, 1968).

24. *The Trial and Death of Jesus* (London: Weidenfeld and Nicolson, 1972).

25. Holger Kersten and Elmar R. Gruber, *The Jesus Conspiracy: The Turin Shroud and the Truth about the Resurrection* (Shaftesbury, Dorset: Element, 1992).

26. *Ha'aretz*, November 11, 1997, p. 8. Hebrew.

27. For example, Norman Golb, *Who Wrote the Dead Sea Scrolls? The Search for the Secret of Qumran* (New York: Scribners, 1995).

28. Matthew 26-27.

29. John Dominic Crossan, *Jesus: A Revolutionary Biography* (San Francisco: HarperCollins, 1994).

30. Luke 20:25.

31. I Kings 22.

32. Amos 7:14.

33. Jeremiah 23:14; 28:16-17; 29:21-23.

34. I Kings 22:28.

35. Amos 7:10-17.

36. Jeremiah 26:20-23.

37. Urbach, p. 559.

38. I Kings, 18, 19.

39. See Ephraim E. Urbach, *The Sages: Their Concepts and Belief,* translated by Israel Abrahams (Cambridge: Harvard University Press, 1987), p. 564f.

40. Quoted in Karen Armstrong, *A History of God: The 4,000-Year Quest of Judaism, Christianity and Islam* (New York: Ballantine Books, 1993), p. 378.

41. Armstrong, pp. xix, 4.

42. David C. Leege and Lyman A. Kellstedt, eds., *Rediscovering the Religious Factor in American Politics* (Armonk, N.Y.: M.E. Sharpe, 1993); Kenneth D. Wald, *Religion and Politics in the United States* (Washington, D.C.: CQ Press, 1992; Stephen D. Johnson and Joseph B. Tamney, eds., *The Political Role of Religion in the United States* (Boulder, Colo.: Westview Press, 1986); Robert Wuthnow, *The Restructuring of American Religion* (Princeton: Princeton University Press, 1988); R. Laurence Moore, *Selling God. American Religion in the Marketplace of Culture* (New York: Oxford University Press, 1994); and Michael J. Lacey, ed., *Religion and Twentieth-Century American intellectual life* (New York: Cambridge University Press, 1989).

43. *Time,* February 6, 1995, p. 48; and Wald, *Religion and Politics in the United States,* p. 12.

44. Harold Bloom, *The American Religion: The Emergence of the Post-Christian Nation* (New York: Simon and Schuster, 1992).

45. Linda Feldmann, "Campaigning for president... or for preacher?: Public's concern over values leads candidates to wear their religion on their sleeves," *Christian Science Monitor,* June 8, 1999. Internet edition.

46. Luke 6:21-22.

47. John 8:8.

48. Exodus 23:2. See Joel Roth, *The Halakhic Process: A Systemic Analysis* (New York: Jewish Theological Seminary of America, 1986), especially chapters 5-7.

49. Exodus 21:24.

50. Isiah 11:4.

51. Matthew 5:7-10.

52. Isaiah 2:11.

53. Sanhedrin 37a, Bava Batra 11a.

54. Daniel J. Harrington, S.J., "The Jewishness of Jesus: Facing Some Problems,"

8. *Jerusalem Post*, January 31, 1997, p. 20.

9. *Jerusalem Post,* July 20, 1990, p. 11.

10. *Jerusalem Post*, January 31, 1997, p. 20.

11. *Jerusalem Post,* June 18, 1997, p. 1.

12. *Jerusalem Post,* June 30, 1996, p. 6.

13. *Ha'aretz*, May 19, 1998, p. 6. Hebrew.

14. *Ha'aretz*, January 9, 1998, p. 10. Hebrew.

15. *Ha'aretz*, February 24, 1998, p. 6. Hebrew.

16. *Ha'aretz*, April 28, 1998, p. 5. Hebrew.

17. *Ha'aretz*, December 30-31, 1998, various articles. Hebrew.

18. *Ha'aretz*, January14, 1998, p. 6. Hebrew.

19. *Ha'aretz*, January14, 1998, p. 6. Hebrew.

20. *Jerusalem Post,* September 11, 1995, p. 1.

21. *Jerusalem Post*, November 1, 1991, p. 6.

22. *Jerusalem Post*, February 29, 1996, p. 12.

23. *Ha'aretz*, August 6, 1998, p. 8. Hebrew.

24. *Jerusalem Post,* June 20, 1997, p. 20; June 27, 1997, p. 18.

25. *Jerusalem Post*, February 14, 1994, p. 12.

26. *Ha'aretz*, June 4, 1998, p. 5. Hebrew.

27. *Jerusalem Post,* June 8, 1989, p. 4.

28. *Ha'aretz,* October 6, 1995, p. 5. Hebrew.

29. *Ha'aretz*, June 9, 1998, p. 6. Hebrew.

30. *Ha'aretz*, February 2, 1999, p. 5. Hebrew.

31. *Ha'aretz,* June 16, 1998, p. 4; July 20, 1998, p. 10. Hebrew.

32. *Jerusalem Post,* November 18, 1996, p. 12

33. *Ha'aretz*, January 29, 1999, p. 1. Hebrew.

34. *Jerusalem Post*, February 23, 1955, p. 1.

35. *Ha'aretz*, April 13, 1995, p 9. Hebrew.

36. Eliezer Don-Yehiya, "Does Place Make a Difference? Jewish Orthodoxy in Israel and the Diaspora," in Chaim I. Waxman, ed., *Israel as a Religious Reality* (Northvale, N.J.: Jason Aronson Inc. 1994), pp. 43-74.

37. *The Jerusalem Post,* January 17, 1992, p. 1B.

38 Charles S. Liebman and Elihu Katz, ed., *The Jewishness of Israelis: Responses to the Guttman Report* (Albany: State University of New York Press, 1997).

39. *Jerusalem Post*, February 9, 1996, p. 6.

40. *Jerusalem Post*, January 22, 1996, p. 1.

41. *Ha'aretz*, February 21, 1999, p. B2. Hebrew.

42. *Jerusalem Post*, May 31, 1994, p. 1.

43. With respect to the situation in the United States, see David C. Leege and Lyman A. Kellstedt, eds., *Rediscovering the Religious Factor in American Politics* (Armonk, N.Y.: M.E. Sharpe, 1993); Stephen D. Johnson and Joseph B. Tamney, eds., *The Political Role of Religion in the United States* (Boulder, Colorado: Westview Press, 1986); Robert Wuthnow, *The Restructuring of American Religion* (Princeton: Princeton University Press, 1988); R. Laurence Moore, *Selling God: American Religion in the Marketplace of Culture* (New York: Oxford University Press, 1994); and Michael J. Lacey, ed., *Religion and twentieth-century American Intellectual Life* (New York: Cambridge Uni-

32. *Jerusalem Post,* November 18, 1996, p. 12

33. *Ha'aretz,* January 29, 1999, p. 1. Hebrew.

34. *Jerusalem Post,* February 23, 1955, p. 1.

35. *Ha'aretz,* April 13, 1995, p 9. Hebrew.

36. Eliezer Don-Yehiya, "Does Place Make a Difference? Jewish Orthodoxy in Israel and the Diaspora," in Chaim I. Waxman, ed., *Israel as a Religious Reality* (Northvale, N.J.: Jason Aronson Inc. 1994), pp. 43-74.

37. *The Jerusalem Post,* January 17, 1992, p. 1B.

38 Charles S. Liebman and Elihu Katz, ed., *The Jewishness of Israelis: Responses to the Guttman Report* (Albany: State University of New York Press, 1997).

39. *Jerusalem Post,* February 9, 1996, p. 6.

40. *Jerusalem Post,* January 22, 1996, p. 1.

41. *Ha'aretz,* February 21, 1999, p. B2. Hebrew.

42. *Jerusalem Post,* May 31, 1994, p. 1.

43. With respect to the situation in the United States, see David C. Leege and Lyman A. Kellstedt, eds., *Rediscovering the Religious Factor in American Politics* (Armonk, N.Y.: M.E. Sharpe, 1993); Stephen D. Johnson and Joseph B. Tamney, eds., *The Political Role of Religion in the United States* (Boulder, Colorado: Westview Press, 1986); Robert Wuthnow, *The Restructuring of American Religion* (Princeton: Princeton University Press, 1988); R. Laurence Moore, *Selling God: American Religion in the Marketplace of Culture* (New York: Oxford University Press, 1994); and Michael J. Lacey, ed., *Religion and twentieth-century American Intellectual Life* (New York: Cambridge University Press, 1989); Wald, *Religion and Politics in the United States;* and Harold Bloom, *The American Religion: The Emergence of the Post-Christian Nation* (New York: Simon & Schuster, 1992). For a more general survey of western societies, see Robert A. Campbell and James E. Curtis, "Religious Involvement across Societies: Analysis for Alternative Measures in National Surveys," *Journal for the Scientific Study of Religion* 33, 3 (1994): 215-29.

Chapter Seven

1. Alan R. Ball and Frances Millard, *Pressure Politics in Industrial Societies: A Comparative Introduction,* (Atlantic Highlands, N.J.: Humanities Press International, (1987); Marcia Drezon-Tepler, *Interest Groups and Political Change in Israel* (Albany: State University of New York Press, 1990); Arend Lijphart, *Electoral Systems and Party Systems: A Study of Twenty-seven Democracies, 1945-1990* (Oxford: Oxford University Press, 1994); Mancur Olson, *The Logic of Collective Action: Public Goods and the Theory of Groups* (Cambridge: Harvard University Press, 1965); Jeremy J. Richardson, ed. *Pressure Groups* (Oxford: Oxford University Press, 1993); Giovanni Satori, *Parties and Party Systems: A Framework for Analysis* (Cambridge: Cambridge University Press., 1976); Alan Ware, *Political Parties and Party Systems* (Oxford: Oxford University Press, 1996); Graham K. Wilson, *Interest Groups in the United States* (Oxford: Clarendon Press, 1981); and Yael Yishai, *Land of Paradoxes: Interest Politics in Israel* (Albany: State University of New York Press, 1991).

2. Satori, p. 155.

3. *Kal Ha'ir,* April 29, 1998, p. 27. Hebrew.

4. *Jerusalem Post,* May 1, 1996, p. 12.

5. *Ha'aretz,* July 13, 1998, p. 12. Hebrew.

6. *Jerusalem Post,* January 15, 1991, p. 2.

7. Shlomo Chosen, "Urban Democracy in Jerusalem," in *Urban Geography in Jerusalem 1967-1992* (Jerusalem: Jerusalem Institute for Israel Studies, 1992), pp. 171-202. Hebrew.

8. *Annual Report* #48 (Jerusalem: State Comptroller, 1998), especially pp. 123-140, 244. Hebrew. For the report of the State Comptroller's press conference that accompanied the publication of the Annual Report, see *Ha'aretz,* May 6, 1998, p. 1. Hebrew.

9. *Ha'aretz,* May 12, 1998, p. 3. Hebrew.

10. The exact numbers defy calculation, insofar as Prime Minister Netanyahu has alienated several former ministers who remain Knesset members formally affiliated with the coalition, but who might not support the government in a vote of confidence.

11. *The Washington Post,* June 4, 1998. Internet edition.

Chapter Eight

1. Deuteronomy 17:14-20.

2. Ecclesiastes 2:16.

3. Ecclesiastes 3:1-8.

4. Exodus 20:13.

5. Numbers 35.

6. Genesis 4:8.

7. Robert M. Grant with David Tracy, *A Short History of the Interpretation of the Bible* (Philadelphia: Fortress Press, 1984), p. 28.

8. Amos Hacham, *The Book of Isaiah* (Jerusalem: Mossad Harav Kook, 1984), pp. 567 ff. Hebrew.

9. Norman Lamm, "Judaism and the Modern Attitude to Homosexuality," in Reuven P. Bulka and Moshe HaLevi Spero, eds., *A Psychology-Judaism Reader* (Springfield, Ill.: Charles C. Thomas, Publisher, 1982, pp. 151-83.

10. *Ha'Aretz,* July 7, 1997, p. 1. Hebrew.

11. Genesis 1:26-29.

12. Gadi Wolfsfeld, *The Politics of Provocation* (Albany: State University of New York Press, 1988); and Sam Lehman-Wilzig, *Stiff-Necked People, Bottle-Necked System: The Evolution and Roots of Israeli Public Protest, 1949-1986* (Bloomington: Indiana University Press, 1991).

13. Norman F. Cantor, *The Sacred Chain: The History of the Jews* (New York: Harper Collins, 1994).

14. See Ecclesiastes 3:1-8.

15. This section relies on my "Religion and Politics in Israel and Utah," *Journal of Church and State,* 39, 3 (Summer 1997): 523-42.

16. See "Selections from the Book of Moses," in *The Doctrine and Covenants of the Church of Jesus Christ of Latter-Day Saints and The Pearl of Great Price* (Salt Lake City: The Church of Jesus Christ of Latter-Day Saints, 1982), 1:6.

17. Interview of Church President Gordon B. Hinckley on Larry King Live, CNN, September 8, 1998.

18. "Brigham Young University Institutional Self Study for Reaccreditation 1985-86: Volume I: An Interpretive Report," February 25, 1986, p. IV-6. Both *Dialogue* and *Sunstone* are publications that deal with Mormon issues. They are not publications of the Church, and are viewed as forums for Mormon creativity and criticism.

19. *Student Review: BYU's Unofficial Magazine*, September 21, 1988.

20. *Churches and Church Membership in the US 1980* (Atlanta: Glenmary Research Center, 1982).

21. One question asked if they accept the *Book of Mormon* as "an actual historical record of ancient inhabitants of the American continent,... translated by the gift and power of God." Armand L. Mauss, John R. Trijan, and Marth D. Esplin, "The Unfettered Faithful: An Analysis of the *Dialogue* Subscribers Survey," *Dialogue: A Journal of Mormon Thought* 20 (April, 1987), pp. 27-53.

22. They comprise seven percent of the state's population, while the Catholics are 14 percent. Mormons comprise eight percent of the population in Clark County (Las Vegas). See *Churches and Church Membership in the US 1980*. On Mormon political activity in Nevada see James T. Richardson and Sandie Wightman Fox, "Religious Affiliation as a Predictor of Voting Behavior in Abortion Reform Legislation," *Journal for the Scientific Study of Religion*, 11, 1972, pp. 347-59; James T. Richardson and Barend Van Driel, "Public Support for Anti-Cult Legislation" *Journal for the Scientific Study of Religion*, 23, (1984): 412-418; and James T. Richardson, "The 'Old Right' in Action: Mormon and Catholic Involvement in An Equal Rights Amendment Referendum," in David G. Bromley and Anson Shupe, eds., *New Christian Politics* (Macon, Ga: Mercer University Press, 1984), pp. 214-33. For a history of Nevada, see Russell R. Elliott, *History of Nevada* (Lincoln: University of Nebraska Press, 1987).

23. Leonard J. Arrington, *The Mormons in Nevada* (Las Vegas: Las Vegas *Sun*, 1979).

24. James Booke, "Utah Struggles With a Revival of Polygamy," *New York Times*, August 23, 1998. internet edition.

25. Stefan Heym, *The King David Report: A Novel* (New York: G.P. Putnam's Sons, 1973); and Joseph Heller, *God Knows* (New York: Alfred A. Knopf, 1984).

26. Such as Robert H. Moss's *The Covenant Coat* (Bountiful, Utah: Horizon Publishers and Distributors, Inc., 1985); S. Dean Wakefield's *Elijah: a Novel of the Chosen Prophet* (Bountiful, Utah: Horizon Publishers and Distributors, Inc., 1982); and Mark E. Petersen's *Three Kings in Israel* (Salt Lake City, Utah: Deseret Book Company, 1980).

27. *Ha'aretz*, December 6, 1996, p. 6. Hebrew.

28. *Ha'aretz*, July 6, 1998, p. 4. Hebrew.

29. See, for example, Louis Ginzberg, *Legends of the Jews* (New York: Simon and Schuster, 1956); and Lillian S. Freehof, *Stories of King David* (Philadelphia: Jewish Publication Society of America, 1952).

30. Jacob Neusner, *Death and Birth of Judaism: The Impact of Christianity, Secularism, and the Holocaust on Jewish Faith* (New York: Basic Books, 1987); and.Calvin Goldscheider and Jacob Neusner, eds., *Social Foundations of Judaism* (Englewood Cliffs, N.J.: Prentice Hall, 1990).

Chapter Nine

1. See Joseph Heller, *God Knows* (New York: Dell Publishing Company, 1984); Stefan Heym, *The King David Report* (New York: G.P. Putnam's Sons, 1973); and Louis Ginz-berg, *Legends of the Jews* (New York: Simon and Schuster, 1956).

2. Job 38-41.

3. Job 40:4-5.

4. Moshe Greenberg, "Job," in Robert Alter and Frank Kermode, eds., *The Literary Guide to the Bible* (London: Fontana Press, 1987), pp. 283-304.

5. Song of Songs 7:5-8; a report about the different responses of the rabbis who were Members of Knesset appears in *Ma'ariv* November 21, 1990 (Hebrew).

6. The relevant passage is II Samuel 1:26.

7. *Ha'aretz*, December 15, 1994 (Hebrew).

8. See II Samuel 12:9. For a summary or rabbinical writings, see Yehuda Kil, *The Book of Samuel: Second Samuel* (Jerusalem: Mossad Harav Kook, 1981), p. 420 ff. Hebrew.

9. *Kal Ha'ir*, April 16, 1998, p. 27. Hebrew.

10. *Kal Ha'ir* April 19, 1991, Hebrew.

11. *Kal Ha'ir,* April 16, 1998, p. 27. Hebrew.

12. *Jerusalem Post,* December 15, 1994, p. 8; *Ha'aretz*, August 1, 1999, p. 1. Hebrew.

13. Ecclesiastes 3:2-8.

14. See Ecclesiastes 12:12.

Bibliography

Aharoni, Yohanan. *The Land of the Bible: A Historical Geography*. Translated by A. F. Raincy. Philadelphia: Westminister Press, 1979.

Armstrong, Karen. A History of God: The 4,000-Year Quest of Judaism, Christianity and Islam. New York: Ballantine Books, 1993.

Asad, Talal. *Genealogies of Religion: Discipline and Reasons of Power in Christianity and Islam*. Baltimore: Johns Hopkins University Press, 1993.

Badone, Ellen, ed. *Religious Orthodoxy and Popular Faith in European Society*. Princeton: Princeton University Press, 1990.

Beckford, James A. and Thomas Luckmann, eds. *The Changing Face of Religion*. London: Sage Publications Ltd., 1989.

Ben-Yehuda, Nachman. *Political Assassinations by Jews: A Rhetorical Device for Justice*. Albany: State University Press of New York, 1993.

Blenkinsopp, Joseph. *A History of Prophecy in Israel: From the Settlement in the Land to the Hellenistic Period*. Philadelphia: The Westminster Press, 1983.

Bright, John. *Covenant and Promise: The Prophetic Understanding of the Future in Pre-Exilic Israel*. Philadelphia: The Westminster Press, 1976.

Cantor, Norman F. *The Sacred Chain: The History of the Jews*. New York: Harper Collins, 1994.

Caplow, Theodore, et al. *All Faithful People: Change and Continuity in Middletown's Religion*. Minneapolis: University of Minnesota Press, 1983.

Charlesworth, Max. *Religious Inventions*. Cambridge: Cambridge University Press, 1997.

Cohen, Stuart A. *The Three Crowns: Structures of Communal Politics in Early Rabbinic Jewry*. Cambridge: Cambridge University Press, 1990.

Dart, John. *The Jesus of Heresy and History: The Discovery and Meaning of the Nag Hammadi Gnostic Library*. San Francisco: Harper and Row, 1988.

Davidson, Robert. *The Courage to Doubt: Exploring an Old Testament Theme.* London: SCM Press, 1983.

Demerath, N. J. III and Rhys H. Williams. *A Bridging of Faiths: Religion and Politics in a New England City*. Princeton: Princeton University Press, 1992.

Ducey, Michael H. *Sunday Morning: Aspects of Urban Ritual.* New York: The Free Press, 1977.

El-Or, Tamar. *Educated and Ignorant: On Ultra-Orthodox Women and Their World.* Tel Aviv: Am Oved, 1992. Hebrew.

Firth, Raymond. *Religion: A Humanist Interpretation.* London: Routledge, 1996.

Frankel, Jonathan. *Prophecy and Politics: Socialism, Nationalism, and the Russian Jews, 1862-1917.* Cambridge: Cambridge University Press, 1981.

Friedman, Richard Elliott. *Who Wrote the Bible?* New York: Harper and Row, 1987.

Garbini, Giovanni. *History and Ideology in Ancient Israel.* New York: Crossroad Publishing Company, 1988.

Geertz, Clifford. *The Interpretation of Cultures.* New York: Basic Books, 1973.

Gilkey, Langdon. *Society and the Sacred: Toward a Theory of Culture in Decline.* New York: Crossroad, 1981.

Gitelman, Zvi, ed. *The Quest for Utopia: Jewish Political Ideas and Institutions Through the Ages.* Armonk, N.Y.: M.E. Sharpe, Inc, 1992.

Golb, Norman. *Who Wrote the Dead Sea Scrolls? The Search for the Secret of Qumran.* New York: Scribner, 1995.

Goldscheider, Calvin, and Jacob Neusner, eds. *Social Foundations of Judaism.* Englewood Cliffs, N.J.: Prentice Hall, 1990.

Gooch, Brison D. ed. *The Origins of the Crimean War.* Lexington, Massachusetts: D.C. Heath and Co., 1969.

Green, John C., James L. Guth, Corwin E. Smidt, and Lyman Kellstedt, eds. *Religion and the Culture Wars: Dispatches from the Front.* Lanham, Md.: Rowman & Littlefield Publishers, 1996.

Hagner, Donald A. *The Jewish Reclamation of Jesus: An Analysis and Critique of the Modern Jewish Study of Jesus.* Grand Rapids, Mich.: Zondervan Publishing House, 1984.

Halpern, Baruch. *The First Historians: The Hebrew Bible and History.* San Francisco: Harper and Row, 1988.

Handy, Robert T., ed. *The Holy Land in American Protestant Life 1800-1948.* New York: Arno Press, 1981.

Harkabi, Yehoshafat. *Israel's Fateful Hour.* Translated by Lenn Schramm New York: Harper and Row, 1988.

————. *The Bar Kokhba Syndrome: Risk and Realism in International Relations.* Translated by Max D. Ticktin, edited by David Altshuler. Chappaqua, N.Y.: Rossel Books, 1983.

Heilman, Samuel. *Defenders of the Faith: Inside Ultra-Orthodox Jewry.* New York: Schocken Books, 1992.

Heym, Stefan. *The King David Report: A Novel.* New York: G.P. Putnam's Sons, 1973.

Johnson, Stephen D. and Joseph B. Tamney, eds. *The Political Role of Religion in the United States.* Boulder, Colo.: Westview Press, 1986.

Josephus, *The Jewish War,* translated by G. A. Williamson New York: Penguin Books, 1970

Lacey, Michael J., ed. *Religion and twentieth-century American Intellectual Life.* New York: Cambridge University Press, 1989.

Lederhandler, Eli. *The Road to Modern Jewish Politics: Political Tradition and Political Reconstruction in the Jewish Community of Tsarist Russia.* New York: Oxford University Press, 1989.

Leege, David C. and Lyman A. Kellstedt, eds. *Rediscovering the Religious Factor in American Politics.* Armonk, N.Y.: M.E. Sharpe, 1993.

Lehman-Wilzig, Sam. *Stiff-Necked People, Bottle-Necked System: The Evolution and Roots of Israeli Public Protest, 1949-1986.* Bloomington: Indiana University Press, 1991.

Liebman, Charles S., and Eliezer Don-Yehiya. *Civil Religion in Israel: Traditional Judaism and Political Culture.* Berkeley: University of California Press, 1984.

Liebman, Charles S., and Elihu Katz. *The Jewishness of Israelis: Resonses to the Guttman Report.* Albany: State University of New York Press, 1997.

McKenzie, John L. S.J. *The Two-Edged Sword: An Interpretation of the Old Testament.* Garden City, N.Y.: Image Books, 1966.

Mendelsohn, Ezra. *On Modern Jewish Politics.* New York: Oxford University Press, 1993.

Mettinger, Tryggve N. D. *Solomonic State Officials: A Study of the Civil Government Officials of the Israelite Monarchy.* Lund: CWK Gleerup, 1971.

Moore, R. Laurence. *Religious Outsiders and the Making of Americans.* New York: Oxford University Press, 1986.

———. *Selling God: American Religion in the Marketplace of Culture.* New York: Oxford University Press, 1994.

Neusner, Jacob. *Death and Birth of Judaism: The Impact of Christianity, Secularism, and the Holocaust on Jewish Faith.* New York: Basic Books, 1987.

O'Dea, Thomas F. *The Mormons.* Chicago: University of Chicago Press, 1957.

Park, Chris C. *Sacred Worlds: An Introduction to Geography and Religion.* London: Routledge, 1994.

Pope, Marvin H. *Job. The Anchor Bible* Garden City, N.Y.: Doubleday, 1973.

Ramet, Sabrina Petra and Donald W. Treadgold, eds. *Render Unto Ceasar: The Religious Sphere in World Politics.* Washington, D.C.: American University Press, 1995.

Rich, Norman. *Why the Crimean War? A Cautionary Tale.* Hanover, N.H.: University Press of New England, 1985.

Roof, Wade Clark and William McKinney. *American Mainline Religion: Its Changing Shape and Future.* New Brunswick, N.J.: Rutgers University Press, 1987.

Samuel, Maurice. *The Professor and the Fossil.* New York: Alfred A. Knopf, 1956.

Sanders, E. P. *Jesus and Judaism.* Philadelphia: Fortress Press, 1985.

Sandmel, Samuel. *Judaism and Christian Beginnings.* New York: Oxford University Press, 1978.

Silberman, Neil Asher. *Digging for God and Country: Exploration, Archeology, and the Secret Struggle for the Holy Land 1799-1917.* New York: Anchor Books, 1990.

Smith, Morton. *Palestinian Parties and Politics That Shaped the Old Testament.* London: SCM Press, 1987.

Steinsaltz, Adin. *Biblical Images: Men and Women of the Book.* New York: Basic Books, 1984.

Storr, Anthony. *Feet of Clay: A Study of Gurus.* New York: Free Press, 1997.

Theissen, Gerd. *Sociology of Early Palestinian Christianity.* Philadelphia: Fortress Press, 1978.

Turner, Bryan S. *Religion and Social Theory.* London: Sage Publications, 1991.

Wald, Kenneth D. *Religion and Politics in the United States.* Washington, D.C.: CQ Press, 1992.

Walzer, Michael. *Exodus and Revolution.* New York: Basic Books, 1985.

Wessels, Anton. *Europe: Was it Ever Really Christian? The Interaction between Gospel and Culture.* London: SCM Press Ltd., 1994.

Wulff, David M. *Psychology of Religion: Classic and Contemporary Views.* New York: John Wiley and Sons, 1991.

Wuthnow, Robert. *The Restructuring of American Religion.* Princeton: Princeton University Press, 1988.

Young, Brad H. *Jesus and His Jewish Parables: Rediscovering the Roots of Jesus' Teaching.* New York: Paulist Press, 1989.

Index

About the Author

Ira Sharkansky has been Professor of Political Science and Public Administration at the Hebrew University of Jerusalem since 1975.